DWELLING IN

AMERICAN

Re-Mapping the Transnational
A Dartmouth Series in American Studies

SERIES EDITOR

Donald E. Pease
Avalon Foundation Chair of Humanities
Founding Director of the Futures of American Studies Institute
Dartmouth College

The emergence of Transnational American Studies in the wake of the
Cold War marks the most significant reconfiguration of American Studies
since its inception. The shock waves generated by a newly globalized
world order demanded an understanding of America's embeddedness
within global and local processes rather than scholarly reaffirmations of
its splendid isolation. The series Re-Mapping the Transnational seeks
to foster the cross-national dialogues needed to sustain the vitality of
this emergent field. To advance a truly comparativist understanding
of this scholarly endeavor, Dartmouth College Press welcomes
monographs from scholars both inside and outside the United States.

For a complete list of books available in this series,
see www.upne.com.

JOHN MUTHYALA, *Dwelling in American:*
Dissent, Empire, and Globalization

WINFRIED FLUCK, DONALD E. PEASE, and JOHN CARLOS ROWE,
editors, *Re-Framing the Transnational Turn in American Studies*

LENE M. JOHANNESSEN, *Horizons of Enchantment:*
Essays in the American Imaginary

JOHN CARLOS ROWE, *Afterlives of Modernism:*
Liberalism, Transnationalism, and Political Critique

ANTHONY BOGUES, *Empire of Liberty: Power, Desire, and Freedom*

BERND HERZOGENRATH, *An American Body\Politic:*
A Deleuzian Approach

JOHANNES VOELZ, *Transcendental Resistance:*
The New Americanists and Emerson's Challenge

Dwelling in American

DISSENT, EMPIRE, AND GLOBALIZATION

JOHN MUTHYALA

DARTMOUTH COLLEGE PRESS
HANOVER, NEW HAMPSHIRE

Dartmouth College Press
An imprint of University Press of New England
www.upne.com
© 2012 Trustees of Dartmouth College
All rights reserved
Manufactured in the United States of America
Designed by Kaelin Chappell Broaddus
Typeset in 10/12 Warnock Pro by Kaelin Chappell Broaddus
5 4 3 2 1

Library of Congress Cataloging-in-Publication Data
Muthyala, John, 1966–
Dwelling in American : dissent, empire, and globalization / John Muthyala.
p. cm. — (Re-mapping the transnational: a Dartmouth series in American studies)
Includes bibliographical references and index.
ISBN 978-1-61168-248-9 (cloth : alk. paper) —
ISBN 978-1-61168-249-6 (pbk. : alk. paper) — ISBN 978-1-61168-250-2 (ebook)
1. United States—Foreign relations—Philosophy. 2. United States—
Civilization—Philosophy. 3. Imperialism. 4. Nation-state and globalization.
5. Culture and globalization. 6. Globalization—Political aspects. I. Title.
E183.7.M88 2012
327.73—dc23   2011049435

In its suspicion of totalizing concepts, in its discontent with reified objects, in its impatience with guilds, special interests, imperialized fiefdoms, and orthodox habits of mind, criticism is most itself and, if the paradox can be tolerated, most unlike itself at the moment it starts turning into organized dogma . . . criticism must think of itself as life-enhancing and constitutively opposed to every form of tyranny, domination, and abuse; its social goals are noncoercive knowledge produced in the interests of human freedom.

"Secular Criticism,"
The World, the Text, and the Critic,
EDWARD W. SAID

CONTENTS

⊸ ACKNOWLEDGMENTS ⊱

This was a difficult book to write because it meant reading against the grain of established scholarship on American empire. I am grateful to Don Pease for giving me the opportunity to think contrapuntally about empire and extend ideas into uncharted terrain; his support is deeply appreciated. Thank you to Michael Bérubé for his collegiality and generosity. Richard Pult guided the publication of this manuscript with the steady hand of an experienced editor. Jeanne Ferris's scrupulous attention to words, syntax, and documentation demanded that I pay close attention to my work, and do so with humility. A big thank-you to Richard and Jeanne. To John Bealle for doing a thorough job of indexing, Amanda Dupuis for keeping track of the project, and to members of the design and marketing team for their collaboration—I appreciate your work. Thanks to Dean Lynn Kuzma at the University of Southern Maine's College of Arts, Humanities, and Social Sciences, for supporting indexing costs.

By doing what they do best, my colleagues Nancy Gish and Kathy Ashley showed that scholarship is about pursuing the life of the mind and a way of living, and they constantly encouraged me to cultivate a restless spirit of inquiry and learning. The readers of the manuscript pushed me to refine my ideas in ways that expanded the horizons of this book's arguments. A few years ago, before this project was conceptualized as a book, Janet Afary read a chapter draft and gave me valuable suggestions for revision. Her scholarship on Iran prompted me to rethink some of my approaches to the study of empire in global contexts. Lindsay Dorney graciously read drafts of two chapters and gave helpful suggestions. Her interest is much appreciated. Over the last six years, I discussed many of the ideas in this book with my students. They questioned me over and over, and for good reason: they took me at my word and held me to the same standards to which I held them. And they did it with a curiosity, humor, and hunger for knowledge that amaze me. They are the reason why I have come to love working at a public university. The daily task of looking up items in catalogs, checking books, and processing library loan requests can pretty quickly become laborious, but the tirelessness with which Loraine Lowell, Bill Sargent, John Plante, and Gabe Stowe performed their work showed that professionalism in academe comes in many forms. For setting the bar so high and living up to it—or at least trying—every day, I thank them. I also thank Kenneth Weisbrode, editor of *New Global Studies*, and Alan Clinton, editor of *Reconstruction: Studies in Contemporary Culture*, for giving permission to revise my essays that appeared there and publish the new versions here. To Mom and Nana, for consistent support and encouragement, and to Hannah, for tolerating many things in the course of my writing this book, many thanks.

It is a truth commonly acknowledged that America is an empire, but its meaning is as varied as it is contradictory. To Chalmers Johnson (*Blowback*), the presence of America's military bases all over the world proves its global dominance; to Noam Chomsky ("The United States Is a Leading Terrorist State"), because the United States has often acted like the states it critiques for their indifference to human rights, it is a terrorist state just like the ones it condemns; to Richard Immerman (*Empire for Liberty*), America has always exercised imperial power inside and outside its national territory, but it has done so to advance the cause of liberty as well as to secure natural resources; to Michael Hardt and Antonio Negri (*Empire*), America's contemporary status as a superpower marks a shift in the structures and logics of rule, in the sense that empire is sustained in the interests of peace, democracy, and liberty through the workings of national, international, and nongovernmental organizations; to Niall Ferguson (*Colossus: The Price of America's Empire*), rather than denying its history as an empire, America should acknowledge it and lead the world as a global hegemon.

These views about America's emergence as an imperial power and rise to global preeminence reveal not only the different methodological and disciplinary approaches these scholars use to study America, but the highly contested meaning of "empire." "Colonialism" refers to the settlement of another country or region and the appropriation of its resources, cultures, and peoples. "Imperialism" is about one region, nation, state, or empire advancing its own interests by directing and managing the internal affairs of another entity, and it does not necessarily involve the settlement of that other entity. "Empire" suggests vast territorial expansion but may not involve direct settlement or even constant intervention; it can be a form of domination and control in which those subjected to imperial rule might have varying degrees of power to direct their affairs—provided they support, directly or indirectly, the ventures undertaken by the dominant power, including waging war to dismantle or protect treaties and alliances. "Control" in this context can mean levying taxes, creating economic and political systems of dependency, using military power to intervene in another nation's territory or negate a threat, providing skills and training to develop industries or institutions designed to further particular ends, and gaining control of or influencing the technologies and realms of cultural production.[1]

In the post–Cold War era, America exerts dominance and control across the globe: it has more than eight hundred bases (broadly defined as sites connected to, if not directly used by, the military) in the world.[2] The real property maintained by the U.S. Department of Defense includes sites in thirty-eight countries, besides the fifty U.S. states and seven territories. The concluding paragraph of the department's *Base Structure Report* states: "Our physical infrastructure provides the framework supporting our military forces globally. . . . Our network of quality operational and support facilities located at sites around the world are *core to U.S. combat power, an inseparable element of the nation's military readiness and wartime effectiveness.*"[3] America, avers Johnson, is actively trying to expand, not scale down, its military network; it is "doing everything in its considerable powers to perpetuate Cold War structures, even without the Cold War's justification. . . . The by-products of this project are likely to build up reservoirs of resentment against all Americans—tourists, students, and businessmen, as well as members of the armed forces—that can have lethal results."[4] This resentment generates "blowback" to empire in the sense that America will reap what it sows, as the effects of empire will have an impact not only on Americans, but on people in countries affected by its policies and military bases; the September 11, 2001, attack on America underscores the prescience of Johnson's arguments, published a year earlier. In *Dismantling the Empire*, Johnson explains that "'blowback' does not refer simply to reactions to historical events but more specifically to reactions to operations carried out by the U.S. government that are kept secret from the American public and from most of their representatives in Congress. This means that when civilians become victims of a retaliatory strike, they are at first unable to put it in context or to understand the sequence of events that led up to it. Even though the American people may not know what has been done in their name, those on the receiving end certainly do."[5] However, even Johnson often uses the logic of guilt by association and counterfactual, or "if only," conjectures to critique American empire, implying that all critical conflicts in the world are somehow, directly or indirectly, connected to the United States, and that their brutality, horror, and tragedy can be explained only by the extent of U.S. involvement or lack thereof. For example, he writes: "But without the United States government's Vietnam-era savagery, [Pol Pot] could never have come to power in a culture like Cambodia's, just as Mao's uneducated peasant radicals would never have gained legitimacy in a normal Chinese context without the disruption and depravity of the Japanese war."[6] Put another way, to understand the savagery of the Cambodians and Chinese, we need to understand the savagery of the Americans and the Japanese—in fact, without American and Japanese savagery, Cambodian and Chinese savagery are inconceivable. The absolute certainty with which Johnson establishes causes and effects about such matters often weakens the valid points he makes about the workings of American empire. He needlessly consolidates American exceptionalism at the same moment that he criticizes its imperial reach, forcing the events of world history into the prison house of American history and waxing eloquent about the perils of empire.

But what do we make of America as an "empire of liberty," a phrase Thomas Jefferson used to characterize the emerging nation's interactions with other powers in the North American continent and across the Atlantic? In a letter to George Rogers Clark written in 1780, Jefferson discusses strategies to counter the advance of the British and the Indians in the western regions, and to take control of Detroit and Lake Erie by using the Illinois Battalion. More significant than the details of military operations, munitions, supplies, and battle plans is the political structure Jefferson authorizes Clark to establish with the new Indian, French, and British subjects: they can "continue under the laws and form of Government under which they at present live, only substituting the authority of this Commonwealth in all instances in lieu of that of his Britannic Majesty," and to the Indians, in particular, Clark is advised to "hold out either fear or friendship."[7] At the end of the letter, Jefferson frames Clark's venture in the larger context of America's struggle to secure territories, expand its commerce, and "add to the Empire of liberty an extensive and fertile Country thereby converting dangerous Enemies into valuable friends."[8] The imperial reach of this enterprise comes across clearly. However, this is not just an imperial act, but a policy to strengthen the new country's power by establishing America as an empire. This is why Immerman maintains that "the extension of America's territory and influence has always been inextricably tied to extending the sphere of liberty."[9]

Almost three decades later, in a letter to James Madison in 1809, Jefferson elaborates on the idea of America as empire in relation to the imperial ventures of the British and the French. Napoleon believed that France needed to take a conciliatory approach to the United States in order to contain the British while maintaining French colonies in the Americas, especially given the fact that Spain, France's European neighbor, was also a colonial power. Jefferson ponders the prospect of French tolerance regarding American incorporation of Cuba as a way to prevent the United States from supporting Spanish colonies like Mexico, which would pose a threat to France's empire:

> [Napoleon] ought the more to conciliate our good will, as we can be such an obstacle to the new career opening on him in the Spanish colonies. That he should give us the Floridas to withhold intercourse with the residue of those colonies cannot be doubted. But that is no price, because they are ours in the first moment of the first war, and until a war they are of no particular necessity to us. . . . We should then have only to include the North in our confederacy, which would be of course in the first war, and we should have such an empire for liberty as she has never surveyed since the creation: and I am persuaded no constitution was ever before so well calculated as ours for extensive empire and self-government.[10]

The expansion of the new nation takes place in a trans-Atlantic nexus, in which various empires scramble to dominate and control territories on both sides of the Atlantic. Warding off threats or yielding a loss here to seize a gain there is the nature of this political calculation that also raises the specter of war and its impact on all empires. But this is not just about a forceful acquisition of foreign territory. It is also about liberty and self-governance; indeed, it's about federalism and republican ideals. This is why Jefferson—who drafted major portions of the Declaration of Independence, with their ringing endorsements of universal values—sees no contradiction in viewing the U.S. Constitution as perfectly suited for the growth of empire, since the sole purpose for empire is the realization of the latent human desire for liberty and self-governance, notwithstanding the highly specific form of economic (nascent capitalist) and political (federal republic) organization in which they would be made manifest.

To Jefferson, empire means a political structure in which different states cooperate in more or less formal submission to a federal unit: empire is a consolidation of states. But Immerman notes, rightly I think, that the nature of this consolidation and the idea of the state have certain features that give us insight into how empire could so directly and unproblematically be connected to liberty: as the United States expanded in the nineteenth century, governance over acquired or acquirable territories became linked to empire. To think and speak of empire means thinking about how states could interact in ways that supported a specific mode of living, and why it was necessary to do so. The question was how the United States "should behave within the constellation of domestic and global actors to promote its national interests . . . while at the same time preserving and frequently expanding a particular definition of individual and collective liberty."[11] Anthony Bogues argues that to conceive of America as an empire of liberty involves privileging two things: first, democracy and individual right as the ultimate mode for social organization; and second, empire as the deployment of power "by which self-regulated, individual subjectivity meshes with the drives of the imperium." Bogues continues: "It suggests that imperial power is also about establishing ways of life that rest on a single truth determined by power as common to human nature."[12]

As noted earlier, the central goal that Jefferson emphasizes to Clark, the general whom he authorizes to advance into alien territory and to govern the subjugated people, is to "add to the Empire of liberty an extensive and fertile Country thereby converting dangerous Enemies into valuable friends." The adverbial phrase illuminates the powerful appeal of the empire of liberty: enemies will be converted into friends not because of the benevolence of American political or military principles, or even because of the unique features of American society, but because America promotes a universal cause intrinsic to human nature—representative democracy—and despite themselves, enemies will become friends because they will be grappling with what it means to be human, and in response to their instinctive desire for liberty, they will become new human subjects, like us. Whereas the civilizing mission of empire was to prevent the natives from becoming like one of us or to carefully control how they mimicked us, the American empire of liberty is about providing the conditions in which the basic human desire for democracy and individualism can be fully expressed and realized. It is this universalizing scope of American empire that allows Americans to conceive of themselves not as an imperial power interested in subjugating the weak, but as one that enables other peoples and countries to achieve two universal goals: the creation of structures of self-governance, and the cultivation of the individual as the embodiment of liberal rights.

The idea of America as empire is not new, to be sure. The concept is integral to the historical formation of the states into a union and, soon thereafter, to the country's expansion in the Americas and the world. In the last two decades, the turn towards the trans- and the postnational in American Studies, in particular, has been marked by a heightened focus on empire. This focus brings to light or traces historical events, processes, and policies that consolidated the growth of empire, and continues to critique America's current role in sustaining a new structure of sovereignty in which its imperial command is actively obscured and denied—or at least reimagined, in the realm of popular culture and political discourse, as a benevolent force for justice and global order. Donald Pease characterizes the tension between the national and the postnational thus: "The image repertoire productive of the U.S. national community can be ascertained through a recitation of the key terms in the national meta-narrative commonly understood to be descriptive of that community. Those images interconnect an exceptional national subject (American Adam) with a representative national scene (Virgin Land) and an exemplary national motive (errand into the wilderness)."[13] To tease out, make visible, name, identify, contextualize, and read or deliberately misread the official symbols, events, and narratives in order to effect displacements and realignments among the subject, scene, and errand—thus reinvesting them with new meanings—is a key aim of the New Americanists, and America as empire has emerged as a dominant counternarrative. The many scholarly works that examine America as empire include Gloria Anzaldúa, *Borderlands/La Frontera*; Donald Pease and Amy Kaplan, *Cultures of United States Imperialism*; Pease, *National Identities and Post-Americanist Narratives*; John Rowe, *Post-Nationalist American Studies* and *Literary Culture and U.S. Imperialism*; Pease and Robyn Wiegman, *The Futures of American Studies*; Rob Wilson, *Reimagining the American Pacific*; Walter Mignolo, *Local Histories/Global Designs*; Amy Kaplan, *The Anarchy of Empire in the Making of U.S. Culture*; Djelal Kadir, "America and Its Studies"; several essays in each of the first issues of *American Quarterly* in 2004, 2005, and 2007; Andrew Ross and Kristin Ross, *Anti-Americanism*; Niall Ferguson, *Colossus*; Thomas Bender, *A Nation Among Nations*; Michael Bérubé, *The Left at War*; Richard Immerman, *Empire for Liberty*; Anthony Bogues, *Empire of Liberty*; and Michael Hardt and Antonio Negri's *Empire, Multitude*, and *Commonwealth*.

While drawing on this scholarship in this book, as chapter 1 explains in greater detail, I argue that sometimes critiques of American empire confuse U.S. history with world history, fail to recognize peoples outside the United States as social actors with agency, and view contemporary globalization as a singular form of American economic, political, and cultural global domination. This book offers an alternate critical model—dwelling in American—and conceives of globalization not only as a complex system with centers and peripheries but as sets of social, cultural, economic, and political processes in which the policies and aspirations of powerful nation-states are enmeshed with the interests of other empires, nation-states, and communities. The book is divided into six chapters.

Chapter 1 lays out the broad argument that dissent about American empire has emerged as a powerful discourse with certain presuppositions, paradigms, and ideological agendas. I examine the dissent from empire offered by several literary and cultural critics, historians, sociologists, writers, and journalists, including Emmanuel Todd (*After the Empire: The Breakdown of the American Order*), Samantha Power (*"A Problem From Hell"*), and David Harvey (*The New Imperialism*). While offering critiques of American empire, these writers, I argue, internationalize U.S. history, thus collapsing the national into the global in ways that privilege the United States as the only symbol of modernity.

Chapter 2 presents an alternate model—dwelling in American—for studying the complex processes of cultural globalization that influence the internationalization of American literature and culture. I revise James Ceaser's proposal (*Reconstructing America*) to wrest control over the real America from the symbolic America by arguing that dwelling in American—as idea and critical model—rejects the notion that non-American experiences and societies gain relevance only insofar as they are seen to be reacting in some way to America. I argue that dwelling in American fundamentally contests the ideology of American exceptionalism, which posits that American history is unique and untainted by world history; that its social and cultural institutions have exceptional characteristics that set it apart from all other societies; and that it has a providential mandate to set the course of world history. I demonstrate how we can avoid these ideological pitfalls of exceptionalism by examining how America is deeply entangled with other nation-states and empires, and studying the complex cultural dynamics of contemporary globalization that have a profound impact on America, even as its foreign policies affect other nations.

Chapter 3 studies the writings of a famous public intellectual, Arundhati Roy from India, who has gained international fame for her critiques of globalization and America. By drawing on Abdul JanMohamed's theory of the border intellectual, I argue that Roy's dissent from American empire and globalization is premised on the idea that intellectuals can provide unproblematic access to non-Western experience and knowledge to people located in the West. I critique her frequent appeals to the binary logic of civilizational difference as she attempts to mobilize antiglobalism sentiment in India and abroad, and I argue that she abstracts culture and aesthetics from economics and politics, a move that blocks the promising directions in which her critiques of globalization could be extended.

Chapter 4 focuses on Azar Nafisi's best-seller *Reading Lolita in Tehran* and argues that most critics who regard her as a cultural apologist for American empire tend to view contemporary globalization as nothing but Americanization, as the seamless and uniform spread of all things American in various parts of the world. I make the case that *Reading Lolita in Tehran* opens up new international perspectives on the Iranian diaspora and helps us understand how migration and relocation affect ideas of home, belonging, cultural continuity, and ethnic solidarity. My discussion demonstrates the irregular, unpredictable dynamics of globalization in which American literature and culture travel through international circuits of intellectual exchange, acquire new readers, and generate diverse interpretations and social uses.

Chapter 5 studies the links between culture and multinational businesses in the globalization of information technology (IT) in Thomas Friedman's *The World Is Flat*. Instead of viewing culture as playing second fiddle to economics and politics, I view it as the site of social, political, and economic struggle, where the legitimation of the logic of globalization is at stake. This legitimation, I aver, is obtained by reorienting world history to American history, just as *The World Is Flat* deploys a New World mythology to develop an account of the contemporary world. I argue that this mythology situates IT globalization in a narrative of European modernity that consolidates Euro-America as the privileged site from which to conceptualize globalization. I examine how this use of New World mythology harnesses the discourse of American exceptionalism to Americanize IT globalization and obscures the role of new transnational classes and cultures linking India and the United States, thus raising the specter of American cultural imperialism at the very moment when *The World Is Flat* heralds a new world order for the twenty-first century.

Chapter 6 looks at how the transnationalization of affective labor has become central to the IT global economy. It studies the role of American culture in call centers in India, a crucial sector of the IT industry linking the United States to technopolises in several countries around the world. In critiquing the documentary *Diverted to Delhi*, which focuses on call center management, I argue that the biopolitical reproduction of culture results in new social classes, which both limit and open up possibilities for individual empowerment and social mobility. Traditional models of globalization as Westernization or hybridization fail to account for the contradictions and paradoxes of transnational cultural production, especially in their gendered dimensions. Although this new dispensation of empire functions with fluid structures, celebrates hybridity, and makes the idea of the other or cultural difference more central to international business, those whose professional and cultural lives are interwoven with business process outsourcing appropriate and manipulate cultural personas while securing a modicum of personal economic initiative, to resist constant surveillance both inside and outside of work locations.

DWELLING IN

AMERICAN

CHAPTER ONE

Empire and Dissent

After the United States went to war against Afghanistan and Iraq in response to the attacks of September 11, 2001, critiques of America as a global
empire gained critical purchase in public discourse, both in the United
States and abroad. This book makes three central arguments about most
of these critiques: they tend to internationalize American national history
as world history; they fail to acknowledge that people outside the United
States are social actors with agency; and they often view contemporary
globalization as a singular form of American economic, political, and cultural global domination. When dissent about empire is transformed into
a disambiguation of empire, as José Limón pointedly observes, "the very
category of empire is itself then up for discussion."[1] When it is left unexamined, dissent can create its own regimes of truth and legitimation, implicate itself in illiberal forms of protest, and engage in ahistorical pursuits
of social and cultural critique. In this chapter, I analyze instances of dissent offered by literary and cultural critics, anthropologists, journalists,
and historians, and I examine the rhetorical maneuvers, critical models,
and ideological motivations that shape their critiques of empire.

AMERICAN EMPIRE AND THE
TRANSNATIONAL TURN

In her presidential address to the 2003 annual meeting of the American
Studies Association, Amy Kaplan examines the rhetoric of war, homeland,
freedom, and liberty in the United States to underscore the "violence of

belonging" in constructing "America as the homeland."[2] Since hasty evo-
cations of America as homeland reify "a sense of racial purity and ethnic homogeneity that even naturalization and citizenship cannot erase,"
immigrants, migrants, undocumented workers, and especially Arabs and
Muslims are targeted for increased surveillance and subjected to illegal
deportation proceedings.[3] Kaplan emphasizes our "obligation to study and
critique the meanings of America in their multiple dimensions, to understand the enormous power wielded in its name, its ideological and affective force, as well as its sources for resistance to empire."[4]

In the issue of *American Quarterly* in which Kaplan's address appears,
the responses to Kaplan by two scholars—Limón and Paul Giles—highlight
the need to think about empire in international and global frameworks.
Giles writes: "Rather than specifically indicting the Bush administration
for the state of American empire, then, a longer perspective might suggest that this state of conflict is an inevitable product of the fraught political relationship between the declining hegemony of United States and the
emerging pressures of what Wallerstein calls the 'world-system.'"[5] World
systems analysis complicates the centrality of the United States since it
examines the historical creation of international economies that produce
and manage centers and peripheries. However problematic Wallerstein's
proposal, Giles's suggestion to historicize the emergence of American empire is valuable. To Limón, General Ricardo Sanchez's role as military general in a foreign country where America is currently exercising its global
power deserves a "translation" of Kaplan's dissent about American empire,
which she articulates in "somewhat abstract terms."[6] How General Sanchez's experience as a Mexican American—growing up as part of a family
raised by a single mother in the border town of Rio Grande City, and getting an education and pursuing a career in the U.S. military—informs his
role in the Iraq war and his perspectives on the ambivalent nature of the
war underscores, to Limón, the need to translate empire. That is, Limón
argues that we must avoid insisting on the United States as the only new
avatar of empire in a global age because "when translated into local specificities, the very ideas of U.S. empire, U.S. violence, and U.S. minorities as
well as the U.S. military *become complicated sites with multivalent social
and moral meanings and outcomes*, frustrating any effort to give them a
singular interpretation."[7]

If we accept Limón's insistence on the need to translate empire, another question emerges: How would our understanding of empire change
if American empire is examined in international frameworks? Unfortunately, it becomes a redundant question in Elaine Tyler May's essay,

"Echoes of the Cold War." May perceptively notes that the heightened de-sire to own guns; view certain ethnic groups with skepticism and, in some instances, hostility; give more power to the government for surveillance and control without also creating mechanisms to prevent abuses of this power; and suppress alternative perspectives articulated in universities and other institutions of learning point to the large-scale social impact of the war on terrorism in the United States. She also notes that it was in declaring the war on terrorism, the Bush administration used contextual frames that referred to the Cold War to respond to September 11. Citing the fear of imminent attacks, using an "us versus them" mentality, and de-claring a state of emergency made the restriction of civil liberties more ac-ceptable to the public. But May finds more useful other precedents for how the United States dealt with terror: the World Trade Center bombings in 1993, which killed five people and injured a thousand; the Oklahoma City bombings in 1995; the Unabomber's plots; and attacks on abortion clin-ics and providers. Internationally, the list is longer: in 1996 a bomb killed 19 U.S. soldiers in Dhahran, Saudi Arabia; in 1998, 224 people were killed when the U.S. embassies in Nairobi, Kenya, and Dar es Salaam, Tanza-nia, were bombed; in 2000, when a bomb blasted into the side of the USS *Cole*, stationed in Arden, Yemen, 17 Americans lost their lives and 39 sus-tained injuries.[8] Although the United States responded militarily to some of these events, May notes that "there was no talk of war." Because the at-tacks on September 11 "were the same sorts of crimes as the earlier attacks, although vastly more efficient and successful," "they, too, might have been handled as the previous attacks had been: through the investigative pro-cesses of the criminal justice system. But the immediate response was to declare war, not to launch a criminal investigation." What May says next is telling: "Declaring war has a number of immediate consequences. It el-evates criminals to the level of a legitimate enemy and recognizes their au-thority as leaders. It provides an opportunity for those who oppose U.S. policies to join armies to fight against us, making them soldiers for a cause rather than accomplices to a crime."[9]

But in May's account, there is not a single reference to the discourse of terror and fear that Osama bin Laden and his followers have circu-lated around the world and turned into a transnational Islamicist move-ment whose primary goal is the destruction of the United States, the an-nihilation of the Jews, and the restoration of an Islamic empire. Even a cursory reading of bin Laden's public pronouncements and letters and Al Qaeda's statements before September 11 shows how adroitly the religion of Islam was used to appeal to young Muslim men to become, to use May's words, "soldiers for a cause." The vision of society that bin Laden and Al Qaeda pledge allegiance to requires their supporters to construct America and the Jews as demonic others whose destruction is authorized by religion. September 11 happened not because some people wanted to engage in crime but because people with a cause, a vision, and a mythology of the good and virtuous life sought to deal a fatal blow to the symbols of global capitalism, American style (the World Trade Center towers), and of the state deemed responsible for waging war against Islam (the Pentagon, the heart of the nation's defense apparatus). To attack the defense departments of Russia, India, China, France, or Chile would not only be a declaration of war, it would be an act of war. To view this as a crime committed by misguided people who can be reined in by police and detective agencies shows a lack of perspective about the relations between social violence and the state.

In modern societies and nation-states, violence is socially acceptable when the state uses, manages, or deploys it. The government, through the institutions of the state, is accountable to the citizens. One of the state's chief responsibilities is to protect its citizens, a notion that is not simply an American idea or a French idea. Should pro-choice groups from other nations and societies have targeted the U.S. Capitol, the White House, the Pentagon, or the Supreme Court during the Bush administration, believing that it was driven by a fundamentalist Christian ideology seeking to spread pro-life values around the world, that would not have been the same as a pro-life zealot targeting U.S. abortion clinics. The difference is not because the clinics are not as important as government buildings, but because the clinics and their medical personnel are not part of the state, which is constitutionally, legally, and ethically obligated to provide for the safety of its citizens. That is why any attempt to destroy the defense departments of Chile, South Africa, or Bangladesh by pro-choice or pro-life groups from France, India, or Japan would more likely invite a military response from the affected states. It should be said that powerful groups within a nation-state can often succeed in winning the consent of citizens to wage war against an enemy if they can be persuaded that the enemy is a threat to the very institutions that the people rely on for safety and protection. However, only a culturalist worldview conflates the symbolic power of the World Trade Center towers with that of the Pentagon: bombing the World Trade Center is quite different from trying to destroy the Pentagon, since the relation of both to the state and the people needs to be seen in multiple, albeit overlapping, perspectives. This is not to deny that close relationships cannot exist between military industries and specific economic policies adopted by the government or big businesses. But the attacks on the Pentagon, not those on the towers, can be more reasonably interpreted as an act against the state and its citizens. May's argument that it was Bush's declaration of war on terrorism that turned bin Laden into a leader is anachronistic: it retroactively gives meaning to a phenomenon that predates September 11 and makes America the birthing ground and the new ground zero for any kind of terrorism linked to the Middle East or Islam. To May, America created bin Laden and, hence, to address the threat of terrorism, we need to critique empire—a move that nicely consolidates America, Americans, and American empire as primary reference points in understanding the significance of the attacks and America's response to them. In this account, there is little need to understand why and how other traditions of resistance and communities of faith can give enormous credence to the fanatical ideas of bin Laden, the Taliban, Al Qaeda, and similar groups.

In a related context, the historian Marilyn B. Young analyzes how "American presidents have routinely drawn on the tropes of World War II to justify their own wars"[10] and goes on to draw a subtle difference between George W. Bush and previous presidents: "And tactics have consequences, certainly to those on the receiving end. There is a difference between the interim bombing of Iraq, *however brutal and futile*, and an all-out war against the country; . . . between the veiled, cautious, unilateralism of the Clinton administration and the naked, crusading version with which we live today."[11] Given the fact that Young's essay appears in *September 11 in History*, an edited volume whose contributors examine whether or not, and to what extent, the event was a "watershed moment," we can appreciate the desire to make distinctions between U.S. foreign policies before and after the attacks of September 11. But the problem with Young's analysis is that her critique implodes with the historical weight of American empire, which she refuses to acknowledge: it is better to engage in "interim bombing[s]" that are "brutal and futile" than to declare all-out war! Perhaps the brutalities of terror and war could be made more palatable if they were "veiled" and "cautious." This, we are given to understand, is what marks the "watershed moment" of September 11. What is even more troubling is that Young makes this comment with regard to how empire may seem to those on the "receiving end." Here, again, a critique of empire can only accommodate a dissent that valorizes earlier forms of empire: we have not so much a dissent from empire as we have the surreptitious management of American empire. In her essay "Explanation and Exoneration, or What We Can Hear," Judith Butler perceptively identifies the problems of such explanations of American empire:

> No doubt there are forms of Left analysis that say simply that the United States has reaped what it has sown. Or they say that the United States has brought this state of events on itself. These are, as closed explanations, simply other ways of asserting U.S. priority, and encoding U.S. omnipotence. These are also explanations that assume that these actions originate in a single subject, that the subject is not what it appears to be, that it is the United States that occupies the site of the subject, and that no other subjects exist or, if they exist, their agency is subordinated to our own. In other words, political paranoia of this kind is just another articulation of U.S. supremacy.[12]

Over the last decade, especially during the Bush administration, a great deal of scholarship critiquing American empire has appeared, but it has not presented a systematic examination of the rhetorical maneuvers, historical methodologies, and conceptual blind spots of dissents offering "closed explanations." By inadequately attending to the symbolic and material powers of states and their apparatuses, May's account tends to exceptionalize the United States, and Young's analysis of September 11 as a watershed moment ends up not so much critiquing empire but managing different forms of empire, conceptualizing one as a transformative moment in American history and roundly condemning another—ironically, at the same time as she privileges one form of empire over another. Such critical tendencies form what Michael Bérubé in *The Left at War* refers to as an "overall intellectual demeanor" that launches criticism from a position that carves the world into regions and societies with clear distinctions between the good and the evil, a world in which non-American peoples and cultures are robbed of all significance, except in relation to their reactive engagement with all things American.[13] He calls this, quite aptly, the tendencies of the "Manichean Left" for three important reasons: the rigidly held view of the media as primarily a propaganda machine; the belief that the masses are so caught up with and within the machinations of the social system that they need to be rescued from false consciousness by enlightened elites like the Left itself; and the notion that culture, politics, and economics are seamlessly connected and often work in tandem, predictably, and uniformly. The first point generates such intense suspicion of the media, in general, and of government agencies, in particular, that the tendency is to search for an out-side space that is untainted and pure in thought, intention, and effect; the second point requires a top-down view of the flow and function of power; and the third point flattens out other important concerns—individuals' age, location, and gender; international relations; state interactions; diversity of thought and tradition; institutional cultures; and many more—to a point where historical context and complexity, people's actual lived experience, becomes invisible. All these undergird a Manichaean view of the world in which the struggle for justice, freedom, democracy, and equality is waged between the forces of good and evil, and the primary purposes of dissent are to convince people of what the right side is, how to be on the right side, and how to affirm their identity by being on the right side.[14] There is another dimension to the manufacturing of dissent that needs to be addressed—namely, the banishing of notions of evil and morality from the vocabulary of dissent in critiques of American empire, and the obscuring of European colonialism in order to resituate the United States as the meta-signifier of global imperialism.

EMPIRE AND POSTMODERN RELATIVISM

In an insightful analysis of David Noble's *Death of a Nation*, Gregory Jay uses the occasion of a book review to paint a picture of the U.S. invasion of Iraq as evidence of the continuing power of American exceptionalism, albeit in forms that co-opt the progressive ideas and practices of minorities and oppressed groups continuing the struggle for recognition, justice, and equality. Although the desire to draw on contemporary events to illumine Noble's arguments is valid, the interpretive maneuvers that Jay performs to achieve his goal need further scrutiny. This is because he imputes motives, desires, and justifications to the powerful Bush administration by drawing heavily on the discourse of exceptionalism. Jay characterizes General Colin Powell's comments that multilateralism should not be used as a ploy to avert war in this way: "Brushing aside concerns from European and Middle Eastern allies, and distancing the U.S. government from possible United Nations advice for more restraint, the general-turned-statesman said bluntly: 'When we feel strongly about something, we will lead. We will act, even if others are not prepared to join us.' And the basis for this John Waynesque bravado? Simply put, America's exceptional command of moral absolutes in its wars against 'evil' empires."[15]

Jay's comments are "decisive assertions," to use Mark Bauerlein's term, because they are "cloaked in a rhetoric of canniness and certainty"; they have a tendency toward "sweeping historical generalizations, or simplistic identifications of x with y."[16] What is striking about Jay's passage—and many similar passages in other works, as I shall soon demonstrate—is its assumption that multilateralism is always, in all contexts, a desirable goal. Jay leaves unexamined the ideological, economic, and political motivations that inflect the "concerns" of Europeans, whose articulations of dissent in the international arena are interpreted as a powerful global movement to contest American empire. Left unexamined is the question of whether these concerns have anything to do with European overseas investments, which were acquired through enduring colonial enterprises. Are the concerns really about European self-protection, or do they reflect a desire to thwart the uncontrolled exercise of power by a belligerent nation? Indeed, in this dissent it seems that Europe had nothing whatsoever to do with the Middle East, except perhaps to play its destined role of taming the great Satan that is America.

Not once does Jay pay attention to the irony of calls for restraint and peace and the need to maintain international stability coming from Europe, mostly Western Europe—a conglomeration of erstwhile colonial powers that plundered and pillaged numerous other nations, uprooting and exterminating millions of people in the name of civilization and modernity, and including countries like England, France, and Russia that even to this day continue to actively maintain neocolonial relations with other nations and communities. It is all the more ironic given *l'affaire foulard*—France's attempt to restrict the use of religious symbols in public schools, an anxiety caused by the view that a growing Muslim population in the country is a destabilizing force.[17] We are just left to wonder why a country that Jay lauds for its "concerns" in trying to restrict the exercise of American power should be so "uneducated" about the ethics of multiculturalism and the ideals of pluralism when it concerns its nonwhite citizens. Indeed, the irony is further compounded by the large-scale violence in France during the fall of 2005, as mostly immigrant youth—protesting economic and cultural marginalization—rioted, resulting in the torching of thousands of vehicles and widespread civic unrest. The point is not that Jay should have predicted this; it would be vacuous to say that he should have. Rather, the point is that in developing a dissent about American empire, all other nations' extensive colonial histories, and their contemporary colonialist tendencies, are easily erased from scrutiny and made irrelevant: dissent about empire is imbued with an unreflective internationalism. In Jay's attempt to situate America in an international context, what emerges is one imperialist nation—the United States. Thus, America retains its manifest destiny of becoming the only object of progressive, liberal critique produced by intellectuals positioned comfortably in First World societies.

When Jay asks why little attention has been given to "what caused nineteen men, many from well-educated 'modern' families in Saudi Arabia, to hijack four planes and fly three of them into the Twin Towers and the Pentagon,"[18] it is clear that in reducing September 11 to the acts of nineteen individuals, the individualistic psychologizing of terror is able to exert its seductive appeal in an analysis of an international event. To be fair, Jay does raise the issue of "American policies in the Middle East," which can be read as an attempt to raise questions that go beyond individual agency. But in critiquing the role of religion in legitimating a narrative of American history that privileges the Puritans of New England, and in linking religion "with racial ideologies of white privilege," Jay undermines religion as a viable analytical category because of its racialized discourses.[19] Since Jay sees religion and racism as seamlessly connected, evil to him becomes an "injunction of Manichean allegories in the narration of national traumas," an injunction that puts Native American and black American experiences in the United States on the same axis as current U.S.-Middle Eastern relations. However, the critical measures used to draw such parallels are not argued for; they are simply posited, with axiomatic certainty. Jay further comments that although Powell "feel[s] comfortable invoking America's sacred right to pronounce timeless judgment on those it would condemn as 'evil' . . . Bush's declaration, 'If this is not evil, then evil has no meaning' exhibits a pathos of religiosity *in the face of postmodern, multicultural complexity*. Against the *purveyors of cultural relativity*, religious pluralism, and postcolonial critiques of the West, Bush reasserts the Calvinistic vision of a world where there is no meaning unless something or someone can be branded as dark or 'evil.'"[20]

What is decried is what is done well—the production of a critical voice that appeals to the ideas and discourses of multiculturalism, postmodernism, and pluralism in order to render invisible the Manichean dynamics that structure the very terms of dissent. Because he stages a Manichean drama in which evil and postmodern complexity are locked in deadly combat, Jay can indulge in an unexamined invocation of cultural relativism resulting in misleading forms of cultural anthropology and political criticism. His appeal to a "postmodern, multicultural complexity" and "cultural relativity" actually raises the stakes since the question becomes, How can we talk about evil in a postmodern world? What is important is not banishing evil in the face of postmodern complexity, but, rather, evil's variegated articulations, manifestations, and groundings in theological, religious, and political discourses. When evil can be "reflexive, creative, adaptive, and cunning . . . in relation to the more technological complex condition of modernity,"[21] inquiring into the "ways in which cultural, institutional, and technological changes have shaped our understanding of what evil is" gains greater urgency.[22]

To the historian John Lewis Gaddis, since "few if any moral standards have deeper roots than the prohibition against taking innocent life in peacetime," the attacks on September 11, which occurred without warning or stated cause and which were calculated to inflict the highest number of civilian casualties possible, can be viewed as evil: "Let there be no mistake: *this was evil*, and no set of grievances real or imagined, however strongly felt or widely held, can excuse it."[23] Along similar lines, Samantha Power characterizes the deaths of more than 16,767 children in the Bosnian war as a grave moral intransigence: "If any event could have prepared a person to *imagine evil*, it should have been this one."[24] Power goes further when she notes that for nations to develop effective international coalitions against genocidal regimes, to "muster the imagination needed to reckon with evil" becomes a necessity.[25] It is noteworthy that while Gaddis grounds his notion of evil not in religious discourse but in discourses of secularism and liberalism, Power strongly encourages the cultivation of a critical sensibility that does not invoke the complexities of postmodern thought and culture to expunge evil from the lexicon of dissent, but one that can "imagine evil" as a distinct worldly possibility that often gets translated into reality.

In contrast, even a cursory reading of the speeches and commentaries of bin Laden and other extremists reveals another dimension of evil that is perversely Islamicized—America is the house of "Jews and criminal Christians," and the God-given mandate to all true believers to fulfill Allah's divine plan of annihilating the "evil" West becomes a global vision, one battle among "the many coming battles of Islam."[26] And some U.S. Christian leaders adopted a similarly binary rhetoric and invoked God's justice on what they commonly referred to as the "evildoers." But such polysemic articulations of evil are unimportant to Jay; instead, postmodernism's exceptional enemy is the Bush administration! Nothing more, nothing less. Whereas Jay posits evil and postmodern complexity as binaries in order to critique empire, Djelal Kadir, in "Defending America against Its Devotees," exceptionalizes the United States. The principle by which this is achieved is belligerence. From this point, Kadir moves to another level of exceptionalism: Americans have to save America because the United States is an exceptionally belligerent empire.[27]

EXCEPTIONALISM IN THE AMERICAS

In questioning the innocence about empire in American exceptionalism, Kadir writes: "And while the frontier wars between Chile and Peru decimated trans-border populations and the genocidal War of Chaco would ravish humanity and cultures on an unprecedented scale, none of the American nations, as it turns out, has been as consistently belligerent and invasive, within and outside the Western hemisphere, as the United States of America."[28] He duly notes other forms of warfare and large-scale oppression, but what he considers important is first and foremost the United States as empire, since it is the only nation among other nations in the Western world that has been "consistently belligerent." But how legitimate is it to use consistent belligerence as a benchmark, and to use the nation-state (in this case, the United States) as the primary category of analysis, to critique empire? Strikingly, the utter decimation on an "unprecedented scale" of certain South American communities and even "genocide," to use Kadir's words, do not matter. What matters is the belligerency of the United States.

In *The Chaco Dispute and the League of Nations*, Margaret La Foy presents perspectives that cannot be accommodated in the dissent from empire that takes the United States as unique in its power and influence and thus worthy of singular focus. Fought between Bolivia and Paraguay over the territory called Chaco Boreal, the Chaco War (1932–35) resulted in more than 130,000 casualties.[29] It was a conflict between the "two most impoverished nations on the South American continent,"[30] which made for "one of the most senseless wars of history."[31] Seven decades earlier, in the War of the Triple Alliance (1864–70) involving the alliance of Argentina, Brazil, and Uruguay against Paraguay, large sections of southern Chaco were ceded to Argentina. The United States, acting as an arbitrator in 1878, seemed— to Bolivia—to favor Paraguay and Argentina in drawing boundary lines, an arbitration referred to as the Hayes Award, after President Rutherford B. Hayes. For the next several years, the disputing parties appealed to the king of Belgium and the president of Argentina for additional arbitration.[32] The War of the Pacific (1879–83) involved territorial disputes among Bolivia, Chile, and Peru, which continued into the 1920s and ended when U.S.

President Herbert Hoover's arbitration in 1929 gave Arica to Chile, Tacna to Peru, and rights of access to the ports to Bolivia but left it effectively landlocked.[33] This increased Bolivia's desire to take control of the Chaco Boreal. There is no doubt that the United States was viewed as a powerful state with immense influence because only three decades earlier, it had begun an expansionist program by successfully annexing Hawaii, the Philippines, Guam, and Puerto Rico.

In *Politics of the Chaco Peace Conference*, Leslie B. Rout Jr. notes that the role of Standard Oil of New Jersey has also been proffered as a main factor in precipitating the conflict. The *Report of the Chaco Commission* to the League of Nations refers to the Chaco Boreal as an "oil-bearing zone," in which Standard Oil Company had begun operations. In 1922 the company had finalized contracts with Bolivia to extract oil, and between 1930 and 1932, it had produced close to 6,000 tons of oil each year. During this period, after Argentina refused Standard Oil's requests for passage across the Chaco to Argentine ports and increased taxes on oil exports from Bolivia, the company started to move its infrastructure outside Bolivia, as noted in the *Report of the Chaco Commission*. The Bolivian government demanded that the company pay taxes on oil it had shipped a few years earlier, and the dispute over back taxes resulted in a stalemate. In 1934, U.S. Senator Huey Long of Louisiana accused Standard Oil of fostering Bolivian aggression in the region, which complicated the U.S. government's attempts to broker peace and gave further credence to Latin American nationalistic charges of American imperialism.

However, reducing the Chaco War to a zero-sum calculation, in which oil companies plus the U.S. government equals war, obscures the nature and scope of their involvement in this dispute. Uruguay, Peru, Chile, and Argentina had complicated relations with Bolivia and Paraguay, as each state tempered its relations with the protagonists in order to balance competing claims of territory, resources, and access to ports.[35] It does not mean that all states interacted with each other on terms of equal power and with common interests. Far from it. What matters is that each war, accord, treaty, and conflict involving nation-states cannot be interpreted simplistically as the result of the actions and desires of the United States and American exceptionalism. State interests and rivalries involving the Grand Chaco region were the legacy of past empires and independence movements, and of nationalism's tendency to selectively imbue events and acts of violence and sacrifice with national significance. As Brian McCormack notes, numerous Native American tribes in the region whose territories cut across several countries had to submit to Bolivia. This 1934 report, issued a year before the war ended, notes that "at present, production appears to have stopped, these deposits being retained as a kind of reserve, which now seems to be attracting the special attention of the Governments concerned."[34] According to Rout, in 1921 Standard Oil had obtained concessions from Bolivia to explore for oil in the region, in 1922 the company had finalized contracts with Bolivia to extract oil, and between 1930 and 1932, it had produced close to 6,000 tons of oil each year. During this decade, after Argentina refused Standard Oil's requests for passage across the Chaco to Argentine ports and increased taxes on oil exports from Bolivia, the company started to move its infrastructure outside Bolivia, as noted in the *Report of the Chaco Commission*. The Bolivian government demanded that the company pay taxes on oil it had shipped a few years earlier, and the dispute over back taxes resulted in a stalemate. In 1934 U.S. Senator Huey Long of Louisiana accused Standard Oil of fostering Bolivian aggression in the region, which complicated the U.S. government's attempts to broker peace and gave further credence to Latin American nationalistic charges of American imperialism.

However, reducing the Chaco War to nothing but a zero-sum calculation, in which oil companies plus the U.S. government equals war, obscures the nature and scope of their involvement in this dispute. Uruguay, Peru, Chile, and Argentina had complicated relations with Bolivia and Paraguay, as each state tempered its relations with the protagonists in order to balance competing claims of territory, resources, and access to ports.[35] It does not mean that all states interacted with each other on terms of equal power and with common interests. Far from it. What matters is that each war, accord, treaty, and conflict involving nation-states cannot be interpreted simplistically as the result of the actions and desires of the United States and American exceptionalism. State interests and rivalries involving the Grand Chaco region were the legacy of past empires and independence movements, and of nationalism's tendency to selectively imbue events and acts of violence and sacrifice with national significance. As Brian McCormack notes, numerous Native American tribes in the region whose territories cut across several countries had to submit to Bolivian and Paraguayan national sovereignty rather than having tribal sovereignty, and had to participate in wars to strengthen the nations where their members lived. Viewing internationalization solely as part of interstate relations can occlude the ideological work performed by the nation to forcefully assimilate indigenous populations, whose notions of tribal sovereignty often conflict with those of the nation-state.[36] Senor Alvarez del Vayo, chairman of the League of Nations Commission of Enquiry into the Chaco Dispute, puts it succinctly: "The Bolivian Indians are asked to die for a State that has sadly neglected them."[37] In Bolivia, the Indians had a strong sense of tribal cultural identity rooted in land and agricultural practices; although they were the largest group in the Bolivian army, their attachment to the nation was very tenuous as a result of its long history of indifference toward them.[38] Similarly, William R. Garner says that "the mass of the Indians had negligible interest in an area so removed from the isolated highlands; and, in spite of the propaganda emanating from La Paz, there was little enthusiasm generated for a Bolivian Chaco."[39]

The Indians in Paraguay were more nationalistic and more likely to support war to protect the nation's interests. "This distinction," notes Garner, "between the extent of national consciousness of the Bolivians and the Paraguayans compensated to a great degree for the military disparity existing between them during the 1930s."[40] In light of the fact that more than 130,000 people died in the Chaco War, most of them Indian peasants and farmers, the ability of governments (both countries had historically been ruled by brutal *caudillos*) and elite groups in Bolivia and Paraguay to adroitly manipulate public sentiment cannot be explained away by any dissent from American empire that—with an opprobrium mingled with fascination—views the United States as the incarnation of imperialism.

This interhemispheric context is further complicated by the transcontinental relations linking different American states to European empires. Powers such as Germany, Spain, Belgium, and Britain also exerted influence, both directly and obliquely. For example, General Hans Kundt from Germany served as chief of the Bolivian general staff for several years between 1911 and 1930.[41] He held the post in 1911, returned to and fought for Germany in World War I, went back to Bolivia to assume various senior military posts, became a Bolivian citizen in 1922, and—although exiled from the country for his supposed participation in a coup in 1930—was recalled by President Daniel Salamanca to assume position of general in chief of the Field Army on the eve of the Chaco War.[42] Later, the Council of the League of Nations played an active role in setting up meetings between the antagonists, but it had to negotiate around the Monroe Doctrine—which, in this context, was about not undermining the American republics to resolve the issue. In the years leading up to the war, a commission of nineteen American nation-states had organized a conference in the United States to address the conflict, but Argentina, Brazil, Peru, and Chile (countries that had some stake in the outcome) had tempestuous relations with Bolivia and Paraguay. Often, these countries' representatives would be opposed by the contending parties or would refuse to participate in negotiations, invoking the principle of noninterference. The League of Nations also set up a special Council Committee of Three (the Irish Free State, Spain, and Guatemala) to investigate the conflict, and issued an embargo on providing arms to any of the disputants. After years of open hostilities, the combined efforts of Argentina, Brazil, Chile, Peru, Uruguay, and the United States in 1935 led to the acceptance by Bolivia and Paraguay of the Protocol of 1935, which decreased open warfare; in 1938 the two countries signed the Treaty of Peace, Friendship, and Boundaries.[43]

Even such a cursory account of the Chaco War clearly shows that to acknowledge it as "genocide" and then shift the focus, as Kadir does, to the United States as empire because it is ostensibly the most belligerent state of all obscures the complex interplay of several American nation-states, the League of Nations, and other inter-American alliances in negotiating access to ports, control over potentially oil-rich land, and trade routes to the oceans. It is in the dynamic interaction among them that we will best be able to examine how international relations among states are formed, broken, and repaired; how nationalist zeal can undermine peace negotiations; and how empires and nation-states, including those with imperial ambitions, engage with each other.

For Paraguayans and Bolivians, it is not enough to develop a sophisticated understanding of American empire in order to grapple with the forces of history, given that thousands of people in both countries were killed in a brutal war. It is not enough to lament the ideology of American exceptionalism. We need to ask if we are willfully blinding ourselves to the "decimation" and "genocide" practiced by numerous communities and nations in the world. Does every conceivable atrocity, genocidal regime, or oppressive nation have to become Americanized for us to take them seriously? This is, indeed, the world according to America, world history according to American history, and planetary consciousness according to the feverish deliberations of scholars unable to imagine anything that does not correspond to what they consider to be real, just, and democratic, or nasty, brutish, and short.

How relevant would such dissents from empire be to the peoples of Bolivia and Paraguay who suffered brutal oppression, or to those who bear the scars of genocidal legacies? What would it mean for such peoples to develop international perspectives? How would they conceive of the turn toward the global and the transnational in the Americas? These important questions cannot even be conceptualized if we continue to treat the historical experience of American empire as a form of history that is unique, lacking all traces of other histories, and absolutely pure in every manifestation or exercise of its imperial desire.

GLOBAL DISSENT AND AMERICAN EMPIRE

In *Power Politics*, Arundhati Roy extends her critique of American empire in a transnational frame when she writes that Osama bin Laden is "America's family secret. *He is the American President's dark doppelganger.*"[44] In equating bin Laden with Bush, and in making their rhetoric equivalent, Roy willfully avoids the labor of historical inquiry and indulges in using the literary device of twinning ideas and personalities to excise the complexities of historical processes. She does so in order to make a circular argument, in which global terror and fear are caused by America because September 11 is nothing but the return of the repressed, the "ghosts of the victims of America's old wars."[45] Roy's attempt at a global analysis of terror begins with America and ends with America.

Like Roy, the sociologist Michael Mann lets rhetorical indulgences mar a suggestive and thoughtful analysis of Bush's foreign policies when he writes, in *Incoherent Empire*, that for two years after September 11, "bin Laden and Bush were to dance their provocative *pas de deux* together, each radicalizing and mobilizing the forces of the other."[46] To Roy and Mann, the peoples of the world are mere players who have only pitiful entrances and exits in a global drama for which the United States writes the script, plots the intrigues, creates the settings, controls the characters, and even issues the final curtain call.

In their introduction to *Anti-Americanism*, Andrew Ross and Kristin Ross distinguish between anti-Americanism from above and from below. To the European intelligentsia of the late eighteenth century, America's attempt to realize Enlightenment ideals in an idealized nation-state signaled a rejection of Europe. Consequently, the emergence of a pervasive critical attitude toward America coalesced into "Americaphobia" that became a "habitual attitude" among certain classes.[47] This, to Ross and Ross, is "anti-Americanism from above" in that it was the privileged and moneyed elite, the educated and powerful classes, that articulated such anti-American sentiment. In contrast, anti-Americanism from below "took root in organic responses to the brutal record of native genocide and plantation slavery and was nurtured by opposition to the territorial expansion that sparked the Mexican-American War (1846–48)."[48] Ostensibly, "organic" implies the non-elite classes, the grass-roots popular movements against U.S. imperial policy.

Anti-Americanism from above and from below are discourses that emerged simultaneously with the new American nation, and in this sense "anti-Americanism is as old as political modernity and could be said to be one of its founding discourses."[49] However, this promising beginning of an explanation for the historical emergence of anti-Americanism becomes a single-minded insistence on narrating the imperial ventures of the new American nation—the Monroe Doctrine, the Mexican-American War, the Spanish-American War, World Wars I and II, the wars in East Asia, and now those in the Middle East. As it moves seamlessly from regional to national to international and global domination, American empire remains the central focus of critique. What Ross and Ross say about September 11 is worth quoting in full:

> The launching of the so-called war on terror in 2001 (this time around, "a war without end") confirmed that it had taken little more than a decade since the collapse of the Communist menace for Washington hawks *to cultivate an enemy fully adequate to their ambitions.* Although the Bush administration has pursued unilateralism in policy making from its first day in office, the events of September 11 presented themselves almost as a tailor-made opportunity to justify the new policy of going it alone.[50]

What happened on September 11 is nothing but America's handiwork—it was busy "cultivating" an enemy, manufacturing a monstrous "enemy" so that it could launch a full-scale assault on the international order. Not a word about the rest of the world; not a word about Islam, Hinduism, or, indeed, any non-Western nations, peoples, communities, cultures, ideas, or traditions. For a book seeking to provide a "more historically informed range of debate" on anti-Americanism,[51] the scope of history is severely restricted, to the United States alone. What others think, say, act, and do about America matters little to this critique of American empire.

Similarly, David Harvey's dissent about empire in *The New Imperialism* cannot resist positioning America at the center of the global world. He distinguishes between territorial imperialism—which he defines as the intent to gain control of a territory and use its resources for social, political, and economic purposes—and "capitalist imperialism"—or the drive to accumulate and manage capital through a process of deterritorialization in time and space.[52] Instead of taking for granted the correspondences between these imperialisms, Harvey makes a case for conceptualizing them in their overlapping dimensions. However, he betrays his inability, and perhaps his refusal, to disentangle himself from the United States in the striking picture by Brooks Kraft of Corbis on the front jacket, which shows President Bush walking back into the Oval Office from the East Room after a news conference. With its framing of the president—his back to the camera, his entire body visible, walking alone on a long carpet of brilliant red that leads to the inner chambers of the White House—the image can signal only one nation: the United States.[53] For all of his insistence on "divin[ing] some of the deeper currents in the making of the world's historical geography that might shed some light on why we have arrived at such a dangerous and difficult conjuncture," and on how the logics of territory and capitalism "intertwine in complex and sometimes contradictory ways . . . and frequently tug against each other, sometimes to the point of outright antagonism,"[54] the only thing that functions as the meta-symbol—the grand, overarching narrative and sign—for globalization is the United States as America, an America that is the apotheosis of modernity and the Enlightenment in all its spectacular singularity.

The dissents of May, Young, Ross and Ross, and Harvey end up Americanizing world history to a point where pivotal events and processes in the world are viewed primarily as responses to the United States. This is a fundamentally America-centric understanding of complex global processes and interconnected social and cultural formations.

CULTIVATING AN IMPERIAL CIVIC ETHOS

A similar orientation to world history and empire is evident in Emmanuel Todd's *After the Empire.* But unlike the authors discussed above, Todd situates his critique of America within a broader trans-Atlantic and Eurasian frame. In both revising and complementing Francis Fukuyama's thesis that the global spread of liberal democracy signals the end of history, and Samuel Huntington's focus on the ideological nature of current international antagonisms that emerge along the fault lines of culture and religion, Todd argues that the spread of mass literacy and the significant drop in birth rates in developing countries, and the growing inability of the United States to negotiate the displacement of the ethic of self-reliance with the ethic of global economic interdependence characterize America's decline as a global empire.[55]

At first glance, Todd's analysis, which is peppered with statistics and charts, offers a refreshing perspective that does not get bogged down in the story of an intractable clash of civilizations. His arguments about Franco-German solidarity, a diplomatically assertive Russia, and an increase in Japanese interest in Asian and European markets point to the waning of the traditional alliance between the United States, Western Europe, and Japan—a change that, he emphasizes, has led the United States to make a "show of empire by choosing to purse military and diplomatic actions among a series of puny powers dubbed for dramatic effect 'axis of evil' and more generally the Arab world—the point of intersection of these two axes, evil and Arab—being Iraq."[56]

To Todd, what denotes a marked shift in post-1989 world politics is America's increasing confusion about its dependence on other nations and economies and its bellicosity in dealing with that confusion, especially after an unprecedented tenure as the world's only superpower. Detailed and persuasively argued, Todd's *After the Empire* avoids the now-familiar choruses of lament and condemnation so pervasive in discourses of empire. However, other points in Todd's critiques of America are troubling. For example, even while contesting Fukuyama's and Huntington's theses, Todd's critiques nonetheless borrow heavily from them. Where and why such borrowings take place in Todd, and how they relate to the perplexing question of grappling with modernity in a global era, should be examined.

Todd writes: "Higher literacy and lower birth rates, two universal phenomena, make possible the universalization of democracy."[57] Although this is quite a departure from his focus on cultural and ideological conflict, Todd's rationale for making this claim deserves scrutiny because, as he later observes, "it is easy to see that these features of human progress are linked to a rise in 'individualism' and the affirmation of the individual within the political sphere."[58] In one stroke, by linking literacy to a decline in birth rates and the rise of an individualist ethos, which together precipitate the spread of democracy across the world, Todd affirms Fukuyama's and Huntington's premises probably more than he would care to admit. Fukuyama's Hegelian individual—"human consciousness thinking about itself and finally becoming self-conscious"[59]—translates into Todd's Third World subject, who, through literacy, realizes her individualism in the "process of emancipating [herself] through contraception,"[60] emerging as a rational subject able to affirm her individualism in the realm of politics.

But what exactly does literacy imply? Is the entire non-Western world mired in illiteracy? What difference does it make to be literate in an indigenous language and illiterate in a global language like English? What cultural, religious, and social practices authorize and permit what kinds of literacies, and what forms of democracies? Without attending to these issues, Todd's "literacy" functions as a universal signifier for the emancipation of the non-West and its entry into the hallowed realm of democracy. More troubling is his delimiting of woman as a separate species, abstracted from history, culture, and the world itself, so that woman can become the new global barometer to calibrate the entry of the non-West into democracy. The ideological force in such a move is of a piece with colonialism and nationalism's harnessing of woman as the primary agent for justifying and measuring the exercise of power and the cultural purity of revolutions, respectively. Furthermore, in appealing to Aristotle, Condorcet, and Tocqueville to frame his argument, Todd is firmly embedded within a European tradition of liberal philosophy and democracy that is extended, proleptically, by Fukuyama, whose final trajectory of universal history begins at the eighteenth century and ends with the demise of the Cold War era.[61]

Even as he seeks to counter Huntington's tendency to view civilizations as closed entities that operate according to inner drives and pressures, Todd takes up a Huntingtonian position when he writes: "'Universal terrorism' is absurd from the standpoint of the Muslim world, which will eventually work its way through its transitional crisis *without outside intervention.*"[62] He even notes that "throughout the world Islam is going through its crisis of modernization, and there is no way to disguise the disruptive aspects of this transition,"[63] a passage that could have been written by Huntington himself. Although Todd says this to explain the West's active attempts to foster democracy in the non-West, when he argues that the "Muslim world" will "eventually" emerge into modernity all by itself, he glosses over the profound upheavals that have characterized East-West encounters over hundreds of years. Such an idea reaffirms Huntington's point that civilizations by and large operate according to inner dynamics that have little to do with encounters between civilizations. Indeed, if the term "civilization" or "Muslim world" itself becomes fraught with loaded meanings, even Todd subscribes to Huntington's idea, but in the different context of Euro-American differences: "Above all, one must speak of the deepest and oldest divergence of the American and European worldviews that derives from the very means by which their respective societies were formed, a level of analysis where it is hardly possible to distinguish customs from economy and thus *it is best to speak of different 'civilizations.'*"[64]

How this differs from Huntington's differentiation among Western, Latin American, Arab, Indian, Chinese, and Japanese civilizations is hard to understand,[65] perhaps because there *is* little difference in the way Todd and Huntington define and use "civilization" to divide the world. Moreover, even as he argues for noninterventionist policies, Todd subscribes to a chronology that is distinctly Euro-American because he views the "transitional crisis" in the "Muslim world" as stages in the evolutionary history of the West that are already finished. Indeed, if the road to democracy in the West is littered with bloody battles, revolutions, violent upheavals, and tense transformations, what else can we expect in the non-West, which is replaying a Euro-American past? But they can make the transition themselves, just as we did. Or so Todd would have us believe.

GENOCIDE: AMERICANIZING THE SORROWS OF THE WORLD

With *"A Problem from Hell,"* Samantha Power's prize-winning critique of genocide and the United States, we move to a different register of dissent altogether. Her deft interlacing of the United States as America with America as global modernity is our central concern because, as I shall soon demonstrate, the historical models she uses to examine the phenomenon of genocide from a U.S. perspective do not so much lead to a false understanding of genocide as they tend to consolidate a world system into a single, international division of intellectual and cultural labor. In this system, the peripheries of the world generate raw material that is processed through centralized Western systems and institutions in order to attain the status of knowledge—all of which secures the superpower status of the United States as America, transforms American national history into global history, and implicitly justifies American imperialism. But first, a few words about what Anthony Giddens identifies as the "consequences of modernity,"[66] to better delineate the problematic conceptual moves that structure Power's dissent about America.

Giddens points to "time-space distanciation," the "disembedding of social systems," and the formation of systems of trust, symbolism, and expertise whose intense functioning, although acutely discontinuous, leads to more radical forms of modernity. This is an argument that views current forms of globalization as engendered by the perfecting, if you will, of modernity, or of modernity's realizing its potential. "Time-space distanciation" refers to the "conditions under which time and space are organized so as to connect presence and absence."[67] The "'lifting out' of social relations from local contexts of interaction and their restructuring across in-

definite spans of time-space" foreground the "disembedding of social systems."[68] The formation of expert systems points to the highly integrated
forms of organizing technical and professional expertise and knowledge
to order daily life, which becomes an elemental part of modernity's "reflexivity" to the extent that the process of reflection itself reproduces and
organizes modernity's institutions.[69] To Giddens, contemporary shifts in
national and international affairs underscore the uneven nature of "disembedding" that seriously challenges traditional and national organizations of space and time. Power's U.S.-based account of twentieth-century
genocide disembeds genocide from local contexts, but where Giddens locates a reordering of relations across "*indefinite* spans of time-space,"[70]
Power reorders a definite, nationalistic time-space—that is, she Americanizes the transnational and validates a modern expert system as manifest in
American democratic institutions.

In presenting a riveting account of governments and peoples that have
engaged in genocide over the last century, and in critiquing the role or noninvolvement of the United States in international affairs, *"A Problem From
Hell"* offers a dissent about America that faults it for its perceived failures,
in some instances, and delayed responses, in others, to intervene internationally to prevent genocide or rein in its perpetrators. Power focuses on
the 1915 massacres of Armenians by the Turks; the impact of the Holocaust
in the West after World War II; the defeat of the U.S.-supported Lon Nol
government in Cambodia and the fall of Phnom Penh to the Khmer Rouge
in 1975, which resulted in the deaths of nearly two million Cambodians,
out of a population of seven million; Saddam Hussein's program of exterminating the Kurds, including using chemical weapons against them, between 1987 and 1991; the "ethnic cleansing" of Muslims and Croats by the
Serbs in Bosnia in the early 1990s and the Muslims of Srebrenica in 1995,
together with the displacement of Kosovo Albanians in the late 1990s; and,
in 1994, the launching of the "fastest, most efficient killing spree of the
twentieth century," as Power puts it, by the Hutus against the Tutsis in
Rwanda, resulting in the death of 800,000 people in just 100 days.[71]

Although Power critiques several U.S. administrations and Congress
for waiting almost four decades before finally passing the Genocide Convention Implementation Act, also called the Proxmire Act, and the belated
setting up of the UN War Crimes Tribunal in 1993, she recognizes the politicized aspects of drafting and implementing foreign policies. This is why
her narrative weaving of Raphael Lemkin's life—his coining of the term
"genocide" in the 1940s; his dogged pursuit of journalists, editors, sen-
ators, and various other officials to recognize its legitimacy; and his ef-

forts to persuade the United Nations to form committees of inquiry into cases of genocide, adopt a charter and create a policy concerning genocide, and have that charter ratified by its members states—into the history of genocide in the twentieth century makes a powerful argument in favor of America's proactive role in the world. But several problems emerge here: the writing of genocide's history primarily in terms of U.S. responses or lack of responses to atrocities in different parts of the world; and the imbrication of discourses of modernity, universalism, and American exceptionalism as validation of dissent about America.

Let's focus on genocide's history first. The book's subtitle is *America and the Age of Genocide*, which forthrightly admits that the book is U.S.-centric. Even its last line appeals not to the peoples of the world but to Americans. However, we would clearly be hard-pressed to find disquisitions on genocide with titles like *Japan and a Century of Genocide, France and the Age of Genocide, Mexico and the Century of Genocide*, and so on. Why? Because there is more to Power's title than a simple clarification of perspective. Since its founding, America has taken a Janus-faced view of the universal significance of its national development, asking in what way a new society should be formed that could effect a fundamental break with the past and announce to the world its task of leading the way into a future, where the ideals of democracy, individual rights, constitutionalism, independence of judiciary, and rule of law would manifest themselves in human institutions and behavior? Right from its inception, this nation has had its eyes on itself and the rest of the world, and in constantly remaking itself, it has moved its gaze between its center, where it ratifies its universalist ideals, and its periphery, where it justifies its right to conquer other peoples and annex territories.

The terms it has used are familiar—"city on a hill," "promised land," "errand into the wilderness," "manifest destiny," and so on—and the discourses they have engendered have solidified into an ideology of exceptionalism. Although critiques of exceptionalism, especially over the last decade, have pungently articulated an acute distrust of the use of the nation-state to represent a national people who embody a coherent national culture whose influence could be sociologically ascertained within a delimited territory, and have made good arguments for recognizing the colonialist ethos and imperialist interests that have informed the nation's history, a crucial problem has continued to plague us. We can speak of the United States as "America" only if we actively suppress the hemispheric dimensions of "America," which have longer, more torturous histories than the specific history of the United States. By the same token, we inevitably end up tracing U.S. history as American history when we historicize "America" in hemispheric terms because for the last 150 years, it is the United States as America, rather than Chile as America or Canada as America, that has emerged as a powerful player in both hemispheric and global affairs. But don't my comments lend further credence to Power's writing about the history of genocide from a U.S. perspective, as U.S. history is thoroughly entwined with world history? Not quite.

My point is not just that Power privileges U.S. perspectives on genocide history; rather, it is that in her entire project, "America" is localized as a nation-state even while, simultaneously and uncritically, the particularizing of America as the United States hinges centrally on the idea that the United States as America is the number one signifier of modernity. To understand how this works, let's foreground her main argument—genocides have taken place in the twentieth century; the United Nations did something about them as early as 1950; and the United States, for numerous reasons argued for and well documented in the book, ratified the UN charter belatedly and, even after having done so, demonstrated an unwillingness to enforce international law, with the result that genocide is a terrible reality even at the end of the twentieth century. Power focuses on the "response of American policymakers and citizens" because, among other things, the United States has "a tremendous capacity to curb genocide," it is "steeped in a new culture of Holocaust awareness," and it has often made public commitments to prevent genocide.[72] I have already pointed out that Power offers a detailed account of the complicated dynamics structuring Euro-American and America-as-super-power global geopolitics; competing national and international interests; and the psychological and social dispositions of bureaucrats, writers, activists, editors, power brokers, policymakers, scholars, journalists, business owners, military planners, and defense strategists who have struggled with the reality of genocide over the last 100 years. However, the issue is not only moral. It is conceptual, although often the conceptual raises the question of the moral.

Genocide is not easy to identify before it happens, while it is happening, or, arguably, after it has happened. As Bernard-Henri Lévy pointedly notes, developing a notion of genocide entails becoming immersed in "an intellectual and political task."[73] To arrive at an understanding of genocide, especially according to Power, several factors have to coalesce; several peoples' voices together need to establish a reasonable framework in which reports about genocide could be verified as violence perpetrated on targeted groups, with the deliberate intent to annihilate them and their culture. Often, initial reports come from the victims themselves, as they flee to avoid being targeted, have survived mass murders, or have heard from trusted sources like friends, relatives, and acquaintances about genocide. The victims then speak and write to politicians, media pundits, social service workers, humanitarian agencies, reporters on assignment—or, with today's advanced communications technology, post reports and images online. To verify and authenticate reports about genocide, it becomes imperative to be fully immersed in modernity's project—how to deal with presence and absence, since the time of genocide is not coincident with the nation's history, and the space of genocide lies beyond the territorial purview of the state.

As the process of collecting and collating reports about genocide and verifying and transmitting information across national borders is set in motion, *"A Problem from Hell"* begins conflating the United States as America with modernity as America. For a variety of disparate reports from numerous sources to come to the attention of those in power, in order to convince governments and public opinion to oppose genocide, all these pieces of information have to become "knowledge." For example, when the Khmer Rouge cloaked itself in a secrecy that was hard to penetrate—given its adroit manipulation of information and elimination of crucial social players like intellectuals, artists, and activists, which allowed its leaders to embark on murderous rampages for four years after they gained power in 1975—the process of collecting, deciphering, verifying, and documenting information about its genocidal activities had to undergo a transformation from "raw, unconfirmed data to the status of knowledge."[74]

This is where we get to the central problem: the rest of the world is where raw data emerge, and that information is transformed into "knowledge" only in the United States, specifically Congress and other institutions and bureaucracies. It is not enough for the United Nations to pass international laws against genocide. What is at stake is what the United States does with genocide. Such a singular focus on the United States is not simply to take a U.S. perspective about genocide. Instead, the United States is important because it is in "America" that undeveloped, hazy, unprocessed information is able to attain the legitimacy of "knowledge" and by extension—in keeping with Power's criticism of the United States for failing to adhere to its ideals—generate moral outrage and governmental intervention. The United States as America is now able to stand in for modernity as well—the discursive space and physical site of reason, knowledge, and the Enlightenment. From this point on, it is but a small step for humankind to address the issue of genocide by historicizing it through the prism of U.S. history.

Power's gripping account of genocide also locates us firmly in the heart of American modernity—the workings of its institutions, its legal discourses, notions of democracy, politics, freedom, and the list goes on. America is able to use its exceptional power as the beacon for the rest of the world by legitimizing its localized history as already imbued with universal angst. Because the United States, more than any other country, has a "tremendous capacity to curb genocide"[75]—although it has often dithered about its commitment to prevent or stem genocide—"when innocent life is being taken on such a scale and the United States has the power to stop the killing at reasonable risk," Power proclaims that it "has a duty to act."[76] But because it has often failed to act, "it is thus no coincidence that genocide rages on."[77] Although genocide was previously located in the world, it has now become part of America's world, and in becoming Americanized, the future of genocide—or, rather, world history itself—depends on America's capability, willingness, and moral courage. Tellingly, what began as an inquiry into U.S. responses to genocide has blossomed into a universal concern with profoundly global repercussions—America is made to carry the burden of the world, and perhaps Americans, by taking genocide seriously, are invited to invest emotionally in the space of global modernity.

Genocide now has an American name, an American moral, an American history. When an appeal is made to Americans in such a context, they are invited to imagine themselves simultaneously in two times at once—an exceptional time in the nation's history, and a universal time in world history. Americans are citizens of the United States and also citizens of the world. In subsuming national history into universal history, *A Problem from Hell* constructs a "house of mirrors"[78] that reflects the anguish of victims of genocide, provided that these peoples' plight is transformed into modern knowledge as it travels an international circuit and reaches American shores, and that their narratives register on American imaginations, tug at American hearts.

Although Power makes a persuasive case for American intervention, a few major premises on which her argument is based are taken as givens, foundational ideas needing no examination, from which to begin a U.S.-oriented historicizing of genocide. Those premises include the following ideas: America is a superpower; it has the capability to prevent genocide; therefore, by creating a moral climate in which narrow national interest can be made subservient to the larger issues of human suffering, America can exercise its awesome power to enforce international law. Only if we accept these premises will the entire argument about America and genocide be convincing, because that is the stated purpose of Power's inquiry into genocide. In other words, what is left unarticulated but implied is the fact of empire, American empire. What makes America a superpower has less to do with global goodwill toward Americans than it does with U.S. military dominance in the world. Currently, the United States has "access to bases" in forty countries, and in a given year its military "will operate in 170 or more countries around the world."[79] It is precisely this that Power takes for granted when she uses America's "capacity to curb genocide" as her starting premise. An appeal for humanitarian intervention predicated on an acknowledged "capacity" to prevent genocide would have a hollow ring were America not a superpower, a fact that Power uses as the basis for an ethics of responsibility. The reality of empire legitimizes American intervention: "Because America's 'vital national interests' were not considered imperiled by mere genocide, senior U.S. officials did not give genocide the moral attention it warranted. Instead of undertaking steps along a continuum of intervention—from condemning the perpetrators or cutting off U.S. aid to *bombing or rallying a multinational invasion force*—U.S. officials tended to trust in negotiation, cling to diplomatic niceties and 'neutrality,' and ship humanitarian aid."[80]

More often than not, to make a case for American intervention is to make a case for war. Power's own account of the history of genocide demonstrates this: it was war that stopped the Nazis; it was war that stopped the Khmer Rouge; it was war that drove Saddam Hussein out of Kuwait; it was war that placed Slobodan Milošević at The Hague. In all probability, it will be war or the threat of war that will stop the next genocide. Hence, it is reasonable to conclude that in the specific context of intervening to prevent or stop genocide, Power argues *for* empire. Why empire? Because one nation's moral vision to prevent genocide is nothing but imperialism in disguise to another nation. From a U.S. perspective, rallying a force and bombing another country to stop genocide may legitimize war, but that is precisely where a deep ambivalence haunts such an appeal for humanitarian intervention—in a global context, humanitarianism is often viewed as the West's desire to impose its values and culture on others, America's desire to fight wars for oil, America's arrogant refusal to respect other nations' sovereignty, or America's internationalist attempts to deny radical cultural, economic, or political differences. In almost every case of genocide that Power discusses, these arguments have been made by those opposing Western or American intervention. At the heart of the argument for moral intervention lies the question of empire—how to justify and monopolize, unilaterally or multilaterally, the use of military power and the application of political and economic force to bring about systemic, structural, institutional, governmental, social, cultural, and political change to prevent, stop, or curtail genocide. Put another way, *"A Problem from Hell"* does not stop at evoking condemnation or national guilt. It places empire at the center of a century of genocide and at the heart of modernity. As Michael Hardt and Antonio Negri note in *Empire*, the "most significant symptom" of the passage to the postmodern global world "is the development of the so-called *right of intervention*. . . . What stands behind this intervention is not just a permanent state of emergency and exception, but a permanent state of emergency and exception justified by *the appeal to essential values of justice*. In other words, the right of the police is legitimated by universal values."[81]

Power's urging Americans to imagine the possibility of evil rests principally on ideas of justice that transcend national, local, tribal, ethnic, racial, and other forms of affiliation. We need to give genocide "the moral attention it warrant[s]," and it is only by cultivating a heightened sense of morality, a sense of horror at the dastardly acts people commit against other people, that the United States can consider "bombing or rallying a multinational invasion force." In the new world order, wars are fought not primarily to protect national interests, but to further universal concerns and sustain global values. At least on this point, Power makes no attempt to call empire by another name: her book textually performs the postmodern empire.

SAVING THE WORLD, AMERICAN STYLE

Like Power's *"A Problem from Hell,"* Djelal Kadir's sharp critique of American empire in his presidential address to the First World Congress of the International American Studies Association—held in Leiden, the Netherlands, in May 2003—appeals to Americans to be more cognizant of the effects of U.S. policies on the world. Kadir offers several insights into globalization's impact on the disciplinary orientations of American studies and the study of America, especially the growing interdependence of the United States and the world. To refrain from making America an object of devotion and turn it instead into a "subject of investigation, scientific scrutiny, and secular criticism" is the challenge facing Americanists.[82] But Kadir, like Power, is too quick to draw parallels between the United States as America and modernity as America when he criticizes the United States for its millennial imperialism, which continues its long tradition of hypocrisy for failing to adhere to its Enlightenment ideals. While urging Americanists to draw distinctions between the "people and the state, between a country and its government, between a nation's myths and its historical reality," and referring to Günter Grass's "The Moral Decline of a Superpower: Preemptive War," Kadir says: "I will do so because Günter Grass's unease is one we cannot help but share as Americanists who dedicate our professional life and intellectual efforts to America, because we consider America a worthy subject and, now, more than ever a *necessary burden we must bear for the sake of both the world and the wellbeing of humanity*, both now in peril, as is every Americanist who might dare interrogate his object of inquiry with any critical scrutiny."[83]

Just as Power invites Americans to invest emotionally in the space of global modernity, Kadir invites Americanists to refashion themselves, their vocation, and their disciplines by Americanizing the world's sorrows and dreams. If indeed the future of humanity and the planet is in jeopardy because of U.S. policies, it becomes the ethical obligation of activists, politicians, scholars, and peace-loving peoples all over the world to desist from any other activity except studying and understanding U.S. history, society, and culture in order to thwart the country's imperial agenda. This dissent produces a state of emergency: to do anything else would be morally unacceptable because the very existence of the planet and "the wellbeing of humanity" are at stake. To Americans, then, the stakes are very high: dissent from empire would mean democratic engagement and saving the human race from extinction at the same time.

Like Power, Kadir makes an argument that legitimizes a worldview in which the rich histories and lives of non-Americans can be safely located in suspended time, a time outside history. Whereas modern colonialism, in variegated ways, sought to marginalize non-Western cultures and histories, dissent from empire in the postmodern world Americanizes global history to the point where history itself cannot be conceived of outside the narrative of America's founding, its growth into an industrial power, and its subsequent rise to global power. John Winthrop's exhortation to his listeners—build a city on a hill, for the eyes of the world are on us—should make perfect sense to all those who dissent from empire because today, as humanity itself is threatened by the United States, it is incumbent on Americans to act responsibly. Not only are the eyes of the world on us, but the weight of the world is on our shoulders. It is this worldview that makes Power remind Americans that it is our "duty to act," and that compels Kadir to encourage Americans to bear "a necessary burden." Such a worldview seamlessly connects U.S. history to international, universal, and planetary history. As each register yields to another, America and Americans find themselves, unwittingly or willingly, playing the role of Captain Steven Hiller (Will Smith) in *Independence Day* or Harry Stamper (Bruce Willis) in *Armageddon*, both of whom eventually save humanity from certain destruction—they act, think, and feel on behalf of all the peoples of the world. All this is for a simple reason: the fate of humanity rests in their hands, making moot any question about whether that fate was created by their nation-state, and rendering inconsequential any understanding of the histories and cultures of non-Americans, whether inside or outside of American empire.

Here again we have the strategy of isolation at work: critiques of American foreign policies, American colonialism, and American empire—which locate America within a global frame—inevitably see America as the center of the universe and the only incarnation of illiberal democracy. Once America is thus positioned, there is no room for any other rhetoric, nationalism, patriotism run amok, alternative political ideology, imperial nations, colonial powers, despotic regimes, tyrannical governments, and fascist ideologies that have little if any sympathy for multiculturalism, pluralism, or democracy. America stands in for everything else. If there is one symbol that can, in all its singularity, embody every conceivable demagogic, antidemocratic and imperialist tendency, that symbol is the United States as America. What is happening here? The whole world is being turned into America. All heterogeneity is being collapsed into a homogeneous and empty time. Amy Kaplan rightly cautions Americanists against "condemning the United States for failing to measure up to its own highest standards" since that "implicitly makes the United States the bearer of universal values."[84] American empire does not gain hegemony or staying power in the world unless other nation-states, communities, elites, and interest groups appropriate, use, and revivify ideas of America and modernity; U.S. power is not exercised in a social vacuum, where nothing exists until America arrives. U.S. power flows out of and across the terrain of American empire as it confronts and interacts with significant power structures that are firmly in place or in a state of disarray or recovery. Indeed, how can we conceive of American empire without also having an understanding of other empires, religious traditions, social perspectives, media and textual representations of life as it is lived in other places, and imaginations wrestling with the complexities of a global world?

For our dissent and our critiques to "resonate and articulate solidarity with the emerging movement for global justice,"[85] as Ashley Dawson and Malini Schueller persuasively argue, we need to rethink the viability of what Daniel O'Hara refers to as the "global point of view": "The global point of view looks at a rapidly modernizing, so-called developing rest of the world outside of Europe and North America and can read into this process of modernization a necessary Westernization, and into this Westernization, it can read in turn an inescapable Americanization. *Modernization, Westernization, and Americanization are the trinity of global capitalism driving the forces of globalization.*"[86]

O'Hara underscores how the turn toward the global in American studies, especially in its critiques of American empire, imposes a critical model—which is also an ideologically determined cartographic grid—onto the rest of the word and posits a direct, unproblematic chain of causal forces linking modernity, the West, and America, which, of course, determine all processes of modernization, Westernization, and Americanization. Once such a model is used or posited as axiomatic, once the world is graphed in this way, it makes perfect sense to discuss any event happening in the remotest part of the world in terms of America and Americanization. This all-encompassing conceptual model renders the entire world knowable as a world outside of the United States only insofar as it can be related to American foreign policy, culture, events, Americans, and so on ad infinitum. This is why Power and Kadir urge Americans to imagine themselves as a people on whom the burden of the world now rests; it is up to Americans to rid the world of genocide and save humanity from itself. The problem is that it is the very critique of empire, coming as it does from a humanistic, secular viewpoint, that positions Americans not only as global citizens but as humanists who occupy the most central position in the world.

For this reason, although most of the writers discussed thus far frequently refer to September 11, their critiques contain almost no carefully thought out arguments that seriously examine the rise of militant Islam in different parts of the world, the noninvolvement of millions of Muslims in the *jihadi* movements whose sole object is the destruction of the United States, and the numerous oppositional movements in the Middle East and elsewhere struggling to create democratic systems of government and desperately trying to avoid the dizzying appeal of militancy and terror preached by people in the name of a "political religion," which Niall Ferguson defines as the "pursuit of worldly goals—for example, the ejection of the United States from Saudi Arabia, or the destruction of the state of Israel—through messianic leaderships and mass indoctrination."[87]

Even as we take up Amy Kaplan's suggestion that we critique the ways in which the American state exercises "enormous power wielded in its [America's] name,"[88] we should make a sustained effort to study the circulation of other meanings of America that are produced, laid claim to, and acted on by people who are not American citizens and who live outside the United States. Put differently, did bin Laden have "enormous power" to create other Americas? Did he draw from other "national and transnational sources"[89] to produce these Americas? Do we need to examine these Americas? If we are to take the route that leads us directly to the United States, the White House, and past U.S. presidents, clearly the answer is no. But when there are other Americas traveling the world and competing with, interweaving, and reevaluating ideas and images of Americas produced by people and their leaders in the United States, then the answer is yes. Absent a sustained examination of these things, our critiques of American empire can end up reinstalling the United States as America as a god worthy of global worship on the altar of dissent.

Are there other ways of thinking about America, of attending to its "multiple dimensions"?[90] I think there are. But to do this we have to make a sustained attempt to address a pervasive problem identified in these dissents—the unexamined conflations and interfaces between the United States as America and America as the master trope of modernity. Rather than driving a neat conceptual wedge between the United States as America and global Americas, in the next chapter I propose an alternative critical model—dwelling in American—that may enable us to avoid these pitfalls by using comparative frames of reference to examine empire, and conceiving of globalization as sets of social, cultural, economic, and political processes in which the policies and aspirations of powerful nation-states are enmeshed with the interests of other nation-states, empires, and communities.

CHAPTER TWO

Dwelling in American

EMPIRE IN GLOBAL CONTEXTS

Whereas critics of American empire, as we saw in the previous chapter, often conflate the United States as America and modernity as America, collapse the national into the international, and do not recognize the agency of non-Americans, in *Reconstructing America*, James Ceaser argues that by differentiating between the United States as a nation-state and America as a symbol of modernity, we can avoid mistaking criticism of modernity for criticism of the United States. This is a promising proposal, but, as I shall soon show, Ceaser's attempt to draw a neat wedge between the two is conceptually problematic. I propose an alternate model—dwelling in American—not to reclaim the real America from the symbolic America, but to examine how they overlap, how their interrelationships create new meanings of America in different parts of the world, and how they require a rethinking of empire in international and global contexts.

Ceaser differentiates between the symbolic and the real America— that is, between America as a trope, sign, and signifier of modernity, and the United States as a geopolitical entity with a specific history of emergence that can be traced to the late eighteenth century. He points out that whereas the United States is a specific sociopolitical entity, discourse about America concerns—to use Felipe Fernández-Armesto's words, the "lost Americas and imaginary Americas," which "multiply in memories and fancies."[1] These Americas, points out Rob Kroes, are a "repertoire of fantasies about America" that includes "those vast areas where America, as a construct, an image, a fantasma, has played a role in the intellectual and cultural lives of people outside its national borders."[2] This "symbolic America" or the "metaphysical America . . . may exist outside of the United

States and involve no actual Americans," says Ceaser, since it "is often used as little more than a front for carrying on a theoretical discussion about modernity and the Englightenment."[3]

Charting the long tradition of discourse about America by sociologists, biologists, politicians, writers, and philosophers that emerged on both sides of the Atlantic, Ceaser contends that this discourse should not be conflated with descriptions of a country but seen as "deductions from the premises of these philosophical propositions."[4] This is why he differentiates between philosophical and historiographical conceptualizations of modernity, on the one hand, and the specific political theories actualized in the societies and institutions established after the American Revolution in the United States, on the other hand. Ceaser traces the popularization, from the mid-eighteenth century to the present, of the "thesis of American degeneracy,"[5] the idea that the physical environment in America was not conducive to fertility and growth, especially of European plants and political traditions. America was about racial discourse, rampant consumerism, rapacious capitalism, technology, unchecked individualism, rootlessness, the primacy of reason and reflection in organizing social life, and the hyperreality of the postmodern present. Propagators and critics of such discourses include Georges Louis Leclerc, the Count de Buffon, the abbé Raynal, William Robertson, the abbé Cornelius de Pauw, Thomas Jefferson, Alexander Hamilton, Friedrich von Schlegel, Georg W. F. Hegel, Arthur de Gobineau, J. C. Nott, George Gliddon, Alexis de Tocqueville, Max Weber, Oswald Spengler, Martin Heidegger, Alexandre Kojève, Leo Strauss, Francis Fukuyama, and Jean Baudrillard.

Ceaser also finds both the postnationalist and transnationalist approaches inadequate for an examination of America as the United States and as modernity because they deemphasize the pervasiveness of America discourse around the world. Since postnationalism entails questioning the legitimacy and viability of the nation in a global world, the impulse is to give voice to those cultures, narratives, and societies marginalized by the nation. This means questioning the nation's claims to organic wholeness. As Ron Robin observes, "the nation is approached as a monolithic power structure that defines and restricts identity and personal agency," which makes the postnationalist look for "alternative, private spaces outside of or hidden from the national framework."[6] In contrast, transnationalists are not quite ready to sing dirges at the nation's funeral and conduct a memorial service where we can reminisce about its glorious or inglorious days. Instead, they resituate the United States in comparative, international frameworks, and develop macrolevel inquiries into trade relations and intercivilizational, cross-cultural commerce and conflicts that have shaped American culture and society.[7] Since these approaches do not explain the disconcerting ways in which different experiences of modernity quickly get tagged with the label "America," thus leading straight back to the "real America," or the United States as a country, Ceaser wishes to make sharp distinctions between the territorially defined, sociopolitical particularity of the United States and the discourse about global modernity.

When Ceaser writes that he "undertook the task of trying to *recapture control of our name*"[8] and "free the real from the symbolic America, thereby liberating a country from the mastery of a metaphor and the tyranny of a trope,"[9] he implies that the United States can control and authorize particular meanings of "America," and that the history of the United States as America has a trajectory quite different from that of symbolic America. But what if we take a different approach, one that does not seek to separate the real from the symbolic but that acknowledges our inability to firmly wrest control of the United States as America and prevent it from becoming hopelessly intertwined with America discourse? This approach, which I am calling "dwelling in American," examines the United States as a nation-state whose exercise of power implicates it in other structures and institutions of power in different parts of the world. Dwelling in American acknowledges the entanglement of American empire with other empires and studies the nature of their interactions and structural forms. By using comparative frameworks to reposition the United States as one among other major actors in the international arena, dwelling in American recognizes non-Americans as peoples with varying degrees of agency and whose worldviews and desires cannot be explained away as responses to American empire. In the rest of this chapter, I provide examples of each of these dimensions of dwelling in American in order to demonstrate its conceptual viability.

ENTANGLED EMPIRES

In "Entangled Histories, Entangled Worlds," the historian Eliga Gould displaces U.S. centrality in the hemisphere by foregrounding the longer history of Spain's imperial expansion in the New World. Rather than treating other empires as epiphenomena, Gould examines the overlapping of imperial interests and antagonisms among numerous social classes as several European powers battled each other and made treaties and compromises in their search for new resources, territories, dominions, and cheap labor.

In 1800 there was only one city in the Americas with a population of over 100,000—Mexico City. Among the fifty biggest cities in the Americas, Spain possessed thirty-seven, while only five could be said to belong to British North America. For colonialism to succeed both inside and outside the borders of the imperial center, the issue of legitimacy is paramount. In 1493 the pope gave all land west of the Azores to Spain in a move to counter the spread of the Portuguese empire. The British sought to differentiate themselves from the Spanish by pursuing a different kind of power, one that was ostensibly less hierarchical and feudal than the Spanish. To the British, what made excursions into the New World a valuable enterprise was their emphasis on cultivating lands not used by the Indians and turning them into productive regions. Unlike the Spaniards, who literally laid waste to the great cities of Tenochitilan and Cuzco, the British were concerned with preventing similar catastrophes in the Americas, which gave them more impetus to expand their colonial program. James Monroe's 1823 declaration that the Americas were off-limits to other imperial powers, on the principle that American autonomy was to be respected, could be viewed as an instance of North America's attempt to parry Spanish encroachments into newly formed nation-states. What these show us, argues Gould, is that "for both Britain and the United States, Spain accordingly remained a potent and hostile antithesis, limiting the ability of either nation to control its imperial project on its own terms."[10] These insights are obtained not by comparing the Spanish Empire with the British Empire, but by using a different methodology—entangled history—to examine those areas, regions, territories, discourses, maritime adventures, religious edicts, and liberal ideas that became entangled in the Americas as various European powers sought to extend their dominion in the New World. As Gould notes, these powers were part of the "same hemispheric system," but their interactions were "fundamentally asymmetric."[11] Gould describes entangled history thus:

> In its most pronounced form, comparative history studies societies that are geographically or temporally remote. Even when the societies in question are closer in space or time, comparative approaches tend to accept national boundaries as fixed, to take the distinctiveness of their subjects as a given, and to assume that the subjects being compared are, in fact, comparable. Entangled histories, by contrast, examine interconnected societies. Rather than insisting on the comparability of their subjects or the need for equal treatment, entangled histories are concerned with "mutual

influencing," "reciprocal or asymmetric perceptions," and the intertwined "processes of constituting one another."[12]

To study American empire, then, is to also study how other empires functioned, where they exercised influence, and which principal actors and groups benefited and which did not. It is in this sense that dwelling in American foregrounds the entanglement of empires in order to avoid folding American international history into world history. To internationalize the study of America, we need to learn so much more about the world, so much more about how other peoples and societies live and exist in this world—rather than assuming that everything related to America is a reaction to U.S. imperialism or a counterbalance to American empire, an idea that imperialistically further consolidates American exceptionalism, even though it is done in the name of liberal critique. Such a decentering of the United States can enable us to better understand how and why peoples coming into contact with American society and culture or affected by U.S. foreign policies actively appropriate—either under varying degrees of compulsion or because of personal or social desire—a plethora of signs, artifacts, symbols, and cultural practices assumed to be American, while simultaneously investing them with new meanings in response to the exigencies of their lives, and creating new ideas of the United States as America and America as modernity. To understand such phenomena, we need to engage with the offshoring of America.

REFRACTION AND VIRTUALIZATION: MULTIPLE ANGLES OF VISION

In asking "Where in the world is America?" Charles Bright and Michael Geyer point to another location of America in a global world, "offshore America"—that complex of "continuing presences, both excesses and products of America beyond the United States," which form "grids of action and interaction that both constituted the United States in a global space and entangled it in the history of globalization."[13] An inquiry into the offshoring of America would lead us to what Paul Giles calls the "virtualization" of America—the use of comparative angles of vision to trace the displacement of mythic representations of America into virtual constructions that emerge at the intersecting sites of history, economy, desire, culture, and identity that mark "transnational interferences and reversals" in the nation's visions of coherence and ideals of stability.[14]

The virtualization of offshore America does not only disturb, in order to deny, the nation's longing for historical transcendence; it also compels a reexamination of how modernity has come to be historicized since that fateful encounter between the Americas and Europe in the fifteenth century. To dwell in American is to engage with the dynamics that structure the interplay of English and American literary cultural traditions, something that Giles does with perspicacity in *Atlantic Republic*. He does not view English and American literatures as repositories of distinct national types, even given America's postcolonial relations with Britain, which spawned a resolute desire to identify, characterize, and affirm a unique American sensibility à la Emerson and Thoreau. In examining the works of writers like Samuel Johnson, Richard Price, Susanna Rowson, Lord Byron, George Ruxton, Arthur Hugh Clough, George Gissing, and P. G. Wodehouse, to name only a few, Giles contends that even their critiques of America are not clear-cut dissents of U.S. foreign policies, whether as empire, new republic, or industrial nation-state. There is a much more multi-faceted engagement with America: although his contemporaries often criticized Byron for his ostensible dislike of England and excessive affection for America, Giles observes that for Byron, this "'penchant' involved a refracted or inverted impression, idealizing a particular image of America as a putative corrective to the ossified institutions of Britain."[15]

To Byron, Washington and Franklin exemplify the admirable qualities of Roman statesmen; Lewis and Clark's expeditions across the continent stir his imagination; the American frontier affords new pursuits; and America's republicanism and Venice's struggles against Austria stand in stark contrast to England's political traditions.[16] There is more to these representations of America than a naive celebration of all things American, as if Byron were a passive person, unable to withstand the dizzying power of American culture. Giles's argument that "Byron's poetry tends always to deploy America as a reflexive mirror, *a spectre of alterity*"[17] sheds a great deal of light on the triangulated dynamics of this poet's cultural politics, dynamics that become part of the "American tradition in English literature," as the subtitle of Giles's book puts it. Hence, it is not enough to use the United States as the primary point of reference to understand how America is being represented in Byron's work. We also need to understand why exactly he thought British institutions were, as Giles puts it, "ossified" and in need of reform. America becomes a site not of reflection but of refraction, digression, oblique reassessment of societies and cultures that lie outside the formal boundaries of the U.S. nation-state. As for Arthur Hugh Clough, notes Giles, for Byron, America becomes a "disruptive influence, an alternative center of gravity."[18] It is to such deployments of America in literary and cultural discourse that we need to attend so that we can resist recentering America in our dissent from its cultures and practices of imperialism.

In a similar vein, Kroes contends that the spread of American culture in Europe should not be read as a clear instance of cultural imperialism. This is because, since the Euro-American encounters in the fifteenth century, America as modernity and America as the United States have permeated European consciousness: "America *is* modernity and the long history of European resistance to America is truly a story of resisting the onslaught of modernity on Europe's checkered map of regional and/or national cultures."[19] Kroes makes this point in analyzing the rise of advertising culture in Europe, which often drew from American media culture in odd, syncretic ways. Advertising culture, for instance, represented America as a boundless land, rich and fertile, affording new possibilities for fashioning society and self. In drawing from such representations of America, advertising cultures often represented Europe as a new, open space in which individual desires could find fulfillment by consuming European goods like liquor, cigarettes, and clothes. This "may well have activated the dream of a Europe as wide and open as America," which is "in itself a sign of a transnational integration of Europe's public space."[20]

The idea of Europe as a stable, unified whole cannot easily be formed unless nationalist longing, cosmopolitanism, and ethnic particularism are rendered insignificant. This instability or lack of clear boundaries does not invalidate Europe as an idea or an agglomeration of various trading blocs in which ethnic and social diversity are not readily apparent. To the contrary, it shows the historical contingency of Europe only as a set of integrated economies in diverse societies with shared cultures. To the nation-states in Europe that are historically linked to or affected by the United States in various ways, America continues to function as a pivotal "reference point to define their positions, either rejecting the American model or promoting it for adoption." With specific reference to the rise of consumption culture, Kroes raises this question: "Now, as images of America's culture of consumption began to fill Europe's public space, they exposed Europeans to views of the good life that Americans themselves were exposed to. To that extent they may have Americanized European dreams and longings. But isn't there also a way we might argue that Europe's exposure to American imagery may have worked to Europeanize Europe at the same time?"[21] Using the United States as America as the only reference point for examining these other "dreams and longings"—which are

shaped by traditions, economies, and histories that are not always or necessarily American in origin or residue from earlier Euro-American interactions—leads us to two imperatives: the need to recognize why and how
ideas of America as modernity and the United States as America are often
interlaced, and the critical necessity of producing a historicized account of
their entanglements and disentanglements. In this context, we cannot just
be critical of American empire, hoping that such a critique will resonate
with other movements for justice and democracy. We must also develop
the linguistic and methodological tools to understand the social and cultural movements and imaginations that draw from "the larger repertoire
of cultural anti-Americanism."[22] It is a repertoire in which the United
States as America is not the only imperial force, the single cultural behemoth, the only nation-state with the power to determine Europe's relation
to its own past and hopes for the future. When critics of globalization and
the United States tend to view almost every conceivable famine, genocide,
war, terror, cultural tension, or national upheaval as primarily and singularly generated by America and the West, it can lead to an "anti-American
psychopathology, which routinely seeks to transform the United States
into a scapegoat burdened with all the sins of the world."[23]

Recognizing the problems of such critiques, Paul Hollander offers a
useful distinction between anti-Americanism abroad and at home. Outside the United States, negative ideas about it are often a direct response to
perceived military threats, U.S. interventions, effects of its economic policies, and the widespread presence of American popular culture. At home,
anti-Americanism emerges as a generalized dissatisfaction with the existing society; it stems from the attempt to link personal anguish to social
conditions, an attempt that is easily achieved in a society that places a high
premium on individual fulfillment.[24] The domestic version of anti-Americanism tends to view America as singularly deficient, almost evil, in some
respects because critics tend to evaluate America in terms of an idealized
set of values of what America ought to be. There cannot be an easy separation between the two since "a proper understanding of anti-Americanism
can only be achieved by balancing two apparently incompatible perspectives or propositions."[25] There are also two views of anti-Americanism that
are often adopted abroad and at home. First, because the effects of U.S.
actions around the world can be identified and experienced, reactions to
America can be viewed as "a direct and rational response to the evident
misdeeds of the United States abroad and its shortcomings and inequities
at home," which are due to the "defects and injustices" of "American social
institutions."[26] The second view considers anti-Americanism to be a form

of irrationalism, something like racism or anti-Semitism, "an expression of a deeply rooted scape-goating impulse, a disposition more closely related to the problems, frustrations, and deficiencies of those entertaining and articulating it."[27] Hollander notes: "The problem of keeping the two attitudes apart intensifies when justified criticism of specific U.S. policies or attributes combines with or culminates in undifferentiated, diffuse, and empirically untenable hostility."[28]

Similarly, Pierre Guerlain distinguishes between two types of anti-Americanism: a "systematic or essentialist . . . form of prejudice targeting all Americans" and "criticism of the Unites States," both of which "are labeled 'anti-American' by supporters of U.S. policies in an ideological bid to discredit their opponents."[29] The essentialist position does not account for differences between the government and the people, and between specific historical events, and it views the desire for and reality of hegemony as a uniquely American phenomenon. Unlike "genuine scholars" who "point out the similarities between historical situations and do not make narrow nationalistic or hateful statements," "the anti-American restricts his or her critique to the United States."[30] Critiques of the United States are often labeled anti-American by those whose administrations or policies are subject to criticism, which at times turns legitimate and reasoned dissent against the United States into unpatriotic behavior or ideas. Anti-Americanism is a "two-sided phenomenon" whose two-sidedness is not always easy to distinguish, as the ideas and positions concerning dissent about America "combine or merge into each other creating a conceptual difficulty."[31] Whether anti-Americanism's forms are domestic or foreign, irrational or essentialist, Hollander and Guerlain both point to the conflation of such terms and the assertive quality of dissent from empire.

STATES, NATIONS, AND POSTMODERN EMPIRE

In *A Nation Among Nations*, the historian Thomas Bender properly locates the history of American imperialism in the context of a global history of empires. The American Revolution "was part of a global war between European powers, it was a struggle for American independence, and it was a social conflict within the colonies."[32] The conflicts among empires during the last three centuries provide the context for conceptualizing the international and global turn in American history. Martin Shaw points out that in the early twentieth century, the United States "was only one among a number of major states,"[33] and became a dominant power not after World War I but after World War II, by countering the imperialism of Japan and Germany. But even this account, notes Shaw, tends to recenter one major power beside another in a burgeoning world economy. Rather than a single nation-state, victorious and gaining total power in the world, what emerged was a new kind of international order, a new world system in which the "autonomous revival of Europe and Japan was nurtured, leading to the complex system of Western and global governance in which the United States is seen as *primus inter pares* rather than an imperial hegemon."[34]

Shaw's point is that the traditional notion of empire—in which one country seeks overwhelming control over and subjugation of another county's people and resources—cannot explain the rise of Europe and Japan as powerful regional blocs and countries, or their close relations with America. Europe and Japan today are not American colonies or countries subject to American imperialism through overwhelming military or economic force. On the contrary, European countries and Japan work more like alliances wherein national autonomy does not become redundant. Calling this the "superiority of the Western system of power," Shaw notes that "a major secret of the Western bloc's success, in contrast, was that despite American dominance (especially in military matters), it was a more or less consensual partnership of states and societies in which nearly all gained in security and wealth. The West offered a model of internationalization that was not forced and, despite, manifest inequalities, offered real benefits to allies and friends."[35]

If we have to use this model to examine America's military ventures over the last two decades, it would be difficult to view the American-led invasion of Kuwait to drive out the Iraqis and the current occupation of Iraq as one and the same. The dissent from empire that critiques the United States as an imperial behemoth since its birth as a new nation analyzes all the wars and skirmishes it fought since 1776 and urges Americans to acknowledge this history of empire and to resist the power of nationalism, patriotism, and exceptionalism—an approach that simply collapses world history into American history. There is one major difference between the two wars: the Persian Gulf War was preceded by the invasion of one nation-state, Kuwait, by another, Iraq. To be sure, both of these nations' possession of oil is not a mere geological fact; it's a fact whose significance for the global economy of the twentieth and twenty-first centuries can be apprehended only in the realpolitik of Europe and America toward Middle Eastern countries.

But what makes the U.S.-Iraq war of 2003 highly problematic is that it was not preceded by conflict between Iraq and another state, leading still other states to marshal forces to evict Iraq from another state's territory. It was the absence of this kind of state conflict that gives a different resonance to the current American occupation in the arena of international politics, where many nation-states work out deals, alliances, and compromises for peace, security, trade, capital, technology, and so on. This does not mean that the Persian Gulf War was somehow more justifiable than the current war. My point is that any critique of American empire that cannot account for the dynamics that shape state alliances and networks, and how state wars over territories can affect international cooperation, makes a leap of logic in which a critique of culture and ideology becomes tantamount to a critique of the state and politics.

Shaw's account of the rise of the United States as a major world power is helpful because it presents a historically informed view of the twentieth century: it takes an international approach that does not simplistically subsume world history into American history. Shaw examines the United States in terms of its entanglements with other nations within the context of "the structure of internationalized state power,"[36] and in terms of the international coalitions of nation-states that emerged at various moments in time. Such an approach helps us examine the cultural and ideological activity engaged in by peoples in different societies and nations to support, displace, undermine, or create such interactions and coalitions.

However, in the second half of the twentieth century, we need to rethink empire, or so argue Michael Hardt and Antonio Negri in their trilogy *Empire, Multitude,* and *Commonwealth.* In Bender's and Shaw's accounts of empire, the world is conceived of primarily in terms of nations, states, civilizations, regional blocs, international zones, East, West, North, South, and continents. The historical basis for such a conceptualization notwithstanding, the large-scale socioeconomic and cultural changes of the last few decades designated by the term "globalization" necessitate, aver Hardt and Negri, a reconceptualization of sovereignty and power for three reasons: the weakening of the nation-state as a mode of social organization; the rapid rise of international and digital technologies that severely compress space and time, leading to a loss of territorial control while simultaneously enhancing the deterritorialized flow of economic and political power; and the increasing convergence of various dimensions of social life, in which cultural processes, economic practices, and legislative, juridical laws and bodies converge in order to classify, organize, delimit, and control vast populations in diverse locations around the globe.

Empire is a "*decentered* and *deterritorializing* apparatus of rule that progressively incorporates the entire global realm within its open, expanding frontiers. Empire manages hybrid identities, flexible hierarchies, and plural exchanges through modulating networks of command."[37] This new form of sovereignty recognizes no boundaries but has a planetary scope; it characterizes the present as an exceptional moment that requires unique and unusual acts of intervention by empire to stabilize the world order, which it does by validating its exercise of power through the ideology of exceptionalism; it seeks to control all aspects of life through biopolitical reproduction; and it professes to eschew war in favor of peace, while waging war to sustain peace.[38]

Given the waning power of the nation-state; the fluid, deterritorialized structures of power; and the expansive networks of labor, capital, law, and information linking cities and peoples across the planet, the political subject of empire is not the people or the mass, crowd, or mob. Rather, it is the multitude that is "composed of innumerable internal differences that can never be reduced to a unity or a single identity—different cultures, races, ethnicities, genders, and sexual orientations; different forms of labor; different ways of living; different views of the world; and different desires. . . . Thus the challenge posed by the concept of multitude is for a social multiplicity to manage to communicate and act in common while remaining internally different."[39]

Hardt and Negri's characterization of the contemporary world less as inter- or transnational and more as postnational—in which the nation-state is reduced to just another node in a global network, if not made irrelevant—is hard to square with events in the last two decades: the Persian Gulf War (1990–91), with its U.S.-led coalition that included several European, Middle Eastern, and Asian countries; the U.S.-NATO intervention in Yugoslavia, sometimes called the Kosovo war (1999); the Iraq War (2003 to the present), with support for U.S. and British forces from European nation-states; the Afghanistan War (2001 to the present), with support for U.S. and British forces again from European nation-states and also the Afghan United Front; and the intervention in Libya (2011 to the present), initiated by France, England, and the United States, with support from other European states as well as Canada and Qatar. These events point not to the declining power of the nation-state but to the interaction among numerous nation-states to forge alliances with each other and with leagues and organizations, including the United Nations, to target specific nation-states to gain territorial control, thwart military aggression, prevent civil war, and maintain the global order.

Formed in large measure by the transnationalization of capital and labor, the multitude seeks to assert difference in order to produce the common—the sites and networks of "communication, collaboration and cooperation."[40] But the radical potential of the multitude, in Hardt and Negri's
formulation, hinges on its desire and ability to "act in common. . . . The
multitude is the only social subject capable of realizing democracy, that is,
the rule of everyone by everyone."[41] They note: "Multitude is a form of political organization that, on the one hand, emphasizes the multiplicity of
social singularities in struggle and, on the other, seeks to coordinate their
common actions and maintain their equality in horizontal organizational
structures."[42] They ignore the possibility that the multitude can simultaneously or alternately be defined as the people, mass, crowd, and working or waged class, and their idea of democracy as the "rule of everyone
by everyone" flattens out differences, not in the sense of producing unity
out of singularity but in the sense of assuming that conflicts between and
among differences can be transcended, not erased, through the common.
How the multitude can resolve conflicting social movements for justice,
revenge, repatriation, equality, and peace without any use of force or without involving the power structures or hierarchical organizations that are
already networked in the multitude cannot be answered in this formulation because it is made irrelevant.[43]

The aspect of empire that directly relates to this book's examination
of globalization is biopower and immaterial labor, which Hardt and Negri
describe as "labor that creates not only immaterial goods but also relationships and ultimately social life itself."[44] Empire obtains sovereignty not so
much by determining life and death but by controlling all realms of life itself; that is, empire exercises its power through administering social life
by bringing all aspects of life under the domain of observation, classifica-
tion, and digitization, and by intertwining the various strands of the social, political, cultural, and economic in complex and pervasive ways. Its
power extends throughout the realms of social existence, and because of
its reach, empire presides over the management of entire groups, classes,
races, masses of peoples, and their living environments.

PATRIOTISM, DEMOCRACY, AND CIVIL SOCIETY

Dwelling in American also departs from current dissents from American
empire in its orientation toward patriotism, citizenship, and renewing our
commitment to the idea of America. There are two main reasons why pa-

triotism, especially to the political Left, according to Todd Gitlin, has become a loaded term—to some, a term to be avoided at all cost. First, after the 1960s, opposition to U.S. involvement in the Far East transformed into, in the academic realm, sustained scrutiny of imperialism's central role in the nation's historical development. To examine how official narratives suppressed the violence integral to the nation's history was a paramount concern, as was recovering those silenced voices and making them part of American cultural and historical traditions. But the second reason why patriotism is suspect has to do with how it undermines individual autonomy. As a cardinal article of faith and practice in social life, individualism viewed society as a mingling of people who understood themselves to be individuals first and members of society second. Moving freely and comfortably across the boundaries of nations and cultures was a cosmopolitan ideal that patriotism—with its focus on the local, the country, and the immediate society—tended to undermine.[58]

But Gitlin cautions that the tremendous outpouring of patriotism after September 11 should not be interpreted narrowly as an expression of nationalist sentiment, a willful erasure of the violence of American history, or a mindless celebration of American power and wealth. No doubt the Bush administration benefited from all these tendencies and in many instances actively encouraged those intellectuals and groups eager to reaffirm, through spectacular displays and unilateral uses of military might, the U.S. position as a global superpower. For many people, patriotism "demands little by way of duty or deliberation, much by way of bravado,"[59] which is perhaps one reason why feverish celebrations of patriotism are indeed feverish, as well as fleeting. But this does not and should not mean that the idea of patriotism and its significance in a democracy are completely subject to the machinations of powerful groups or presidents, or that all displays of patriotism indicate only blind belief in the state and affirmation of official culture.

After September 11, many people did indeed experience and give voice to patriotic sentiments because the attacks undermined the United States as a nation, a state, and a cultural and political community. Gitlin writes: "Lived patriotism requires social equality. It is in the actual relations of citizens, not symbolic displays, that civic patriotism thrives."[60] For a nation to cultivate and sustain a democracy, its people have to actively participate in its practices and forms of governance, but this desire to participate cannot come about unless there is a strong attachment to the nation, unless there is a "citizenry that takes pride in its identity as such."[61] Patriotism in this sense can be and has often been an affirmation of belonging to a nation and trusting its institutions. "The work of civic engagement is the living out of the democratic commitment to govern ourselves," Gitlin points out, and patriotism can play a pivotal role in sustaining this commitment.[62] A patriot in this sense is not the person who is the loudest and brashest celebrant of national culture. A patriot is one who has sacrificed for the national community and actively participated in its social life for the common weal. True, "undemocratic societies require sacrifice, too, but unequally. There, what passes as patriotism is obeisance to the ruling elite. Democracy, on the other hand, demands a particular sort of sacrifice: citizenly participation in self-government."[63] It is this patriotism that we need to affirm and celebrate today. But how can this patriotism find attachment to the nation in a global world?

AMERICA AND ITS DISCONTENTS

This is precisely the question that concerns Alan Wolfe, who—in his much-publicized review essay "Anti-American Studies"—argues that the turn toward the international and the focus on empire among contemporary Americanists, sometimes called the New Americanists, has allowed criticism to devolve into a "hatred" of America: "Yet the third generation and the fourth generation of scholars in the field not only reject the writers who gave life to the discipline, they have also developed a hatred for America so visceral that it makes one wonder why they bother studying America at all."[64] Multiculturalism, diversity, celebration of identity, opening and subverting the canon, uncovering the work of ideology in a literary text or cultural artifact, substituting or downplaying the national for the inter- or transnational—these critical tendencies do not view the nation as having any viability in the postmodern present.

Like Wolfe, the prominent Americanist Leo Marx—in "On Recovering the 'Ur' Theory of American Studies," an essay that Wolfe refers to in his article—charges the New Americanists of constructing a grand narrative when they historicize American studies by making the 1960s a paradigm-shifting moment: before the 1960s, most Americanists were busy identifying and creating an American canon—which was duly deconstructed by the New Americanists, who examine the role of ideology and empire and the nexus of race, class, and gender in shaping the discipline and its pedagogy.[65] In his response to Marx and Wolfe, George Lipsitz downplays the importance of the national in favor of the international when he says that "to work exclusively within the terrain of citizenship and national purpose only exacerbates the citizen/alien distinction and abdicates our moral responsibility to engage with the concerns, injuries, and aspirations of a world wider than any one nation."[66] But Lipsitz does not address the more important point made by Marx—namely, that the New Americanists do not adequately emphasize "the remarkably positive, even celebratory view of American culture" in the work of earlier scholars who "were untrained, unaffiliated, unspecialized writers whose common trait was a fascination with the idea of America."[67] This is not an exclusivist revival of the nation-state and citizenship, but an attempt to explain why, how, and whether America as idea matters at all and warrants our commitment to celebrating and realizing it. To Marx, the idea of America is about the Enlightenment project as manifest in political modernity, the reorganization of society based on contract, consent, and republicanism. It is a worthwhile project to situate all this in transnational and hemispheric frameworks, as Lipsitz would have it, so that we can counter the ideology of exceptionalism and also make connections to other ideas of America in literary and cultural traditions in different parts of the Americas. But such connections obtained in international contexts do not necessarily invalidate Marx's point. What is outside of the United States is not just "a world wider than any one nation," as Lipsitz notes, but a world in which there are many nations, many models of citizenship, and in all these nation-states, nationalism and citizenship are not dead but very much alive. It would be worthwhile to examine what kinds of nationalisms legitimize "citizen/alien distinction[s]" in these nations, and how those nationalisms have historically been part of U.S. history or have intersected with it in some way.

In her response to these writers, Amy Kaplan, dismayed that Marx sides with Wolfe, calls Wolfe's piece an "insidious diatribe" since he "label[s] American studies scholars he disagrees with 'anti-American' and 'America haters,'" which is "irresponsible and inflammatory, especially during this time of crisis."[68] In light of the Bush administration's tendency to label strong critiques of its policies anti-American, Wolfe's characterization of the work of contemporary Americanists as anti-American runs the risk of inviting similar criticisms from the government; at the very least, it fails to offer a way to discriminate between critiques and outright or indirect aiding or abetting of the enemy, to use official parlance. That Wolfe's rhetoric is charged is readily apparent, and his discussion of the New Americanists hardly needs bolstering by charges of hatred. In *Return to Greatness*, published two years after the essay appeared, Wolfe—wisely avoiding such loaded terms—notes that there is a general "hostility towards the idea" of America, and makes an argument for revitalizing the nation and restoring America to greatness: "Achieving national greatness involves three tasks: articulating a meaningful vision of the American purpose; assembling the political capacity to transform that vision into reality; and demonstrating a willingness to use force if necessary to protect that vision and that reality from international enemies and, on occasion, to spread it around the world."[69]

Similarly, Marx writes: "Among the radical ideas of the revisionists, none more compellingly bears out this hypothesis than their conviction that the US as a whole—the nation-state itself—no longer is a worthy subject of teaching and research."[70] This does not mean that Americanists are not studying the United States as a nation-state, but rather that their study does not come close to "articulating a meaningful vision of the American purpose," as Wolfe would have it. Marx is not, as Lipsitz says he is, "confus[ing] criticism of the nation-state with contempt for the nation and its culture";[71] rather, Marx is arguing that this criticism does not, refuses to, or is unable to commit itself to the idea of America and actively work toward its material and sociopolitical realization. And what about Amy Kaplan's rumination? "Today especially I wonder—with my own embarrassment—whether I do believe enough in the idea of America to want to protect democracy, civil liberties, racial equality, the Bill of Rights, checks and balances, and international obligations from the dismantling of these institutions by the Bush administration."[72] What Kaplan enumerates as articles of belief that animate the idea of the America are what Marx and Wolfe would call the values and heritage of national American culture. But does this mean that Kaplan, in calling for a truce, is embracing the nation-state and subscribing to American exceptionalism? Does her entire analysis of empire and ideology become redundant? Indeed, in *Who Are We?* Samuel Huntington makes the same point, while arguing for renewing American culture by celebrating the American creed: "I believe that America can do that and that Americans should recommit themselves to the Anglo-Protestant culture, traditions, and values that for three and a half centuries have been embraced by Americans of all races, ethnicities, and religions and that have been the source of their liberty, unity, power, prosperity, and moral leadership as a force for good in the world."[73]

By the American creed, Huntington means the idea of individual dignity and individualism, the emphasis on the rule of law, the valuation of liberty and equality, the notion of popular sovereignty, and the desire for limited government. Kaplan's and Huntington's passages are paraphrases of each other. So what does this mean? To say or imply—as Kaplan, Marx, Wolfe, and Huntington do—that there are certain ideas that "America" represents and that, historically, the United States of America as a nation-state and Americans as a people were actively involved in creating and building institutions embodying these ideals does not mean that this idea of America is nothing but another version of exceptionalism. Arguing that the United States is part of a larger hemispheric history does not make any of this insignificant or false. It is true that, historically, America actually meant much more than the United States. But it is just as true that specific ideas of modern governance, individual rights, equality, balance of powers, and democracy crystallized in certain ways as several social experiments and independence movements played out on the North American Eastern seaboard. It is to this that "America" has become attached most resolutely. It is this that appeals to millions of people all over the world who seek to come to America. Although America can refer to the hemispheres, it does not mean that those dreaming of America are actually lining up to go to Brazil, Cuba, or Mexico. In fact, to people in those countries, the passage to America means finding a way to travel across Mexico and cross the border into the United States. To them, America is very much a distinct nation-state, quite unlike what they find in South America and the world outside the United States.

The problem is that although Kaplan and Huntington agree that there is this idea of America, how they go about imagining it historically and making a case for its significance in the present are very much at odds. To Huntington, the American creed is a product of a unique Anglo-Saxon Protestant culture, and to revitalize national culture is to get back to those cultural roots. As a New Americanist, Kaplan stresses the history of imperialism and empire building, which propelled the United States into the world and subsequently saw its rise to superpower status at the end of the twentieth century. These histories of expansion and dispossession do not figure prominently in Huntington's formulation of America. So when Wolfe argues for restoring America to greatness and Marx calls for reaffirming the idea of America, they are not rejecting Kaplan in favor of Huntington. They are not calling for a mindless celebration of the nation-state and Anglo-Saxon Protestantism at the expense of all things secular, international, and global.

TRANSLATING EMPIRE

I think that Ernest Renan's idea of the nation can help us better understand Wolfe's and Marx's argument that we need to return America to
greatness and celebrate it:

> A nation is therefore a large-scale solidarity, constituted by the
> feeling of the sacrifices that one has made in the past and of those
> that one is prepared to make in the future. It presupposes a past; it
> is summarized, however, in the present by a tangible fact, namely
> *consent, the clearly expressed desire to continue a common life. A*
> *nation's existence . . . is, if you will pardon the metaphor, a daily*
> *plebiscite*, just as an individual's existence is a perpetual affirma-
> tion of life.[74]

Renan points to two powerful tendencies in how nations are formed
and how they survive: the idea of a common past and the desire to continue that past. But this continuation cannot be achieved unless the people consent to it. In turn, that can happen only when the people agree that
there *is* a common past, and that there are values, ideas, and histories
worth preserving and perpetuating. They need to desire to continue the
past and the present. The idea that the nation is a plebiscite means that the
nation is continually engaged in the process of ensuring its survival. It is
constantly trying to reproduce itself.

Here we run into a problem. We know that the past is not simply there
waiting to be discovered. The past, or history, is the work of human beings and the product of human imagination and ingenuity. The past can be
twisted to suit the present. When Renan notes that wars or major events
can unify communities into a nation, he is also saying that the past is created by and around such pivotal events. History, or the past, comes to us
in terms of specific events, which means that some events become important and others do not. This is why memory becomes central to the formation of a nation. The nation can survive not only on what people remember
about the past but also on what they choose to forget about it. This is why
when historians examine the past, sometimes what they find can conflict
with the national version of history. Renan goes on: "Forgetting, I would
even go so far as to say historical error, is a crucial factor in the creation
of a nation, which is why progress in historical studies often constitutes a
danger for the [principle of] nationality. Indeed, historical enquiry brings

to light deeds of violence which took place at the origin of all political formations. . . . Yes, the essence of a nation is that all individuals have many
things in common, and also that they have forgotten many things."[75]

In a general sense, it would seem that the work of the New Americanists emphasizes empire, ideology, race, gender, class, and how they
all shape the politics of remembering and forgetting, whereas Marx and
Wolfe stress the impulse of the nation to renew itself constantly and pro-
vocatively ask if Americanists, in particular, have any stake in perpetuating, celebrating, and affirming national culture, and doing so in order
to bequeath it to later generations. The absence of such affirmations leads
Marx and Wolfe to view the critical work of the New Americanists as in-
fused with hatred. But what they mistake for hate is rather an inability
or sometimes a refusal—conceptually, methodologically, ethically—to
develop a coherent worldview that takes account of the ideals and values
worth preserving and celebrating about America today. It is significant
that restoring America to greatness involves, to Wolfe, making a case for
how American power might be used. This means that empire, understood
as the awesome power of the U.S. military, and the ability of America to
project that power worldwide and deploy it for specific ends, is again at the
heart of the program for renewing American national culture. Wolfe is not
being an imperialist or an apologist for empire. He is issuing a challenge to
those who dissent from American empire to clarify how exactly they understand and would use American power. The problem is that if we work
with the conceptual models that have often been used to dissent from empire, as we have seen in the previous chapter, it would be very difficult to
even attempt to answer Wolfe's challenge in any affirmative way because
that response could just as reasonably be condemned for being outrightly
imperialistic. But that quandary is just what Marx and Wolfe anticipate,
which is why they urge a renewing of American national culture so that
we—the people, an agglomeration of groups—can have some understanding of what values and ideas of America are worth celebrating and affirming—even fighting and dying for.

Two things gain significance, then, for the project of dwelling in
American—translating empire and accounting for America as a signifier
of modernity and for America as the United States. If we are to celebrate
America today, either by critiquing its imperial histories or restoring its
progressive social visions, as José Limón contends, we need to translate
empire: "When translated into local specificities, the very ideas of U.S.
empire, U.S. violence, and U.S. minorities as well as the U.S. military *become complicated sites with multivalent social and moral meanings and*

outcomes, frustrating any effort to give them a singular interpretation."[76] In studying American empire, rather than viewing the entire world as a tabula rasa on which the United States exerts itself imperially, we need to pay careful attention to what is already in the world: to existing institutions, communities, nation-states, empires, social movements—in short, to human and ecological conditions. Short of the decimation of entire populations or a biopolitical endeavor to control and eventually wipe out an entire race or community of people, for American empire to work, it has been and will continue to become entangled with other power networks, empires, and hierarchical institutions and structures. Empire becomes a site of struggle—it's the site where empire is subjected to new articulations, appropriations, and outcomes. We cannot be content to use a giant vacuum that sucks up the world's diversity so that we can produce a singular interpretation of American empire, as if nothing else mattered; as if what other peoples did, thought, and said about America and themselves and their worlds were irrelevant; as if the entire world possessed a reactive consciousness, so that their difference is always and only rendered intelligible because of its relationship to America.

As we have seen in the first chapter, such ideas and methodologies have a powerful hold on contemporary dissents from empire. Dissent is able to establish its own regime of truth and power because it refuses to translate empire, refuses to come to terms with other perspectives and ideas about American empire, and refuses to appreciate its complex entanglements with other empires.[77] Dwelling in American insists on translating empire and attending to its involvement with other structures and institutions of power. Dwelling in American views those whose histories, countries, and lives have been affected in some way or another by America as active social beings with a stake in responding to U.S. initiatives as a nation-state, while also creating and deploying ideas of the United States as America and America as modernity for various purposes.

In the next chapter, I extend these ideas in analyzing the nonfictional writing of Arundhati Roy. Drawing on Antonio Gramsci's idea of the organic intellectual and Abdul JanMohamed's notion of the syncretic and specular intellectual, I examine the rhetorical ploys Roy uses to appropriate the role of the subaltern in order to gain representational authority, and the ethical quandary she faces when intellectuals like Noam Chomsky apply the critical apparatus she uses to dissent from American empire in order to influence parties on the Left and activists in northern India to desist from opposing a government headed by a Marxist party. I aim to show that the turn toward the international or the global requires grappling with the entangled histories of nations and communities who have their own sociopolitical agendas, and that dwelling in American—as idea and critical model—is an attempt to learn more about the peoples and societies who come into contact with American culture, reflect on how and why they respond to it, and develop a more expansive understanding of the motives and passions that animate their engagement with America.

CHAPTER THREE

Dissent on the Border

ARUNDHATI ROY

Arundhati Roy, author of the Booker Prize–winning *The God of Small Things*, has also penned a series of essays—collected in *The Cost of Living*, *Power Politics*, *War Talk*, *An Ordinary Person's Guide to Empire*, *Field Notes on Democracy*, and *Broken Republic*—that have gained international recognition for their pungent critiques of exploitative multinational corporations, international organizations like the International Monetary Fund and the World Bank, and the complicity of India's national and state governments in marginalizing millions of *adivasis*[1] and the rural poor by displacing them, submerging their lands, and alienating them from their cultures by a forced imposition of industrial development. In this chapter, I analyze Roy's nonfictional writings and, drawing on Abdul JanMohamed's theory of the border intellectual, I advance the following arguments: (1) Roy views herself as a public intellectual who has direct access to non-Western experience and knowledge; (2) she affirms civilizational difference to mobilize antiglobalism sentiment in India and abroad, and she disingenuously abstracts culture from economics and politics; and (3) she uses an interpretive grid that enables her to frame international events as integral to a world system dominated by the United States and the West, whose power is exerted with such penetrative force that almost every conceivable large-scale problem in the non-Western world—such as poverty, drought, genocide, and corruption—can be explained with reference to this grid. Roy, I argue, risks becoming an exoticized, authentic voice of the Third World in the First World, and being co-opted as an intellectual who can transparently represent the interests of the subaltern in the global arena.

PUBLIC INTELLECTUALS ON THE BORDER

JanMohamed distinguishes between a syncretic border intellectual who, positioned between cultures, chooses to "combine elements of two cultures in order to articulate new syncretic forms and experiences," and a specular border intellectual who, "caught between several cultures or groups, none of which is deemed sufficiently enabling or productive . . . subjects the cultures to analytic scrutiny rather than combining them." The difference between the two types is in the "intentionality of their intellectual orientation." He identifies "four different modes of border crossings" by border intellectuals: "the exile, the immigrant, the colonialist, and the scholar."[2] The exile—unlike the immigrant, who is eager to become part of the host society—sustains the memory of home, which may make the subject "indifferent to the values and characteristics of the host culture." Without any "structural nostalgia," the immigrant emphasizes assimilation into the host society. In contrast, unlike the exile and the immigrant, the colonialist and the scholar view culture "not as a field of subjectivity, but rather as an object of and for their gaze."[3]

Not having to choose between the life of an exile and an immigrant does not automatically cancel out the ambivalence of cross-cultural encounters that inform Roy's nonfiction, which could be characterized as protest literature. Although a novel like *The God of Small Things* is syncretic in the sense that it embodies what might be called Indian English, which combines elements of the Queen's English with regional dialects and idiolects, and the tensions of cross-cultural histories, traditions, and interactions, her nonfiction takes clear ideological and political stances and embodies a sense of specularity—a "willed homelessness"[4] that subjects indigenous, national, and international politics, societies, and cultures to scrutiny and judgment. This kind of specularity is not so much about an unwillingness to be Indian as it is about the intentionality of her dissents and politics. Those dissents generate a condition of homelessness, an uprooting from the stable ground created by the myths of modernity, development, nationhood, and globalization.

To Pablo Bose, Roy is—like Medha Patkar, a famous activist associated with the Narmada Bachao Andolan (Save Narmada Movement, hereafter the NBA) in India—a "popular intellectual" or critic.[5] The difference between what Michel Foucault calls experts and critics is applicable to Roy and her writings, notes Bose. The experts are the engineers, administrators, and planners whose work gains authority by the imprimatur of governments and institutions, while the critics include students, activists, workers, villagers, and the poor. "Through their empirical research, critical reflection, and careful analysis" of "the complex processes of nationalism, international development, and globalization that are intertwined and affect life in the valley," critics like Roy are also "popular intellectuals" who have become "the public faces of the Narmada struggle, much more so even than the many thousands of villagers scheduled to be displaced by dams."[6]

Making a different distinction, Antonio Gramsci notes that organic intellectuals elaborate the needs and aspirations of their class and direct them to particular political ends, while traditional intellectuals exercise their power to the degree to which they "represent an historical continuity uninterrupted even by the most complicated and radical changes in political and social forms."[7] The latter derive their power by seeming to transcend social changes and class formations, a transcendence obtained by obscuring their investments in perpetuating those social classes that support them and whose interests they represent. Given her extensive support of the NBA and her organizing and planning for the organization, as well as speaking for and representing poor and indigenous people affected by industrial development, Roy functions as an organic intellectual, and her dissents acquire an identifiable ideological orientation. Having taken strong positions against dams, dispossession and displacement of indigenous peoples, economic globalization, privatization, and American empire, Roy rejects the labels of writer-activist, which tends to view her fiction as nonpolitical and her nonfiction as political writing:

> My thesis—my humble theory, as we say in India—is that I've been saddled with this double-barreled appellation, this awful professional label, not because my work is political, but because in my essays, which are about very contentious issues, I take sides. I take a position. I have a point of view. What's worse, I make it clear that I think it's right and moral to take that position, and what's even worse, I use everything in my power to flagrantly solicit support for that position.[8]

Despite her disavowals, there is ample evidence in her work and her extensive involvement with the NBA that she plays the role of the representative intellectual and that her dissent has a social function in the public arena, in the Gramscian sense. Roy is not a professional but an amateur, to use the distinction Edward Said makes in *Representations of the Intellectual*: the amateur intellectual eschews specialization in a field of knowledge, does not depend on the authority vested in the certifying power of an institution or accrediting process, and refrains from direct employment by governments, parties, or think tanks in order to publicly espouse and pursue a party line or policy—not in the belief that these activities are in and of themselves illegitimate, but because the vocation of the intellectual is to subject tradition, religion, nation, and the state to critical investigation. Said observes: "The intellectual today ought to be an amateur, someone who considers that to be a thinking and concerned member of society one is entitled to raise moral issues at the heart of even the most technical and professionalized activity as it involves one's country, its power, its mode of interacting with its citizens as well as with other societies."[9] Roy harnesses her dissent to the idea of civil society governed not only by technicians, politicians, professionals, businesses, academic institutions, and political organizations, but by anyone who is affected by them and who cares to question, expose, and hold them to account for their exercise of power, their use of knowledge and expertise to justify public policies, and their claim to act on behalf of or for the people, justice, prosperity, and security. As an amateur intellectual, Roy takes up what Said identifies as a key issue for the intellectual in the modern world: "The dominant norms are today so intimately connected to (because commanded at the top by) the nation, which is always triumphalist, always in a position of authority, always exacting loyalty and subservience rather than intellectual investigation and re-examination of the kind that Woolf and Walter Benjamin speak about."[10] When the nation is viewed as an organic community—bound together by an easily obtained national culture, whose difference from other nations and cultures is posited as natural, traditional, primordial and thus beyond dispute—the intellectual's responsibility is to submit the nation to analytical scrutiny and "to show how the group is not a natural or god-given entity but is a constructed, manufactured, even in some cases invented object, with a history of struggle and conquest behind it, that it is sometimes important to represent."[11]

Roy has often chided the central government of India and its highest courts for their apathy toward the poor who have been displaced by big dam projects; Indian officials for their corrupt involvement with multinational corporations; the rhetoric of extreme nationalism used by the Indian and Pakistani governments to justify the testing of nuclear bombs as a step toward regional stability; the Hindutva-suffused national Bharatiya Janata Party (BJP) for inciting communal tensions; the neocolonial mentality of President Bill Clinton for presiding over nontransparent business negotiations between Enron and the Maharashtra state government; and

President George W. Bush for taking preemptive steps to combat terrorism. Roy's political stances and ideological orientations cannot easily be
bracketed with neat labels—liberal, left-wing, right-wing, Dalit representative, feminist, or any of the other terms common to political and social
discourse. The central purpose of such critiques is to generate public interest about corruption at high levels, the abuses of influence and power by
governments and corporations, and the importance of democracy to civil
society, albeit with a journalistic panache that is made memorable for its
artful use of a pun, a pointed simile, and a colorful metaphor. At least, that
is what the purpose seems to be, at first glance.

However, a closer analysis of her writings that address issues of globalization, transnational and multinational corporations, and America's
role in the world reveals a certain predictability of argument: a world system exists that separates East from West; because the United States is the
sole superpower in the postmodern world, it is the meta-signifier of global
morality or, better still, immorality; the flow of political and economic
power is unidirectional from West to East, but cultural exchanges operate
on a level that leaves them less tainted with realpolitik; and globalization is
just a euphemism that permits the First World to pillage, exploit, oppress,
and colonize the peoples of the Third World. Within this global context
Roy's own positionality and location emerge: she is an intellectual from
the East playing a mediating role between the First and Third Worlds, and
in that process giving voice to the oppressed, the marginalized, and the
subaltern.

SYNCRETISM OR SPECULARITY

At issue in Roy's *The Cost of Living* is India's dogged pursuit—as the "world's
third largest dam-builder"—to continue building big dams: 3,600 big dams
already built, and 1,000 more being constructed.[12] Although the goals of
dam building include the irrigation of agricultural lands and provision of
water for people and livestock, the results are alarming: 600 million Indians do not have sanitation, and 200 million do not have water that is safe
to drink. Of immediate concern to Roy are the proposed dams on the Narmada, a 1,300-kilometer-long river running through the states of Madhya
Pradesh, Maharashtra, and Gujarat.

The massive displacement of 30 to 40 million people, submersion of
villages, and destruction of ecosystems; the callous attitudes of the state
and central governments toward the needs of the displaced and the lack

of compensation for their losses; the higher courts' politicized judgments in support of the ruling parties; the utter lack of transparency in the civic and political process—these are the objects of Roy's critique. Evident at numerous points in the process of proposing, evaluating, negotiating the terms of, and building a dam is the influence of multinational corporations and international organizations like the World Bank—which formed committees of inquiry, some led by a former head of the United Nations Development Program—and the pressures of a global system of banking, loans, and the channeling of monies for various projects.[13]

Roy's involvement with the NBA and the publicity surrounding the fact that a winner of the Booker Prize was writing about big dams and the displacement of the poor generated such controversy that the Indian Supreme Court in 1999 took umbrage at her essay titled "The Greater Common Good" and publicly chastised her for her undignified attitudes toward the courts and her "objectionable writings."[14] In 2001, Roy, Medha Patkar, and Prashant Bushan, the attorney for the NBA, were charged with "committing criminal contempt of court by organizing and participating in a demonstration outside the gates of the Supreme Court," a charge that the justices of the court felt merited their attention.[15] Roy was sentenced to a day in jail, which she served.

These incidents point to the tremendous publicity that Roy's involvement with the antidam movement has generated. In a series of judgments, the courts demonstrated that they can glibly subvert the principles they are charged to uphold and blatantly pander to the demands of powerful political parties, businesses, and other vested interests. It is in Roy's criticisms of such power plays and the subversion of democracy that we see JanMohamed's two roles vis-à-vis the authorial position emerge for the public intellectual, the syncretic and the specular: first, the role of the elite intellectual, who mediates between the large numbers of villagers who have been and will be adversely affected by dam building and government bureaucrats, court officials, and business leaders; and second, the role of the Third World critic who mediates between the non-West and the West as she travels a global circuit.

The question of representation thus becomes pivotal in understanding the syncretism and specularity of Roy's activism. She notes: "I think it's vital to de-professionalize the public debate on matters that vitally affect the lives of ordinary people. It's time to snatch our futures back from the 'experts.' Time to ask, in ordinary language, the public question and to demand, in ordinary language, the public answer."[16] Not quite playing the role of the organic intellectual in the Gramscian sense, who emerges from within an identifiable class formation, Roy—in her role as a public intellectual—could be considered syncretic in the sense that she makes a conscious effort to direct her activism against specific institutions in order to represent the interests of aggrieved groups of people and make public demands for justice and equality. In this sense, she syncretizes—literally, brings together—the disparate interests of the poor, working class, *adivasis*, and subalterns in order to create a public platform from which the marginalized voices can be heard and, in her own writing, to create an alternative voice embodying the aspirations of the dispossessed and displaced. Despite the different needs of these disparate groups, Roy syncretizes their experiences by giving their demands for redress, recognition, and rights social and moral coherence insofar as the groups, communities, and classes can be located within a specific geopolitical structure of international relations, and can change their oppressive conditions by drawing on movements and traditions of anticapitalism, antiglobalization, antinationalism, and anticolonialism.

With respect to the second role, that of Third World subject representing the interests of the non-West to the West, the fact that most of Roy's opinions are accessible in the West, especially in North America—in the form of books published by South End Press and online publications of her essays in *Salon*, *The Guardian*, and the left-wing webzine *Z*; frequent lectures at U.S. campuses and other venues such as the famous Riverside Church in New York, later broadcast by C-SPAN; other public appearances on, for example, *Nightline* with Ted Koppel; and her association with intellectuals like Noam Chomsky and Howard Zinn—underscores the role of publishers and lecture circuits in the United States, the leftist political orientation of the editors, journalists, and publishers with whom she has worked, and the multimedia venues that both give audiences in the United States and Britain access to her writings and facilitate the circulation of her ideas and provide a public space for her to articulate her politics. The republication of Roy's numerous essays by Western presses for audiences outside India points to "the creative recycling of her publishing catalogue and the extension of her brand in the republishing of Chomsky's work," argues Julie Mullaney, who goes on to add that Roy's dissent is often co-opted "by a publishing industry keen to make capital and not just cultural capital out of her interventions."[17]

However, this second role is specular, in JanMohamed's terms, because even as Roy mediates between First and Third World audiences and peoples, her determined effort to generate a "willed homelessness" is more prominent in her second role as a specular intellectual: Roy is often critical of actions not often strenuously examined by most U.S. liberals—namely, the immense expansion of global business in the Clinton years, the active interference of the State Department during the Clinton administration in India's business relations with Enron, John Kerry's policies of imperial dominance, and his toeing the liberal ideological line. Indeed, one of her essays in *Power Politics* is sarcastically titled "The Reincarnation of Rumpelstiltskin," based on President Clinton's visit to India in March 2000. Those who consider Vice President Dick Cheney's affiliation with Haliburton after he left office as proof that the Republicans are hand in glove with big business—while the Democrats are ostensibly for the working class and the poor—would have to contend with Roy's "King Rumple" striding like an imperial colossus on the international stage while proclaiming the virtues of open markets and deregularization.[18] In short, to Roy, Clinton's policies epitomize the viciousness of capitalist greed on a global scale, although their exploitative power is masked in a discourse of friendly international cooperation, treaties, cultural give and take, and so on. It is in this sense that we could view her role as having specularity, with her unwillingness to find a "home" in ideological camps and her insistence on a critical intervention that does not engage in critique only to justify her political leanings, or to legitimate a discourse of liberalism. The dichotomies of liberalism and conservatism or Democrat and Republican do not adequately explain Roy's specular activism and politics.

AUTHENTICITY OR SUBALTERNITY

However, there is a particular conceptual orientation to Roy's dissent that deserves scrutiny, first because she views the intellectual as having unproblematic access to non-Western experience and knowledge, and second because she conceives of globalization as a world system dominated by the United States and the West to such an extent that their domination can be used to explain almost every problem in the non-Western world. As Todd Gitlin points out, such "anti-Americanism is one of those prejudices that musters evidence to suit a conclusion already in place."[19] It is a hermeneutic engagement that often strives for closure by appealing to rigid dichotomies in a neatly organized world system, and that reinscribes what Roy's politics strains to undermine—namely, the logic of civilizational difference and West-oriented ideas of modernity.

Instead of addressing the problems of mediation and representation involved in the role of public intellectual, Roy's desire to polemicize leads her to make claims of authenticity not as a subject on the border who mediates among different cultural constituencies and audiences—in the process producing contingent, fractured knowledge—but as a subaltern subject who possesses authentic knowledge that is accessible to those who are willing to trust her to share it with them. As she invites her readers to rely on her—that is, on Roy the subaltern—to lead them to an enlightened state of consciousness about the non-West, the dispossessed, and the poor, she stakes her claim to authenticity: *"Allow me to shake your faith. Put your hand in mine and let me lead you through the maze.* Do this, because it's important that you understand. If you find reason to disagree, by all means take the other side. But please don't ignore it, don't look away. . . . *Trust me.* There's a story to tell."[120]

A crucial displacement has occurred here: the border intellectual is no longer mediating, syncretically or specularly, and producing contingent knowledge; instead, the borders of mediation have been erased from scrutiny, as Roy becomes the producer of authentic knowledge because she speaks and writes and thinks as the subaltern subject. No longer is the role of the mediator at play here; the authentic subject herself is available. Only prejudice, bias, and unwillingness to learn can prevent the reader's acquisition of the consciousness possessed by Roy as the subaltern. The subtler implication is even more compelling: to refuse to acquire this consciousness is not so much to disagree with Roy, but to disbelieve in her. Far from countering hegemony, such dissent is solely concerned with creating a community of true believers in which the spirit of skepticism is made subservient to the obligation to believe. Only belief can lead to absolute, authentic knowledge. Such is the power of Roy's imperative: "Trust me." Equally problematic is Roy's total lack of skepticism regarding the nature and power of her representational claims. In response to a question from David Barsamian about her celebrity status, Roy says:

> As a rule I never do things because I'm a celebrity. Also I never avoid doing things because I'm a celebrity. . . . I know that there's a very fine balance between accepting your own power with grace and misusing it. When I say my own power, I don't mean as a celebrity. Everybody, from the smallest person to the biggest, has some kind of power, and even the most powerless person has a responsibility. I don't feel responsible for everybody. Everybody is also responsible for themselves. *I don't ever want to portray myself as a representative of the voiceless or anything like that.* I'm scared of that.[21]

The contradiction is self-evident—Roy cannot urge people to place their hands in hers and trust her to lead them to enlightenment about the plight of the subalterns and at the same time disavow her explicitly stated intention to assume the role of intellectual mediator keen on giving voice to the voiceless, both in India and abroad. In "An Open Letter to Arundhati Roy," Gail Omvedt cautions Roy that her dissent and activism have significant representational qualities that need to be responsibly addressed:

> There is nothing wrong with going out to organize people, with throwing oneself into a cause or supporting a cause, with rallying world opinion. NBA has succeeded in giving great power to a "no big dam" position and in putting a big question mark before the whole issue of "development." You have every right to support them. But in doing so, please think about one thing: when you go as leaders to people in the valley, or when you represent people in the valley to the world outside, what are the consequences for them of the arguments you make? What does it mean when you put your own arguments, either explicitly or implicitly, in their mouths? Are you so sure your sweeping opposition to big dams is in their best interest, or that you are democratically representing their real feelings on the matter?[22]

Rather than examining the complex dynamics of representation and the questions of accountability they raise, Roy takes recourse in belief, trust, and sincerity as if greater belief, deeper trust, and keener sincerity were bulwarks against ideology and politics, a position that is itself ideological and political. What we see here are the operations by which the instability inherent in the role of mediating intellectual is rendered stable in order to grant purity of thought and motivation to the representations that ensue.

What the Brazilian educator Paulo Freire says about such displacements of the space of the subaltern by elite intellectuals—when the border intellectual, in standing in for the subaltern, ends up speaking and talking *as* the subaltern, is relevant in this context. Freire's caveat about becoming aware not just of consciousness but of consciousness as consciousness calls into question Roy's claims to authenticity and subalternity: "Liberating education . . . epitomizes the special characteristic of consciousness: being *conscious of*, not only as intent on objects but as turned in upon itself in a Jasperian 'split'—consciousness as consciousness *of* consciousness."[23] To Freire, knowledge is liberating only insofar as the conditions of enablement—the entire gamut of systems, institutions, and conditions of knowledge production and circulation, and the power dynamics that inform the very formation of that consciousness—are acknowledged and renegotiated, not simply handed down from generation to generation, individuals to individuals, teachers to students, and intellectuals to publics. The positionality of the border intellectual in critical engagement with structures of knowledge acquisition and systems of knowledge production is a more pressing issue than the pursuit of the ideal pedagogical situation. Notice that, to Freire, consciousness is not a matter of putting one's hand in another's and following her; it is not simply a matter of trust, as it is to Roy. Every claim to knowledge, every act in which knowledge becomes part of an economy of learning, should necessarily be accountable to its own conditions of production. But that is not what we have in Roy's dissent. What we do have are strenuous attempts at a forced displacement of the subaltern by the border intellectual. Tellingly, that displacement obscures the privileged positionality of the border intellectual in the economy of mediation, as the next example illustrates.

In "The Loneliness of Noam Chomsky," Roy criticizes the ideologies that fueled the Cold War, which made the rest of the world a battleground for two supreme powers. A paragraph that she writes about herself is worth quoting in full:

> As a child growing up in the state of Kerala, in South India—where the first democratically elected Communist government in the world came to power in 1959, the year I was born—I worried terribly about being a gook. Kerala was only a few thousand miles west of Vietnam. We had jungles and rivers and rice-fields, and communists, too. *I kept imagining my mother, my brother, and myself being blown out of the bushes by a grenade,* or mowed down, like the gooks in the movies, by an American marine with muscled arms and chewing gum and a loud background score. *In my dreams, I was the burning girl in the famous photograph taken on the road from Trang Bang.*[24]

It is unclear what social, economic, political, and cultural conditions create a climate of fear in which a girl from Kerala, South India, should have dreams of being blown up by Americans. Once again, the problem of mediation, the vexatious problem of negotiating the positionality of the border intellectual in a global economy, is skillfully excised: Roy is no longer mediating; in the literary imagination, she *is* the burning girl on the road from Trang Bang. The border intellectual now speaks as the subaltern: once again, we need to trust her. Roy implores us to put our hand in hers as she leads us to a greater consciousness. Just believe, just trust, just hold onto the hand of the girl from Trang Bang. As Mullaney points out, Roy's self-identification with Phan Thi Kim Phuc "suggests a less self-reflexive appropriation of Kim Phuc's life-story than one would expect" and exemplifies an "uncritical deployment of simplified figures of female oppression."[25] Roy's writings produce a state of emergency: readers are invited and even expected to take a stand. What is urgent is not a critical examination of the issue but the identification of one's self with the stated position of the text and the writers. The architecture of such dissent, points out Emilienne Baneth-Nouailhetas, which connects Roy's fiction and nonfiction, involves making explicit the connection between the small and the big, and individualizing the small through emotional rhetoric while depersonalizing the state, democracy, modernity as the big. The suffering of the small is caused by a plurality of factors that "form a coalition of oppression," and since it "implies a uniformization of the manifestations of power,"[26] the central aim of Roy's dissent is to compel readers to identify with her, her position, and the subjects of her writing: "the text functions as an ultimatum, for once it has been read it cannot be annulled, and neither can knowledge be erased. The aim of such a rhetoric is to cancel critical distance or the possibility of objection through the forging of a chain of affect between portrayed victim and reader or, occasionally, between the prophetic 'I' and her interlocutor."[27] This is why Roy urges readers to put their hands in hers and accompany her on a journey to truth, justice, and freedom. We are to trust her. We are to believe in her. We are to identify with her. And through her, with the many others who deserve our sympathy, and with whom we can join to fight the big in the world.

Another instance of such dissent is her prefatory comment in a lecture she gave at Riverside Church, in New York:

> Since I am a writer, I have written out what I want to say because they are complicated things and *we must be precise about our politics*. . . . Some of you will think it bad manners for a person like me officially entered in the big book of nations as an Indian citizen to come here and criticize the US government. But speaking for myself, I am no flag waver, and I am fully aware that venality, brutality, and hypocrisy are imprinted on the leaden soul of every nation. But when a country ceases to be merely a country and becomes an empire, then the scale of operations changes dra-

matically. So may I clarify that tonight *I speak as a subject of the American empire. I speak as a slave who presumes to criticize her king.*[28]

Aware of herself as a public intellectual, aware that her audience at Riverside Church is different from the ones she has in France, Brazil, or India, Roy wants to be "precise about our politics," because her outsider status as a non-American could potentially create a distance between herself and her audience. Given that in a few moments her lecture will offer a harsh critique of the American government, this rhetorical strategy seeks to reassure the audience of the speaker's awareness of her positionality. But when being precise about politics merits the labor of historical inquiry, the now-familiar displacement mechanism that enables her to transcend her border positioning goes into operation—Roy becomes the subject of American empire, and thus she has the right to offer a critique just as a slave could "criticize her king." With one fell stroke, all struggles for freedom and justice through the archives of history are made commensurable, accorded equal weight, so that postmodern pastiche can reign supreme— everybody in the world can become everybody in the world, since everybody is the subject of American empire. By collapsing all differences, by erasing every conceivable historical change and material reality, all identities and roles can be easily exchanged: those who have, historically, never borne the brunt of American empire can now have the same standing apropos empire as those who have suffered its brutality: the African slaves, the Irish, the mulattoes, the victims of Hiroshima, the dispossessed natives of the Americas, the interned Japanese Americans, the hunted border crossers of the Southwest, and the numerous peoples in various parts of the world who have at one point or another been directly affected by America.

Are the Dalit youths who were killed for skinning a dead cow in Haryana, India, victims of American empire?[29] Were the thousands of Muslims and Hindus who were slaughtered over the last ten years, as communalism enacted its drama of blood and revenge, the victims of American empire? Were the hundreds of Muslim women who were disfigured and mutilated in Gujarat the beneficiaries of American empire?[30] All of these events happened in Roy's country, India. By what historical fiat, by what principle of methodology, does she claim that she is the subject of American empire? However, answering this question is unnecessary because Roy's dissent is predicated on two important ideas—world history is the global history of America, and globalization is a synonym for Americanization. No

other empire, no other nation, no other people deserve to be taken into account because they all come under the banner of empire, American style.
Cambodia, Vietnam, Iran, Iraq, Chile, and Japan are all different names
for India; history is only a word game. Roy retells the creation myth, making America the god that created the millions of Adams and Eves running
loose all over the world. Their only hope for historical consciousness is
America, the giver and taker of all life—indeed, the creator of the global
world. The ideological force of Roy's dissent consolidates American exceptionalism on a global scale. Having locked the entire world in the prison
that is America, Roy throws away the keys in order to produce a dissent
about American empire so that she can become the apotheosis of the oppressed in Afghanistan, the displaced in Palestine, the dispossessed on the
banks of the Narmada, the sweatshop workers of the Third World. As her
readers and listeners, all we need to do is trust her to lead us from this moment of secular transfiguration—the radiant metamorphosis of the border
intellectual into the authentic subaltern—into the realm of higher consciousness. Indeed, the subaltern cannot speak unless Roy becomes the
subaltern.

CLASH OF CIVILIZATIONS

Coterminous with Roy's Americanization of the world is her making democracy and modernity equivalent, a move that betrays a naive understanding of modernity as processes and conditions with no bearing on
material situations, institutional structures, and ideological movements.
In opposing the Indian government's dogged pursuit of big dams, Roy observes: "The NBA believes that Big Dams are obsolete. It believes there are
more democratic, more local, more economically viable and environmentally sustainable ways of generating electricity and managing water systems. It is demanding *more* modernity, not less. It is demanding *more* democracy, not less. And look at what is happening instead."[31]
     Far from clarifying the difference between less and more moder-
nity, linking modernity with "environmentally sustainable ways" further
nudges modernity into the realm of politics and technology. It would be
hard to argue that the technology used in building a dam—whether big or
small—is inherently less modern, unless one were to adopt an evolutionary scale for measurement. Why the NBA believes that big dams are "obsolete" and therefore less modern is the question to consider. Because the
pursuit of big dams by the government has been undemocratic, nonpartic-

ipatory, and hierarchical, and its decisions have been arbitrarily imposed on the inhabitants of places affected by dams, big dams have become less modern. Although it would be possible to speak of refining dam technology and managing water systems, Roy's concern is with the imbrication of dam building with nation building, the influence of caste-based politics and communal passions on modernizing India. It is this dangerous nexus of power politics that underscores why Roy's pleas for more modernity are linked to local governance, indigenous ways of managing the environment, and participatory forms of decision making.

More crucially, Roy undercuts her laudable attempts to effectively intervene in this nexus and undermine its politics when she subscribes to the logic of civilizational difference to counter the global threat of Americanization, as we have seen earlier. Simultaneously pleading for more modernity and insisting on the Indian nation as a dazzling manifestation of an essentialized, non-Western civilizational difference demonstrates not just a simplistic understanding of modernity but the systematic use of oriental ideas to prop up the nation-as-civilization in order to counter an already flawed conception of world history and American empire.

Roy finds India's obsequious response to President Clinton's visit embarrassing: "He was courted and fawned over by the genuflecting representative of this ancient civilization with a fervor that can only be described as indecent."[32] Emblematic of First World greed disguised as liberal humanism, Clinton's visit is, to Roy, yet another public extravaganza staged on an international scale by multinational corporations, U.S. diplomats and businessmen, and Indian government officials and businessmen. But in positing an "ancient civilization" that stands in stark contrast to what she views as predatory globalization, Roy affirms as an essential India frozen in space and time: India, with all of its immense cultural, religious, and social plurality is reduced to a single ancient civilization. This reductive move counters Roy's earlier emphasis on the cohabitation of modernity and tradition in India and its "schizophrenic nature."[33] Only by denying the heterogeneity of India and the tenuous relations between modernity and tradition can Roy affirm the existence of an ancient civilization, which stands in sharp contrast to modern globalization.

Again, in criticizing the establishment of call centers in Gurgaon, near New Delhi, Roy deploys the same stable category—"ancient civilization"— to oppose modernity in the form of globalization: "I thought it would be interesting for a filmmaker to see how easily an ancient civilization can be made to abase itself completely."[34] In "Democracy," an essay that scrutinizes the Indian government's propensity to view Pakistan as its most deadly enemy—particularly in the aftermath of the Pokrahn nuclear tests of 1998, in which the Indian test was promptly followed by Pakistan's test as if they were running a relay race—Roy writes: "With each battle cry against Pakistan, we inflict a wound on ourselves, on *our way of life, on our spectacularly diverse and ancient civilization,* on everything that makes India different from Pakistan." She adds: *"Can we not find it in ourselves to belong to an ancient civilization instead of to just a recent nation?* To love a land instead of loving a territory?"[35]

It would be worth taking the trouble to ask the people working at these call centers—Muslims, Hindus, Christians, Jains, the scheduled classes, members of indigenous tribes, and others—if they all emerged organically from a single, ancient civilization. What is especially disturbing is that it is just this kind of single-minded insistence on historical reductionism that the Bharatiya Janata Party's central government of India has encouraged among its ardent followers, who believe that all non-Hindu communities in India should be subservient to the rule of the Hindu majority. The Hindutva fundamentalism of the BJP and its affiliated organizations like the Shiv Sena and the Rashtria Swayamsevak Sangh (National Volunteer Organization) have all publicly used the same idea—India as an ancient civilization, albeit a Hindu one—to reclaim India from non-Indian Muslims, Sikhs, Christians, Jains, and other minorities. It is all the more ironic that Roy's antiglobalization rhetoric, in this particular instance, overlaps neatly with the Hindutva fundamentalist plan to purify the nation. Roy affirms the existence of an ancient civilization to reclaim an untainted India from the impure forces of globalization, while the Hindutva traditionalists seek to purge India of its non-Hindu impurities. The bond that links them is never in question—the glorious civilization of ancient India. Outside of this grand narrative of globalization and civilization, the subalterns stand as subjects outside history.

THE TERRORIST STATE AND
THE TERRORIST

Much of Roy's dissent has a dual focus, as it both examines the rise of corporate culture in India and critiques American empire. This is evident in several of her essays, when she moves quickly from talking about India to commenting on U.S. multinational corporations and then shifts back again to the Indian context. In one sense she occupies the subject position of the syncretic border intellectual, straddling two worlds—textually, intellectually, culturally—and although she lives in India, her essays on American empire show a familiarity with domestic American cultural and political affairs that make her comments more persuasive than they would be otherwise. This dual focus is syncretic in the sense that it leads her to use a comparative perspective that does not so much examine each nation in its context as it identifies specific social issues—governmental abuse of authority, poverty, and so on—in order to draw out common-alities of power's operations and effects "to reclaim the space of civil dis-obedience."[36] This comparative context allows her to frame her dissent as resistance to global forms of capitalism and empire. But Roy is some-times so deeply invested in maintaining and legitimizing this conceptual apparatus that she obscures crucial distinctions, ascribing a universal character to very different movements of resistance. In "Peace Is War," a speech given in 2003 at the Center for the Study of Developing Societies in New Delhi, India, there is a reflective tone to her dissent that is absent in earlier essays. This welcome development enables her to keep a criti-cal distance from practices of dissent and forms of protest that she argues have succumbed to the powerful logic of media cultures that today de-pend on crises to generate news and, in the absence of crises, easily man-ufacture them: "While governments hone the art of crisis management (the art of waiting out a crisis), resistance movements are increasingly be-ing ensnared in a sort of vortex of crisis production. They have to find ways of precipitating crises, of manufacturing them in easily consumable, spectator-friendly formats."[37]

Roy argues that movements of resistance tend to operate like political campaigns, such as L. K. Advani's Rath Yatra and the *kar seva* (volunteer-ing for a religious purpose), which eventually resulted in the demolishing of the Babri Masjid in Ayodhya, and demands for rebuilding the temple of Ram in 1993. In Bombay alone, more than a thousand people died in the ensuing riots. In maintaining law and order, the state operates in dif-ferent ways, Roy points out, ignoring forms of violence like those in the Babri Masjid example, but quickly cracking down on protest meetings by the *adivasis*, as it did in April 2001 against the Adivasi Mukti Sangathan in Madhya Pradesh, and two months earlier in Jharkhand, when *adivasis* protested the building of the Koel Karo hydroelectric plant. In 2000, in the states of Gujarat and Orissa, police opened fire against *adivasi* demonstra-tors. But these are examples of the state and the media generating crises and inflaming people's passions, with disastrous results.

Roy gives two examples of resistance movements that were turned into spectacles—the threat of *jal samarpan* (suicide by drowning, as pro-

test) in India and the September 11 attacks on the United States. In response to the Supreme Court of India's ruling that allowed dams to be
built on the Narmada River, some protestors threatened to commit suicide
by drowning as a sign of ultimate resistance. Roy does not say directly that
all of this was a spectacle created by the movement, but she does say that
the media and the government treated such responses as another crisis to
be turned into a spectacle: "People resisting dams are expected to either
conjure new tricks or give up the struggle."[38] About the September 11 attacks, Roy writes: "We have entered the era of crisis as a consumer item,
crisis as spectacle, as theater. It's not new, but it's evolving, morphing, taking on new aspects. Flying planes into buildings is its most modern, most
extreme form."[39] There is an implied contrast made between an ostensibly premodern, indigenous use of suicide by drowning as protest and the
modern technique of using planes as weapons to bring down buildings. It
is significant that suicide is the operative mode of resistance in both examples. Although Roy provides detailed comments on the NBA in this
and other essays, she does not explain why she characterizes the taking
of thousands of innocent lives by the hijackers as protest by a resistance
movement.

To Roy, the poor people's struggles for democratic governance in India and the fight against the West led by Osama bin Laden and Al Qaeda
have the same meaning: they are both resistance movements, one resisting the state, and the other resisting empire. Such an equivalence is hard
to justify, both historically and ethically. However, the problem here is
not that Roy loses sight of ethics in drawing such equivalences, but that
there is a certain logic in how and why she arrives at such conclusions.
This logic is the ideological scaffolding of the critical apparatus that she
sets up uncritically, in order to produce her two-pronged dissent against
the Indian government and American empire. The histories of globalization are reduced to a single-stranded history of U.S. empire, and Indian
movements of civil disobedience become important footnotes to such a
historicization of the world. Thus, resistance against the state in a country
like India has the same social and ethical import as Al Qaeda's war against
the United States because India and its central and state governments are
but a small manifestation of the larger whole—the West and modernity.
American people and Indian people, American governments and Indian
governments, are all part of a world system that is managed by a single
nation-state—the United States—and they are all subjected to one single
culture—corporatism—which, of course, emanates from America. Such
a conception of world history and contemporary globalization creates an

axiology that erases profound differences in social circumstance, socio-economic demands and plans, rights of recognition, and strategies for articulating, mobilizing, and enacting resistance. Roy's dissent uses a meretricious reasoning that collapses stark differences in the ideologies and social commitments of a vast grass-roots movement like the NBA and bin Laden's methods of contesting empire by forming and inspiring groups like Al Qaeda.

Roy is hardly oblivious to the many dictators and oppressive regimes in various parts of the world. But because she believes that most of them were "installed, supported, and financed by the U.S government," and that the entire world is managed by a world system with the United States as its core and the rest as the periphery, all other despotisms and genocidal movements, governments, and peoples pale in comparison to the threat posed by the United States:

> Regardless of what the propaganda machine tells us, these tin-pot dictators are not the greatest threat to the world. The real and pressing danger, the greatest threat of all, is the locomotive force that drives the political and economic engine of the U.S. government, currently piloted by George Bush. Bush-bashing is fun, because he makes such an easy, sumptuous target. It's true that he is a dangerous, almost suicidal pilot, but the machine he handles is far more dangerous than the man himself.[40]

By characterizing Bush as an "almost suicidal pilot," Roy craftily compares him and the U.S. government with Al Qaeda and the suicidal pilots who hijacked four planes and killed thousands of people on September 11. The U.S. invasion and occupation of Iraq is hardly a decision that is unanimously accepted, but the point here is not about the U.S. military response to September 11, nor is it about U.S. support of dictators. It is about the United States being the most dangerous power to all the peoples of the world and, Bush—because he is president of the United States—becoming more dangerous than bin Laden. It is this conception of global processes, histories, and conditions that makes Roy liken Bush to bin Laden. Indeed, she sees them as twins, two sides of the same coin:

> But who is Osama bin Laden really?
> Let me rephrase that. What is Osama bin Laden?
> He's America's family secret. He is the American President's dark doppelganger. The savage twin of all that purports to be

beautiful and civilized. He has been sculpted from the spare rib
of a world laid to waste by America's foreign policy. . . . Now that
the family secret has been spilled, the twins are blurring into one
another and gradually becoming interchangeable. Their guns,
bombs, money, and drugs have been going around in the loop for
a while."[41]

In anticipation of President George Bush's visit on March 2, 2006, to
Rajghat, a memorial site, to pay tribute to Mahatma Gandhi, Roy notes
that Bush, the "world nightmare incarnate," is "by no means the only war
criminal who has been invited by the Indian government to lay flowers at
Rajghat. . . . But when George Bush places flowers on the famous slab of
highly polished stone, millions of Indians will wince. It will be as though
he has poured a pint of blood on the memory of Gandhi."[42]

In these passages, Roy explicitly equates Bush and bin Laden, allowing
one to stand in for the other, as "interchangeable" as a twin. She explains
away September 11 as nothing but the return of the repressed, the ghost
of America's support of dictators and wars. America is now experiencing
the violence and fear that she perpetrated on many governments and peoples around the world. The central cause of September 11 is America; she
is solely responsible for it. Nothing more, nothing less. Roy tells the inter-
viewer David Barsamian: "It's more like America is the hub of this huge
cultural and economic airline system. It's the nodal point. Everyone has to
be connected through America, and to some extent Europe."[43] Corporate
globalization's pursuit of free markets and capitalist expansion has led to
the "economic terrorism unleashed by neoliberalism, which devastates the
lives of millions of people, depriving them of water, food, electricity. Denying them medicine. Denying them education. Terrorism is the logical extension of this business of the free market. Terrorism is the privatization of
war." Today, both governments and terrorists do things that affect innocent
people, which is why "Osama bin laden and George Bush are both terrorists. They are both building international networks that perpetrate terror
and devastate people's lives. Bush, with the Pentagon, the WTO, the IMF,
and the World Bank, Bin Laden with Al Qaeda." To Barsamian's observation that the United States has "three or four percent of the world's population, yet it's consuming about a third of the world's natural resources, and
to maintain that kind of disparity and imbalance requires the use of force,
the use of violence," Roy responds: "The U.S. government is now speaking
about putting down unrest from space. It's a terrorist state, and it is laying
out a legitimate blue-print for state-sponsored terrorism."[44]

Ian Buruma contends that "her demonology of the United States takes on the foaming-at-the-mouth, eye-rolling quality of the mad evangelist. Unfortunately, it is this side of her, and not the campaigning against dam projects, that has found a worldwide audience. Roy has become the perfect Third World voice for anti-American, or anti-Western, or even anti-White, sentiments."[45] America becomes the meta-signifier of modernity and globalization; thus, to criticize any aspect of modernity is to criticize the West's complicity, largely due to the legacy of colonialism, and to criticize any dimension of globalization is to implicate the United States because it is the current superpower. This is why the most urgent, dangerous threat to the world is the United States. It is easy to conflate the United States as America and America as modernity. Once this conflation is postulated as an incontestable premise, the logical outcome is to render world history meaningful only insofar as it is interpreted through the prism formed by the machinations, tribulations, and anxieties of America and Americans. Hence, almost everything that "tin-pot dictators" do in the world pales in comparison to what the United States has done, is doing, and will do. To counter Roy does not mean discounting the extent of U.S. involvement in wars and coups in the more than 200 years of its history. What it does mean is making American empire not the sole cause, but one powerful strand, one important layer, a crucial pivot point in the webs of commerce and imperialism, in the networks of resistance and cultural give and take that have shaped the world over the last four hundred years—if we take the Renaissance and the settlement of the Americas as the beginning of modernity.

The problem with Roy's dissent is that although it makes a much-needed critique of the abuse of power by modern institutions of democracy and by the state in India, and although it gives the protest movements of rural, tribal peoples a broader appeal and public face, it conflates America with modernity and American history with world history, ending up with an ethical framework that is as crippling in its relativism as it is careless in its history. Roy's critique of American empire ironically relegitimizes American exceptionalism—American history as a manifestation of providential destiny—as it recenters Americans by universalizing their anxieties, actions, and desires. About the worldwide opposition to the U.S. invasion of Iraq, Roy writes:

> Most courageous of all are the hundreds of thousands of American people on the streets of America's great cities—Washington, New York, Chicago, San Francisco. *The fact is that the only insti-*

tution in the world that is more powerful than the American gov-
ernment is American civil society. American citizens have a huge
responsibility riding on their shoulders. How can we not salute
and support those who not only acknowledge but act upon that
responsibility? They are our allies, our friends.[46]

The argument that civil society in America is the "only institution in
the world that is more powerful than the American government" echoes
the myth of the "city on a hill"—set apart, unique, untainted by worldly
events—that shaped American culture and history from the time of the
nation's founding. Since Roy's affirmation of American society further re-
inforces the tendency to navel gaze, it can justify the U.S. national preoc-
cupation with the here and the now, a presentism that is unmindful of history. Internationalism demands an outward orientation, a curiosity made
uncomfortable by but interested in what lies beyond the nation's borders,
outside of the purview of official culture. It would make perfect sense for
Americans to imagine themselves as so utterly indispensable to the world
that some of them become feverish with the desire to bring democracy
and freedom to unfortunate peoples. The U.S. invasion of Iraq was often
justified on these grounds. The more Americans imagine themselves to be
at the center of the universe, the easier it is for the state to obtain public
consent for its interventionist, militarist policies.
    Roy's dissent generates a state of emergency and a state of exception-
alism: the American government is the greatest threat to the world, and
American society is the best hope for the world. Both states are viewed as
unique, out of the ordinary, or exceptional, which requires the suspension
of the normal. America as empire and America as civil society are in suspended animation: historically, ethically, and politically. The paradoxical
nature of these states of emergency is that they cannot and need not become entangled with all that is deemed non-American. And when the return to normalcy is predicated on the exceptional valorization of American society, the complex struggles and histories of the peoples of the world
become mere footnotes to American history. The rich history of the NBA
in India and Roy's own involvement with it offer persuasive correctives to
this paradox. Indeed, they call into question its requirement of American
self-isolation from history and universal representation of all humanity.
But since Roy's dissent exceptionalizes American empire and centralizes
American society as the emerging model and hope for the world, empire
can now artfully manage its dissent and produce its critiques while simultaneously perpetuating its own existence.

Given how this paradox structures Roy's dissents and the axiology they produce and legitimize, it is all the more important to subject her, her subject positions, and her dissent to close scrutiny. Not least because the admirable work she has done and continues to do can, despite her best intentions and disavowals, undermine the promising directions in which her critiques could be extended. We cannot let the crippling paradox of her dissents against American empire render superfluous the important work done by various groups, movements, peoples, and communities in India, across the divides of caste, religion, and language, in successfully inserting into the public imagination new ways of thinking about progress, new ways of conceiving of human rights, democracy, ecology, and sustainability. We need to understand the nature of those movements that cannot be reduced to effects of American empire. We need to reject Roy's paradox that grants universal hegemony to "the only institution in the world more powerful than the American government"—American civil society. We can avoid succumbing to the seductive power of such exceptionalist visions of America by developing a world-mindedness that has greater awareness of American imperialism without Americanizing the rich and varied histories and cultures of the world. This approach can also help us reject the paralyzing relativism of Roy's dissents that makes the NBA and Al Qaeda commensurable, the *jal samarpan* of anguished *adivasis* equivalent to the murderous rage that took around 3,000 lives on September 11.

WATER AND RESISTANCE: RETHINKING DEVELOPMENT

Originating in Amarkantak, Madhya Pradesh, the Narmada River flows more than 1,300 kilometers across the states of Gujarat and Maharashtra. The Sardar Sarovar Project on the Narmada in Gujarat comprises an "irrigation network" covering 40, 920 miles, 3,344 villages, and 4.4 million acres that include parts of Rajasthan. There are already 4,050 dams in India, and 475 more are in the process of being built. They are categorized as large (covering an area of 10,000 hectares or more), medium (covering 400 to 10,000 hectares), and minor (covering under 400 hectares).[47] Constituted in 1969, the Narmada Waters Dispute Tribunal released its report ten years later, providing an ambitious river management scheme that included 30 major dams, 125 medium dams, and 3,000 minor dams.[48] The Sardar Sarovar Project was to have a reservoir 124 miles long and 1.24 miles wide, covering 86,440 acres in the states of Madhya Pradesh, Maha-

rashtra, and Gujarat, which included 248 villages inhabited by 66,593 people—of whom two-thirds were identified as *adivasis*.[49] Later estimates put
the number of people between 145,000 and 170,000.[50]

According to the World Commission on Dams, as of 2000 between
sixteen and thirty-eight million people had been displaced by large dams
in India.[51] Public opposition to further dams quickly followed the report's
publication, but a point needs clarification here. Roy gained prominence as
a socially conscious writer following the publication of her essays "The End
of Imagination" and "The Greater Common Good" in *Outlook* and *Front-
line*, respectively (both essays were republished in *The Cost of Living*). Before she published these essays, which are highly critical of the dam building projects, she won the 1997 Booker Prize for *The God of Small Things*.
Given her rise to international fame as a novelist, *The Cost of Living* generated extensive interest in the rise of mass protest movements such as the
NBA and in its emphasis on environmentalism, sustainability, and democratic protest. Although socially engaged celebrities generally attract a
wide audience domestically and internationally, celebrity culture tends to
personalize major social events and processes to the point where complex
historical contexts are simplified, and individual agency either on the part
of the celebrity or the people associated with the movement is publicly
lauded or decried. Especially to readers located in the West, then, the challenge is to avoid equating the NBA with Roy or public mobilization against
governmental apathy and injustice with Roy's dissents, and to avoid granting her and her work a kind of Third World authenticity and unproblematic representational function. The following sketch of the rise in opposition to dam building in India can help address this challenge.

The Forest Conservation Act of 1980 gave the central Department of
Environment the authority to assess the plans of the governments of Gujarat and Madhya Pradesh to address the environmental impact of the
Sardar Sarovar Project. In 1983 the department determined that they failed
to meet its requirements, and only four years later did the state government get clearance to proceed. Various people, groups, and organizations
began seriously examining and criticizing the actions of the state and national governments: Dhirubhai L. Sheth from Lokayan (meaning "transformation"), an organization formed by the Centre for the Study of Developing Societies in Delhi; Bhanubhai Adhvariyu and Achyut Yagnik from
Vishamata Nirmoolan Samiti (the Disparity Eradication Committee), the
Centre for Social Knowledge and Action, and the Centre for Social Studies
in Gujarat; Ambrish and Trupti Mehta from Chhatra Yuva Sangharsh Va-

hini (the Student Youth Struggle Force); Anil Patel from Action Research in Community Health and Development; Father Mathew Kalathil from the Rajpipla Social Service Society; Harivallabhbhai Parikh from Anand Niketan Ashram (House of Joy); Girish Patel from Lok Adhikar Sangh (the Association for People's Authority); and Baba Amte and Medha Patkar from Narmada Ghati Dharangrastha Samiti (the Committee for the Dam-Affected of the Narmada Valley, Maharashtra) and Narmada Ghati Navnirman Samiti (the Narmada Valley New Awakening Committee, Madhya Pradesh).[52]

In *Deep Water*, Jacques Leslie's account of the life and work of Medha Patkar, the most prominent member of the NBA, it is amply clear that she and others like her play a mediating role between the people affected by dam building (mostly tribal and indigenous people who make their living by farming and fishing) and government officials, politicians, judges, police, writers, reporters, and the public at large. They conduct workshops, sit-ins, and informal seminars for rural people to educate them about threats of dispossession, promises of relocation, and their civil rights, and inform them about anti-dam movements in other countries. This pedagogical role involves two levels of representation—one vis-à-vis the tribal people, who are given information and taught strategies and skills of protest, and the other vis-à-vis the wider society, which is educated about the injustices of industrialization.[53] As noted above, the challenge for Western readers of Roy's writings on the NBA is to avoid conflating the NBA with Roy and to develop a richer understanding of the long struggle against big dams and governmental apathy led by other Indian activists, of whom Patkar and Baba Amte are notable for the high esteem in which they are held by Indians.

Several nongovernmental organizations (NGOs) eventually merged to form the NBA. There were significant disagreements among the various antidam groups over strategies and, eventually, over their views on modernity and development. Since the four states of Gujarat, Rajasthan, Maharashtra, and Madhya Pradesh had different priorities and needs, and since their governments related in different ways to the central government, an approach that worked well in one state often did not work as well in another. The demands for recognition, rehabilitation, and accountability often pitted peoples and groups from these states against each other. For instance, the government of Gujarat set up a Grievances Redressal Authority, which examined 14,158 complaints from April 1999 through December 2000, and found 10,725 of them to be favorably determined. But in

Madhya Pradesh, when dam construction began at Bargi, Mann, and Maheshwar, the NBA protested the action of S. Kumars Ltd., the private construction company involved, and the state government intervened by arresting hundreds of protestors.[54]

Although these efforts have often been framed in terms of dam development and the relocation and rehabilitation of *adivasis* and other affected people, the complexities of water management raise different social, political, and economic issues, all of which have varying degrees and kinds of impact on people, who themselves live in different states and face different challenges and needs. People need water for drinking, irrigation, sanitation, fishing, controlling floods, hydroelectricity, and industrial purposes, among other uses. And because these uses involve territorial rights, community rights, the nature of river flows, the quality of water, and the kind of dams built for purposes ranging from irrigation to the provision of drinking water, they become part of the region's and country's politics. Specific demands made by those opposing and supporting dams are related to questions of participation and the openness of decision-making processes: for example, the height of a dam determines how much land will be submerged and how many people displaced; claims to protect tribal cultures or ways of life must be assessed to make sure the tribal people are being fairly represented; both governments and residents must benefit from the final agreement. And who will decide issues concerning navigation, risks of earthquakes, waterlogged or salinized soil, mercury formation, water-borne diseases, greenhouse gas emissions, and the maintenance of machinery and facilities?[55] Hundreds of NGOs and activist groups take positions on these issues that often put them at loggerheads with each other and make it difficult to develop a single pro- or anti-dam movement. In some cases, tensions have been so high that other activists have vandalized NBA offices in Gujarat.[56]

Since 1981, the central and state governments had received loans for the Sardar Sarovar Project from the World Bank. It commissioned an independent review of the project, and when the resulting report came out in 1992, it strongly opposed the project, faulting its inadequate planning and implementation. This increased opposition to both the project and the report. In September 1992, a World Bank team headed by Pamela Cox submitted another report that overlooked several problems the independent review had raised, which further increased tensions among opposing camps within the NBA. Some moved beyond seeking fairness and equity for those whom the dam had displaced to total opposition to the dam, seeking to stop all construction.[57] Spurred on by the withdrawal of the World Bank, the NBA filed suit in 1994 in the Supreme Court to stop the project, and the court agreed to suspend construction. But in 2000, the court issued a judgment in favor of Sardar Sarovar, while making several recommendations for addressing the issues raised by the NBA. In 2006, the NBA filed a motion against the Narmada Control Authority for raising the height of the dam, but the court decided to wait for another report before ruling on the motion.[58]

Over the last two decades, in light of blatant governmental ineptitude, lack of information, unclear policies, lack of transparency and accountability in governments and courts, and shoddy implementation of relocation and rehabilitation programs, the NBA's emphasis has shifted to stopping the construction of big dams completely. Roy asks: "Is it unreasonable to call for a moratorium on the construction of Big Dams until past mistakes have been rectified and the millions of uprooted people have been truly recompensed and rehabilitated? It is the only way an industry that has so far been based on lies and false promises can redeem itself."[59]

Such has been the large-scale impact of the NBA, both in drawing worldwide attention to the plight of the displaced and the inefficiency of big dam projects, that with its rejection of such massive state-sponsored, partially privatized projects, it has put into question the philosophy of development and its relation to modernity and nationalism. Ramaswamy Iyer avers that "the NBA is a great mass movement, one of the most important since independence; it—and the Tehri movement—have forever altered our understanding of such projects."[60] In *Dams and Development*, Sanjeev Khagram says that it was because of the movement's impact that the World Bank was forced to commission, for the first time, an independent review of one of its projects. But the report was so critical of the entire Narmada plan that the bank, along with Japanese funders, was forced to withdraw financial support. The transnational dynamics of all this, including the globalization of human rights discourse, the rise of environmentalism, and the rapid increase of NGOs all over the world, created a critical mass that enabled this resistance movement to question the hegemonic idea of development—"large-scale, top-down, and technocratic pursuit of economic growth through the intense exploitation of natural resources"—and give legitimacy to experimenting with alternative ideas of development—"bottom-up and participatory processes directed towards socially just and ecologically sustainable outcomes."[61]

Two points need to be noted here: first, the nature of this protest movement's operations, strategies, and policies; and second, the movement's significance for reconceptualizing modernity and development. The

fact that there was no destruction of government property; kidnapping, in-
timidating, or killing of state officials and civic leaders; and complete and
forceful takeover of machinery, infrastructure, or finances from prodam
agencies underscores the civic and nonviolent nature of the movement.
Besides publicizing its cause, providing information, and generally raising awareness of related problems in villages and cities, the NBA used acts
of civic disobedience like *rasta-roko* (blocking roads), *gherao* (encircling),
dharna (staging a sit-in or fasting) to register dissent in the public arena.[62]
In asking for studies, reviews, new assessments, changes, revisions, and
annulments of charters, policies, and court judgments, this grass-roots
movement eventually compelled a rethinking of development and modernity. Given that social, economic, and political forces had been accelerating the process of globalization for several decades, the movement's questioning of basic assumptions is all the more laudatory. By linking the fight
against dams to issues of environmental protection, ecosystems, the use of
natural resources, displacement of people and reparations to them, institutional and governmental power, civic obligations, and the civil society,
the movement garnered the attention and support of other groups and
peoples around the world and acquired global significance. It has led to
what John Wood calls the "revival of traditional water harvesting systems": the use of *kunds* (underground tanks that store water from catch-
ment areas); *kuhls* (streams that divert water toward fields); *phads* (small
canals that channel water from a nearby tank to irrigate an area divided
into small zones); *virdas* (wells dug in low-lying areas); *vavs* (step wells);
talavs (small reservoirs); managing the watershed through increased participation by those directly affected and widespread leveling of fields and
planting of trees; check dams (which collect rainwater for wells); *nalla*
plugs (smaller check dams); and collecting rainwater on roofs.[63] These alternatives should not be taken to indicate the absence of politics in water
management, but to show that a different kind of power balance can exist
between people and governments, the elite and the poor, the educated and
the illiterate.

Let me be clear: the arguments I am making are primarily about the
failure of the border intellectual, or about the need to not trust Roy or other
border intellectuals. In numerous ways, the wide publicity that her writings
have generated has put the spotlight on issues of great importance for people and communities in India and the world. I have already pointed to several positions that Roy has adopted and actions she has taken—especially
her active involvement with the NBA—that are worth publicizing. But as I
hope this discussion has shown, as Roy has risen to prominence as a rep-

resentative of the Third World in the global cultural circuits and enclaves where her work, speeches, and lectures have gained legitimacy as the genuinely alternative, anti-global voice of dissent and revolution, she has unwittingly become complicitous in the First World's efforts to produce an authentic, non-Western voice and presence. She has also constantly reaffirmed the clichéd verities of fundamentalist, antidemocratic movements. Underpinning her work is a predictable tautology of assumed intentions and presumed reactions, which lead her to further legitimize, through her dissent, the workings of empire and the ideological machinations of the powerful. Roy's critical apparatus of dissent—the displacement of the subaltern by the elite; the claims to absolute and pure knowledge; the easy interchangeability of historical differences; the consolidation of exceptionalist discourse to legitimize dissent about empire; the collapsing of world history into American global history; and the insistence on the stability of the border intellectual's role—must be rigorously examined.

When, in some instances, the difference between a critique of fundamentalist fervor and multinational corporations pivots around the axis of exclusivist ideas of national belonging and civilizational otherness, it becomes even more urgent to scrutinize the border intellectuals' power to co-opt the space of the subaltern and to speak in the name of, and as the complete embodiment of, the poor and the disenfranchised. It is this sense of urgency that propels my discussion. To that end I have tried to articulate important concerns about border intellectuals in a global economy. Roy's critique can be effective in weakening the nexus of power politics if modernity can be conceptualized in more complex ways. A fairly recent example demonstrates an important shift in Roy's approach to dissent and resistance. It involves Nandigram, India.

BLOWBACK: THE COST OF MANUFACTURING DISSENT

On March 14, 2007, fourteen people were killed and several wounded in Nandigram, in the state of West Bengal, when police confronted hundreds of farmers, peasants, and activists protesting the state government's attempt to gain control of thousands of acres to allow the Indonesian Salim Group to build chemical plants. Under the Special Economic Zones Act ratified by the Indian Parliament in 2005, state governments could mark specific zones in which complex and advanced infrastructure could be built, industries set up, and thousands of new jobs created. The aim was to spur exports and attract foreign investments with a view to creating large-scale employment opportunities. Over the last three decades, the Left Front, an alliance of several Communist and progressive political parties, has held power in West Bengal, and in 2007, the Communist Party of India (Marxist) (CPI[M]) was heading the government, with Buddhadeb Bhattacharjee as chief minister.

That the Left should be actively seeking to industrialize parts of the state and contracting with foreign companies to establish new industries is important in the Indian context. But more significant is the fact that state violence was used to quell demonstrations against government policies, although the situation appears to be less a clear-cut instance of state versus farmers and more a confrontation between the CPI(M), which was part of the government, and other political parties like the Trinamul Congress Party and Maoist organizations vying for political control. Several thousand inhabitants of Nandigram, some of them supporters of the CPI(M), had been displaced before March 14, in several episodes of violence, intimidation, and forced removal. The government's attempt to relocate other peoples on March 14 was met with opposition. Protestors argued that the close connections between the police and the CPI(M) activists compromised the government's ability to act as an independent, unbiased organ of the state charged with maintaining order and peace.

In response to the events of March 14, famous Leftist intellectuals including Noam Chomsky, Howard Zinn, and Tariq Ali, published an open letter in the *Hindu*, a major Indian national newspaper, on November 22, 2007. It reads:

> To Our Friends in Bengal:
>
> News travels to us that events in West Bengal have overtaken the optimism that some of us have experienced during trips to the state. We are concerned about the rancour that has divided the public space, created what appear to be unbridgeable gaps between people who share similar values. It is this that distresses us. We hear from people on both sides of this chasm, and we are trying to make some sense of the events and the dynamics. Obviously, *our distance prevents us* from saying anything definitive.
>
> We continue to trust that the people of Bengal will not allow their differences on some issues to tear apart the important experiments undertaken in the State (land reforms, local self-government).

We send our fullest solidarity to the peasants who have been forcibly dispossessed. We understand that the government has promised not to build a chemical hub in the area around Nandigram. We understand that those who had been dispossessed by the violence are now being allowed back to their homes, without recrimination. We understand that there is now talk of reconciliation. This is what we favour.

The balance of forces in the world is such that it would be impetuous to split the Left. We are faced with a world power that has demolished one state (Iraq) and is now threatening another (Iran). *This is not the time for division when the basis of division no longer appears to exist.*[64]

This is a remarkable piece of dissent because the logic of critique against empire—which Roy and others like her passionately espouse—leads to this impasse, in which the dispossessed farmers of Nandigram become small players in the planetary drama between the champions of the downtrodden, those elite, media-savvy, prodigious producers of scholarship and knowledge, and the ostensibly cabal-driven, terror machine called America led by fundamentalists like Bush, Cheney, and their acolytes. Some of these intellectuals have visited India, and although they are located in the West, they have presumably, through their visits, gained adequate knowledge about the imbroglio. They have also received news from others, which shows the flow of information between East and West. They have heard from "people on both sides of this chasm," indicating that their position is neutral. They express sympathy for all those adversely affected by violence and, in anaphoric sentences, state the assurances they have received from the government that the chemical plants will not be built, that the affected people can return, and that gestures of "reconciliation" have been made. The last paragraph is where the full force of American exceptionalism is in blatant display—because America has occupied Iraq and is "threatening" Iran, this is not the time to "be impetuous [and] split the Left," since "the basis of division no longer appears to exist."

Like Roy, who finds no difference between bin Laden and Bush and who calls America a terrorist state, these intellectuals develop their dissent and their understanding of world history by unquestioningly centering America in a global system in which anything that is not directly related to the United States becomes supplementary. "This is the type of left politics," writes Martha Nussbaum in "Violence on the Left," "that holds that the enemy of my enemy is my friend, no matter how many rapes and murders that friend has actually perpetrated."[65] Nandigram once again becomes just another footnote to the magnificent fight between good and evil, between enlightened intellectuals like Chomsky, Zinn, Ali, et al. and unenlightened ones like Bush et al. The sufferings of the dispossessed of Nandigram can be ameliorated only insofar as they can be made relevant to fighting the United States. Anything short of that is an "impetuous" distraction.

But here is the problem: there is nothing in this dissent that can help Nandigram's victims understand why and how the CPI(M) and the government of West Bengal used state machinery to threaten, coerce, rape, and kill people in violent confrontations, or learn how to contest the party and the government politically and ideologically. There is nothing in this dissent that can help CPI(M) workers victimized by opposing parties in West Bengal understand and resist intimidation. These intellectuals want those fighting against injustice in Nandigram to know that what really matters in today's global world is America. To these intellectuals, there is no "basis of division" in the Left. But what kind of intellectual blindness proclaims that there is no basis for division when the CPI(M) and other political parties have engaged in thuggish brutality and illegality? To the grieving families of those killed in Nandigram, there is too much basis for division because what they see is the color of blood, what they touch is a mangled corpse, what they lament is injustice. But to the writers and signers of this open letter, all this can lead to an undesirable and "impetuous" splitting of the Left, that one great hope for humankind.

The irony of the events in Nandigram, in the context of this chapter's focus on dissent and Roy, is that luminaries like Chomsky, Zinn, and Ali have been publicly chastised by Roy, Mahasweta Devi, Sumit Sarkar, and other Indian activists for precisely the reasons I have just criticized the open letter, and more ironically, Roy herself. The first paragraph of their statement "A CPI (M) Public Relations Coup," a response to the open letter, reads:

> We read with growing dismay the statement signed by Noam Chomsky, Howard Zinn and others advising those opposing the CPI(M)'s pro-capitalist policies in West Bengal not to "split the Left" in the face of American imperialism. We believe that for some of the signatories, their distance from events in India has resulted in their falling prey to a CPI(M) public relations coup and that they may have signed the statement without fully real-

ising the import of it and what it means here in India, not just in Bengal.[66]

They further note that with its commitment to industrialization, the CPI(M) has strayed from the cherished goals of the Left and has resorted to propaganda, an example of which is the very statement signed by Chomsky and others. Complicating matters further is the largely anti-Muslim rhetoric of the government and its indifference to the disproportionate unemployment of minority groups. The statement ends:

> History has shown us that internal dissent is invariably silenced by dominant forces claiming that a bigger enemy is at the gate. Iraq and Iran are not the only targets of that bigger enemy. The struggle against SEZ's [Special Economic Zones] and corporate globalization is an intrinsic part of the struggle against U.S. imperialism.
>
> We urge our fellow travellers among the signatories to that statement, not to treat the "Left" as homogeneous, for there are many different tendencies which claim that mantle, as indeed you will recognize if you look at the names on your own statement.[67]

These Indian intellectuals caution those in the West against assuming that the Left has throughout history had a set of common concerns, and against setting up hierarchies of injustice by using the West, especially its policies toward and actions in the East, as the principal yardstick for measuring to what extent people can criticize the Left and fight against oppression. Although Susan George, one of the signatories of the open letter, later issued a statement apologizing for and withdrawing her support for the document,[68] the response by Chomsky and others reassured their critics that they were neither supporting the government's policies nor condoning its actions, but only trying to "implor[e] a restoration of unity among the left forces in India" and not "dismiss [the CPI(M)] wholesale as an unredeemable party."[69] Missing from this response is any mention of their earlier advice to critique the more important enemy, America; to them, the problem seems to be more a matter of clearing up a misunderstanding.

Such is the blinding power of their ideological commitments that they cannot recognize that what led them to issue a statement about Nandigram was their uncritical reliance on a world system with a single power—America—at the center, and everything and everyone responding to it, relying on it, or resisting it. It is this notion of history and the dynamics of contemporary globalization that produce the kind of dissent promulgated by Roy, Chomsky, and others. A mark of Roy's courage is that, to her credit, she took a public stand against Chomsky and his allies and refused to subordinate the resistance movement against the Left in West Bengal to the larger worldwide resistance to the United States. However, there is in her critiques of the Indian government as an occupying power in the state of Kashmir, and the government's interaction with the armed rebellion of Maoist-Naxalite groups in India, a distinct shift in her idea of social change, a shift that can best be characterized as the Fanonian turn.

DECOLONIZING INDIA:
THE FANONIAN TURN

A leading figure in anticolonial movements in the twentieth century, Frantz Fanon gained worldwide attention for, among other things, his views on the relationship between colonizer and colonized, which he argued is always fraught with an odd mix of desire, anger, envy, and pride; the psychological turmoil that grips colonizer and colonized; and the role of violence in independence movements—in particular, its exhilarating, almost cathartic power to liberate the oppressed by vanquishing the colonial enemy and completely dismantling oppressive society. The power and appeal of Fanon's writings such as *The Wretched of the Earth* and *Black Skin, White Masks* lie not in his idea of colonial society as fundamentally Manichaean, but in his insights into the psychic dimensions of colonization, the role of violence in forestalling annihilation or complete domination, and the need to think beyond binaries of good and evil, right and wrong, colonizer and colonized, servitude and freedom. As Homi Bhabha puts it, Fanon "not only changes what we understand by a *political* demand but transforms the very means by which we recognize and identify its *human agency*," and in this sense, Fanon's idea of social transformation "emerges, not as an assertion of will nor as an evocation of freedom, but as an enigmatic questioning."[70] In several essays collected in *Field Notes on Democracy* and *Broken Republic*, Roy, like Fanon, examines how oppressed peoples respond to their conditions of oppression, but there is a difference: whereas Fanon pitted colonized against the colonizer and the native against the foreign, colonial invader or settler, Roy relocates the phenomenon of armed rebellion within the national context in order to expose the Indian state's colonial relations with its minorities (Muslims, Jains, Buddhists, Christians, lower castes, and *adivasis*), and its systematic suppression, through military means, of the Kashmiri people's struggle for self-determination.

In these recent essays, Roy highlights the following developments in order to show the transformation of Indian democracy into a theater of farce. When Prime Minister Indira Gandhi was assassinated by her Sikh bodyguards in 1984, indiscriminate assaults on the Sikhs left 3,000 of them dead. The Babri Mosque, in Uttar Pradesh, was demolished in 1992 by Hindu zealots in order to reclaim the birthplace of Lord Ram for the Hindus, and hundreds of people were killed in the ensuing riots. The BJP—whose leaders, including L. K. Advani, launched a campaign called the Rath Yatra in support of a Hindu takeover of the Babri Mosque site—was in power from 1998 to 2004, and it was followed by a government led by the Congress Party, from 2004 to the present. In 2002, fifty-eight Hindus, a majority of whom were returning from a visit to Ayodhya, were killed when carriages of the Sabarmati Express train were set on fire. The retaliatory attacks that followed resulted in gang rapes; the brutal murder of Ehsan Jafri, a Muslim who had been a member of Parliament; the deaths of 2,000 people; and the displacement of 150,000. Narendra Modi—who was chief minister of Gujarat when these communal riots occurred, and who has often been criticized for his administration's lackadaisical stance toward preventing and controlling social unrest, and at times for giving free rein to Hindu mobs intent on attacking Muslims—has been reelected twice and is currently in his third term.

In 1999, Graham Stains, a missionary from Australia, and his two sons were burned alive by Hindu radicals. Supported by Islamic extremist groups in Pakistan, militants attacked the Indian Parliament in 2001; the suspects who were arrested, tried, and convicted included Kashmiris, one of whom—Mohammed Afzal—was sentenced to be hanged. Roy argues that because his trial was marred by procedural and evidentiary flaws, Afzal should be retried and the government should conduct a thorough examination of all reports, documents, legal proceedings, and other evidence pertaining to the attack. In 2008, in Karnataka, a state led by the BJP, young women wearing jeans and dresses or visiting pubs were verbally and physically attacked by Hindu extremists. The state and federal governments in India agreed in 2008 to transfer up to 100 acres of forest land to the Amarnath Shrine Board, to facilitate access and enhance pilgrimage to holy sites in Kashmir. After large-scale protests and killings due to police firing on protestors, the agreement was rescinded. Over the last few years, there have been several Maoist-Naxal uprisings in Dantewada, Chattisgarh, Orissa, West Bengal, Jharkhand, and Andhra Pradesh, against the state governments' policies to relocate people in order to spur economic growth—euphemistically called modern development—by creating Special Economic Zones, building dams and manufacturing plants, and giving mining rights to companies that made it impossible for *adivasis* and other poor people to continue their traditional socioeconomic practices. In Chattisgarh, the state government worked with the Salwa Judum (Peace March), a loose association of various anti-Naxal groups that included the poor and *adivasis*, to counter Naxalite influence in the villages. This initiative has been criticized for its extralegal use of violence against Maoists, its use of young *adivasis* as special police officers, and its role as an instrument of the state to sustain, through undemocratic means, the rule of law and democracy. In "Walking with the Comrades," Roy distills her arguments thus:

> Almost from the moment India became a sovereign nation, it turned into a colonial power, annexing territory, waging war. It has never hesitated to use military interventions to address political problems—Kashmir, Hyderabad, Goa, Nagaland, Manipur, Telangana, Assam, Punjab, the Naxalite uprising in West Bengal, Bihar, Andhra Pradesh and now across the tribal areas of Central India. Tens of thousands have been killed with impunity, hundreds of thousands tortured. All of this behind the benign mask of democracy. Who have these wars been waged against? Muslims, Christians, Sikhs, Communists, Dalits, Tribals and, most of all, against the poor who dare to question their lot instead of accepting the crumbs that are flung at them. *It's hard not to see that the Indian State is an essentially upper-caste Hindu State (regardless of the party in power) which harbours a reflexive hostility towards the "other."*[71]

The idea of the nation as a powerful ideological force that fashions unity out of immense diversity—often through marginalization, repression, denial, forgetting, and violence—is underscored in this passage. What makes it controversial, given that it was written in 2010 and that it focuses on contemporary events more than sixty years after India's independence, is Roy's claim that the "Indian State is an essentially upper-caste Hindu State." Because of this long history of violence against minority groups—including the Kashmiri Pandits (Hindu inhabitants of Kashmir) and especially the Muslims of Kashmir, the majority of this state's population—Roy moves a step further: "India needs Azadi [freedom] from Kashmir just as much—if not more—than Kashmir needs Azadi from India."[72] In a speech on October 24, 2010, at a seminar organized by the Jammu and Kashmir Coalition of Civil Society, Roy notes that, when a reporter asked her if Kashmir was an integral part of India, she had responded: "Kashmir has never been an integral part of India. . . . This is not something I've invented. It's not some radical position that I am taking. It's a historical fact . . . even the Indian government has accepted it."[73] Three days earlier, at another seminar, Roy had said that India had "waged protracted war against its own people or what it calls its own people relentlessly since 1947," particularly its minorities. As the "most militarized zone in the world," with close to 700,000 military personnel managing social order in Kashmir, this was an "endless war by an upper caste Hindu state," which is the "modern history of our country." For these remarks, the BJP party urged the central government to bring sedition charges against Roy and Syed Ali Shah Geelani, a Kashmiri leader, and in November 2010, a formal complaint was registered by the police.[74]

The Fanonian turn in Roy's support for the Kashmiris' self-determination and Maoist rebellion is evident in her focus on the role of violence in a democracy, the abuses of the state, and the armed response to such abuses by the victims. Bemoaning the farcical condition of Indian society—in which electoral democracy is often viewed as the only viable guarantor of progress, development, and equality—Roy criticizes majority rule and democratic elections between political parties that go on to take nondemocratic, forceful measures against various ethnic, tribal, and religious groups and get reelected by adroitly spreading disinformation, controlling access to the media and technology, engaging in propaganda, and using covert force to quell opposing ideas or groups. She argues that "the system of representative democracy—too much representation, too little democracy—needs some structural adjustment."[75] Powerful political groups have "realized that a democratic mandate can legitimize their pillaging in a way that nothing else can."[76] In a situation where the "Muslim community has seen a sharp decline in its fortunes and is now at the bottom of the social pyramid, along with the Dalits and Adivasis," and 70,000 people in Kashmir have died between 1989 and 2006,[77] it is understandable why people are engaging in armed resistance:

> People who have taken to arms have done it with full knowledge
> of what the consequences of that decision will be. They have done
> so knowing that they are on their own. They know that the new
> laws of the land criminalize the poor and conflate resistance with

terrorism. They know that appeals to conscience, liberal morality, and sympathetic press coverage will not help them now. They
know no international marches, no globalized dissent, no famous
writers will be around when the bullets fly. Hundreds of thousands have broken faith with the institutions of India's democracy. Large swathes of the country have fallen out of the government's control.[78]

In seeking to understand the reasons for Maoist resistance and in providing a broad national context within which the failures of Indian democracy are inextricably linked with the exploitation of the poor and *adivasis*, Roy, like Fanon, locates the role of social violence on a continuum
of historical and material contradictions that have pitted a state intent on
pursuing policies of modernization against various people who—without recourse to the institutions of modernity, and finding themselves on
the brink of forced displacement, incarceration, or annihilation—take up
arms as a desperate act of resistance. As Fanon writes in *The Wretched
of the Earth*, "on the logical plane, the Manichaeism of the settler produces a Manichaeism of the native."[79] Each dreams of a future in which the
other is absent, while both are locked in deadly combat. To Roy, the Indian
state and the Naxalites are locked in a Manichaean conflict: the state uses
the police, the political and judicial apparatus, the media, and its institutional power to further the program of modernization but subverts processes and principles of fairness, equity, freedom of expression, and equality, which in turn generates anger, fear, mistrust, and desperation that is
translated into armed rebellion against the state. The oppressed peoples
refuse integration into the national body and mainstream society, through
processes that take from them their rights, territories, and desires and fail
to supply their needs, and that are subsumed within an official narrative
in which to resist the state is tantamount to sedition, and the spread of
social anarchy can be controlled only by the legitimate exercise of large-
scale force. This is the intractable conflict. This is the agonizing drama in
which a democratic nation yields to its baser instincts and, in the name
of progress and justice, subverts its own hallowed institutions and thus
turns its citizens into enemies of the state. It is not surprising that Roy
contends, echoing Malcolm X, that *"people believe that faced with exter-
mination they have the right to fight back. By any means necessary,"*[80] a position that she reiterates in an interview with the writer Amitava Kumar:
"So, my position is just that it would be immoral of me to preach violence
to anybody unless I am prepared to pick up arms myself. But I think it is

equally immoral of me to preach nonviolence when I am not bearing the brunt of the attack."[81]

BEYOND GANDHI AND GANDHIANISM?

Written after Roy lived for a few days with the Maoists in the Dantewada jungles, talking to men, women, and children in the group, and observing their habitats and efforts to mobilize themselves into an effective insurgency, "Walking with the Comrades" offers a view of *adivasi* life that is detailed, sympathetic, and contextually specific. She eats with them, talks with them, listens to them, sleeps in their huts and on their *jhillis* (mats), treks with them, and seeks to understand their obduracy toward the state and modern development. Her courage and interest in rendering the *adivasis* and *dalits*—the neglected, discarded, or disdained sections of Indian society—as people with humanity and dignity is worthy of high praise. To Roy, the Indian government's four-decades-long civilizing mission—its attempt to bring the poor, illiterate, *adivasi* and *dalit* peasants into mainstream society—is a history of ruthless exploitation, as more than sixty million people have been "displaced by rural destitution, by slow starvation, by floods and drought (many of them man-made), by mines, steel factories and aluminum smelters, by highways and expressways, by the 3300 big dams built since independence, and now by special economic zones (SEZs). They're part of the 836 million people of India who live on less than twenty rupees a day, the ones who starve while millions of tons of good grain is either eaten by rats in government warehouses or burnt in bulk (because it's cheaper to burn food than to distribute it to poor people)."[82] The intersecting discourses and movements of national progress and democracy have led to conditions in which state policies for land allotment, relocation, displacement, compensation, equity, and allocation of resources for farming, ranching, and village-based industries and economies were unevenly applied, if applied at all—resulting in nepotism, land grabbing, forced relocation, lack of compensation, murder, pillage, looting, and even the near total destruction of *adivasi* communities. State governments have colluded with big business and enacted policies to gain access and control regions of Orissa, West Bengal, Chattisgarh, Jharkhand, and Andhra Pradesh that are rich in timber, minerals, bauxite, iron ore, and uranium and are covered with thick vegetation and rivers.[83] Referred as the Red Corridor, these places—inhabited by the *adivasis* and *dalits*—became hotbeds for the growth of Naxalism, which spread across the region in the form of powerful movements that continue to exert potent political and economic force in India. For example, they have succeeded in success-fully slowing down or preventing corporate initiatives by the Tatas, Posco, and Vedanta corporations in Kalinganagar, Jagatsinghpur, and Niyamgiri, respectively.[84]

Among other attacks by the Naxals against the police, Roy refers to the Naxal attack on a barrack in Rani Bodili Kanya Ashram, a hostel for girls used as a police outpost in Chattisgarh, on March 15, 2007, which resulted in the deaths of fifty-five policemen. Although there are no at-tempts to cover up Naxal violence in the essay, the manner in which Roy interweaves her descriptive sociological narrative with critiques of Ma-hatma Gandhi and Gandhianism warrants close scrutiny. Roy writes ap-preciatively of the Naxals' ability to move from one location to another with only the most necessary tools and utensils to help them eat, sleep, hunt, gather food, and, most important of all, fight the state:

> I looked around at the camp before we left. There are no signs that almost a hundred people had camped here, except for some ash where the fires had been. I cannot believe this army. As far as consumption goes, it's more Gandhian than any Gandhian, and has a lighter carbon footprint than any climate change evangelist. But for now, it even has a Gandhian approach to sabotage; before a police vehicle is burnt, for example, it is stripped down and ev-ery part cannibalised. The steering wheel is straightened out and made into a *bharmaar* [barrel], the rexine upholstery stripped and used for ammunition pouches, the battery for solar charging. (The new instructions from the high command are that captured vehicles should be buried and not cremated. So they can be res-urrected when needed.) Should I write a play, I wonder—Gandhi Get Your Gun? Or will I be lynched?[85]

Roy uses "Gandhian" as an adjective to describe a simple lifestyle based on recycling things for other uses. Her use of irony—the commitment of the Naxals to resist the state through violence and their simple way of liv-ing, which recalls Mahatma Gandhi's commitment to a nonconsumer-ist and noncapitalist mode of social organization—has been interpreted as an empathetic reading of tribal insurgency, one that seeks cultural and social legitimation through an explicitly positive comparison of the spe-cific activity of recyling a police vehicle. The ironic retooling of a machine used by the state to oppress *adivasis* is deconstructed: it is stripped bare and refashioned for everyday use and as a resource for armed conflict. The irony, double-entendre, mockery, and implicit satire of governmental ineptitude in this passage are obvious. There are four facts that make it complicated, however: later in the essay, Roy disparages Gandhi's idea of social redistribution while offering a sympathetic perspective on Charu Mazumdar, one of the early leaders of the Naxal movement; the essay appeared in Outlookindia.com with the subheading "Gandhians with guns?"; this essay follows the one on Kashmir in which Roy empathizes with armed rebellion as a logical and, arguably, inevitable and thus reasonable outcome of state oppression; and on April 6, 2010, hardly a month after the essay was published, the Naxals attacked a group of the Central Reserve Police Force and killed seventy-six people.

On Bhumkal Day, observed by the Naxals to commemorate the Koya rebellion against the British in 1910 and to honor the memory of slain comrades and leaders, the Naxals wave banners bearing images of comrades and Marx, Mao, and Charu Mazumdar, about whom Roy muses, "Charu Mazumdar, the founder and chief theoretician of the Naxalite Movement. His abrasive rhetoric fetishises violence, blood and martyrdom, and often employs a language so coarse as to be almost genocidal."[86] She points to the irony of a Naxal leader heralding China as a country worthy of emulation for its commitment to Communism during the Cold War, while today, it's the Indian government, the media, and the middle class that look to China as a model of integration into the new global economy based on information and technology. Roy notes that Mazumdar and the Naxals in general have often downplayed or simply ignored the violence perpetrated by the Chinese and Russian governments and General Yahya Khan in Bangladesh because China supported Pakistan and the Khmer Rouge in Cambodia. Roy observes:

> And yet, despite these terrifying contradictions, Charu Mazumdar was a visionary in much of what he wrote and said. The party he founded (and its many splinter groups) has kept the dream of revolution real and present in India. Imagine a society without that dream. For that alone, we cannot judge him too harshly. Especially not while we swaddle ourselves with Gandhi's pious humbug about the superiority of "the non-violent way" and his notion of Trusteeship: "The rich man will be left in possession of his wealth, of which he will use what he reasonably requires for his personal needs and will act as a trustee for the remainder to be used for the good of society.[87]

Roy juxtaposes Mazumdar's tendency to gloss over the crimes committed by Communist governments and Gandhi's idealistic characterization of social equity as resulting not from principles of equity but from the supposed generosity of the rich with the Indian people's propensity to "swaddle ourselves with Gandhi's pious humbug." In response to criticisms that she was supporting Naxal violence and calling them "Gandhians with guns," Roy issued a disclaimer:

> Whoever infers from this that I have called the Maoists Gandhians with Guns is either a little slow or has no sense of irony or both. Do I really have to spell out what I was alluding to—of Maoist guerrillas who combine Gandhi's principles of spartan consumption with their own very un-Gandhian belief in sabotage and armed revolution? Perhaps the confusion arises because the Indian elite would love to prescribe the opposite: conspicuous consumption for the rich and non-violent satyagraha for the poor.[88]

Roy also cites the sections from her essay in which she refers to Mazumdar and Gandhi and ends: "Does this sound as though I'm calling Maoists 'Gandhians with Guns'? Honestly, I'm almost embarrassed to have to write this letter."[89] The confusion over Roy's views about Naxal violence are not only, as she argues, the possible result of the Indian elite's eagerness to marginalize the poor, but a result of the manifold ways in which she uses the term "Gandhian" in her essay. Notwithstanding her disclaimer, Roy and readers of her essay have to admit that the subheading of the essay when it appeared in Outlookindia.com is "Gandhians with a gun? Arundhati Roy plunges into the sea of Gondi people to find some answers." Although Roy dismisses this as a "copywriter's blurb" that should not be construed as her own words or views,[90] she explicitly uses the term "Gandhian" to describe how the *adivasis* live a life devoid of consumerist trappings: their habits, activities, and tools are spare, light, lean, mobile, and reusable.

In "Trickledown Revolution," Roy elaborates on the point:

> The decision whether to be a Gandhian or a Maoist, militant or peaceful, or a bit of both (like in Nandigram) is not always a moral or ideological one. Quite often it's a tactical one. Gandhian satyagraha, for example, is a kind of political theatre. In order for it be effective, it needs a sympathetic audience, which villagers deep in

the forest do not have. When a posse of 800 policemen lay a cor-
don around a forest village at night and begin to burn houses and
shoot people, will a hunger strike help? . . . Sometimes, tactics get
confused with ideology and lead to unnecessary internecine battles. Fortunately ordinary people are capable of breaking through
ideological categories, and of being Gandhian in Jantar Mantar,
militant in the plains and guerrilla fighters in the forest without
necessarily suffering from a crisis of identity. The strength of the
insurrection in India is its diversity, not uniformity.[91]

In these passages, Roy uses the term "Gandhian" in a manner that is
both descriptive and ironic in its references to the content of Naxal beliefs
and the material practices of their collective vision. This specificity can
and often does get lost in a political discourse where taking sides, defending party lines, or espousing ideologies takes priority. But the essay also
needs to be examined as a piece of writing, a discursive act that involves
elements of composition; rhetorical maneuvers; the use of tropes, metaphors, and comparisons; the analytical rigor of terms, concepts, and arguments; the distillation of secondary sources and their use to support, deny,
or contextualize the political ideologies, philosophies, and discourses that
are drawn on, contested, or affirmed; and difficult choices such as any
writer faces when addressing many audiences even as he or she espouses
taking stances toward an issue, practice, people, nation, or institution.

Is it necessary to use "Gandhian" as a synonym for recycling and daily
life in the forest? Perhaps not, since the point about the austerity of Naxal
life can just as easily be explained by words like "recycling," "retooling,"
and "reusing." But since Roy seeks to counter the idea of Gandhi as a fault-
less icon of nonviolence, she deliberately uses his name to describe not an
entire social movement, as in the struggle for independence from the British, but specific acts of recycling and sparse living. She also wishes to draw
out the irony of a people engaged in armed rebellion, who seem to follow
Gandhi's precepts of simplicity but undermine his belief in nonviolence as
a way to generate social change. This irony is pushed further as she compares Mazumdar and Gandhi: both are criticized, and both are praised.
Roy goes even further when she contends that Mazumdar should not be
dismissed as an extremist intent on destroying the state because "the party
he founded (and its many splinter groups) has kept the dream of revolution
real and present in India. Imagine a society without that dream. For that
alone, we cannot judge him too harshly." But this injunction has an adverbial clause from which it draws its moral force: "especially not while we

swaddle ourselves with Gandhi's pious humbug." In other words, as long as we accept Gandhi's humbug, we cannot judge Mazumdar harshly. As long as the state oppresses its citizens through violence, the oppressed will use violence against the state. As long as Indians venerate Gandhi and his humbug, they should also accept Mazumdar as a visionary. Such a vision of social contradiction and conflict locks the government and the people into a mortal embrace that threatens to annihilate both. It's a dialectic with an endgame whose terms can be determined only within an either/or framework, with each side completely convinced that the other is the primal instigator and beneficiary of their misfortunes.

Having called President Bush a "nightmare incarnate" and likened Osama bin Laden to "the American President's dark doppelganger. The savage twin of all that purports to be beautiful and civilized," it is surprising that Roy does not use the same twinning device to characterize Mazumdar as Gandhi's ideological and converse twin but with a difference: Mazumdar, like Gandhi, is a visionary. Or perhaps the state and the Naxals are twins, each mirroring the worst in the other, but each worthy of praise for great accomplishments. Mazumdar, notes Roy, "fetishises violence, blood and martyrdom, and often employs a language so coarse as to be almost genocidal," but his legacy is that his idea of obtaining social justice through violent means continues to be accepted by the poor and *adivasis*. The problem is that in the same essay in which Roy argues that certain Indian states are guilty of genocide against minorities, and cites Article 2 of the United Nations Convention on the Prevention and Punishment of the Crime of Genocide to bolster her case that the *adivais* and *dalits* are victims of state genocide, she applauds Mazumdar's legacy as a key intellectual leader of Naxalism while criticizing his penchant for violence and using "language so coarse as to be almost genocidal." "Walking with the Comrades" performs the cultural work of rescuing Mazumdar from himself, rescuing his ideals of equality and justice from his genocidal vision of a society in which these ideals can be realized. Inserting Gandhi and Gandhianism into such a rhetorical structure turns Roy's otherwise insightful critique of state abuse, extreme nationalism, religious fundamentalism, and modernization into a text pockmarked with mixed metaphors, strained comparisons, and slippery logic that confound the meaning, purpose, and idea of dissent—without which no democracy can survive, except as farce.

The question is not whether Gandhi is pure or impure, or whether his ideas were sound or illogical, or whether his nonviolent approach created the conditions for the reification of servitude and dispossession. If the key goal of Roy's essay is to decanonize Gandhi, make him more human, and address his weakness as well as his strength, that is fine. But the essay does not demonstrate that Gandhianism or Gandhi is used by the state to justify violence against its peoples, and thus Roy's Gandhian references—with all their varied, recontextualized applications (Baba Amte as Gandhian, recycling police vehicles in the forests as Gandhian, Mazumdar's propensity for violence, Gandhi's humbug, the Indian middle-class's anti-Gandhian consumerism)—leave us confused about Gandhi and Mazumdar, the state and Maoists, dissent and Roy. In the essay "Knocks on the Door," Roy points out that it is futile for the Naxals to use nonviolence as a strategy of resistance since "people who lived deep inside forest villages could not resort to Gandhian forms of protest because peaceful satyagraha was a form of political theatre that in order to be effective, needed a sympathetic audience, which they did not have."[92] What she misunderstands about Gandhianism, suggests David Jefferess, is that "*ahimsa*, as theorized by Gandhi, involved much more than the use of tactics of nonviolent civil disobedience; rather, ahimsa was a way of understanding power and struggle that illuminated injustice while performing an alternative to it."[93] It rests with Roy as the writer to show that humbugs, pious or not, operate or have been forced to operate on the same social plane as fighting a class of people or the state to the point of eliminating it. Or whether "sympathetic audiences" emerge in isolation in society, have a priori status, or are created through persuasion, popular culture and media technologies, and religious, political, and cultural traditions. The presumed absence of an audience sympathetic to nonviolence cannot in and of itself invalidate nonviolence as a mode for social change. Audiences are discursively constructed; they are not born with genetic dispositions for violence or nonviolence.

It is not for nothing that the people whom Roy has often castigated publicly with admirable passion and intellect use exactly the same logic of her dissent: Narendra Modi, who was and still is Gujarat's chief minister, and during whose tenure the horrors of Godhra unfolded (the burning of the Sabarmati Express train was followed by mass killing, looting, and destruction), is much admired and applauded for his economic vision in privatizing and liberalizing the state's economy. Indeed, Roy faults the chief executive officers of Indian megacorporations—Mukesh Ambani of Reliance Industries and Ratan Tata of Tata Ltd.—for glossing over Modi's culpability in failing to stop the reign of terror in the aftermath of the burning of the Sabarmati Express on February 27, 2002, and supporting Modi's economic policies. But where Roy sees Mazumdar as a visionary whose dreams, despite their genocidal potential, sustain a revolutionary spirit among the Naxals, Ambani and Tata see Modi, despite his administration's indifference to large-scale massacre, as keeping alive the nation's dream to lift millions of Indians from poverty and hopelessness. Roy's critiques seek to construct a moral universe in which principled dissent can shed light on the horrors of state-sanctioned violence and the machinations of a democracy emptied of content. She wants to persuade readers to support policies that can be carried out with necessary checks and balances to ensure the greater common good. But her essays often end up as artfully constructed prose in which historical, ethical, conceptual, and epistemological clarity and integrity vanish into passionate equivocations.

In an interview that took place after the Naxals had killed seventy-two members of the Central Reserve Police Force, and after the publication of Roy's "Walking with the Comrades," which appeared before the Naxal attack, Sagarika Ghose of Cable News Network's Indian Broadcasting Network (CNN-IBN) asks Roy: "Should people like you not be raising their voices against the cycle of violence or should you actually be trying to find rationalizations for it? Because you have been called an apologist for the Maoists, the BJP has called you the sophisticated face of Naxalism. If you don't raise your voice against their violence, and simply see it as a morally acceptable, as a morally legitimate counter to the state . . . are you not actually failing as a member of civil society?"[94] Roy replies:

> No, I am not, because I think it suits the status quo right now to have everybody saying, Oh, this is terrible and this is also terrible, so let's just keep on without taking into account the terrible structural violence that is actually, I mean I don't use this word lightly but actually creating a genocidal situation in those tribal areas. If you look at the levels of malnutrition, if you look at the levels of absolute, abject desperation there, you, any responsible person has to say the violence will stop when you stop pushing those people. When you have a whole community of tribals, which, by the way, is a population larger than the population of most countries, which is on the very brink of survival, which is fighting its own annihilation, I cannot equate their reaction, their resistance, to the violence of the state. I think it's immoral to equate the two.[95]

A month after the Naxal attack, an explosion caused by a land mine resulted in the death of thirty people traveling in a bus whose passengers included civilians, regional police officers, and special police officers. Two days later, Roy issued this statement:

> Media reports say that the Maoists have deliberately targeted and killed civilians in Dantewara. If this is true, it is absolutely inexcusable and cannot be justified on any count. However, sections of the mainstream media have often been biased and incorrect in their reportage. Some accounts suggest that apart from SPOs [special police officers] and police, the other passengers in the bus were mainly those who had applied to be recruited as SPOs. We will have to wait for more information. If there were indeed civilians in the bus, it is irresponsible of the government to expose them to harm in a war zone by allowing police and SPOs (carriers of the mantle of all the crimes of Salwa Judum) to use public transport. Also, for a sense of perspective, let's not forget that right at this moment, in Kalinganagar and Jagatsingpur in Orissa, hundreds of police are firing on unarmed people protesting the corporate takeover of their land.[96]

Mullaney points out: "However potent Roy's arguments, their place in wider systems of debate and interrogation is often undermined by attendant, problematic 'rhetorical' conflations which appear in what can best be described as her 'hyperbolic' style and her use of dangerous moral equivalences."[97] In these comments, because state violence becomes the only prism through which to view Naxal violence, it stands to reason that critical attention be directed at the state, first and foremost. Everything else becomes secondary. The failed Indian state in which democracy is a sham becomes the originator of violence. The state becomes the first cause. The state is the locus of original sin, which explains the reluctance to criticize Naxal violence and examine whether or not the millions of *adivasis* whom the Naxals claim to represent are indeed spoken for adequately and have their needs and aspirations represented fairly, and whether or not the Naxals use their clout, knowledge, and power democratically among the *adivasis*. As we saw earlier, when Chomsky urged Indian leftists not to get caught up in internal problems within the Left and in India when the entire world system was being managed by imperial America, he was using the same analytical framework that Roy uses to criticize the Indian state: Naxal violence occurs within the "terrible structural violence" of the state; therefore, dissent against the state becomes imperative. Chomsky simply broadens the context from the national to the international, making America, rather than the Indian state, the first cause, the site where violence is planned and executed. This is why the struggles within the Left or those among the Naxals, *adivasis*, and leftist governments cannot be equated with the oppression unleashed by American empire. The great irony of their adoption of such parochial and dichotomized understanding of globalization is that when Chomsky applied his framework to the Indian context, Roy—normally one of his most ardent supporters—indignantly and publicly distanced herself from his position. The key to moving out of the double bind that Roy's dissent creates for her and her many supporters is to rigorously question the conceptual framework she uses to understand complex social phenomena such as the role of the state in a democracy and the potential for violence, whether against *adivasis* or the state, to create conditions of tremendous suffering and injustice; and the ethical responsibility of leaders of movements, who raise armies against empires or illiterate peasants against the state, to subject their own ideas and practices to public scrutiny, to be held accountable, and to create structures of justice within which their programs for social transformation can be assessed, rejected, or revised for the greater common good. It is for the border intellectual to eschew the politics of willed homelessness that constructs abstract, universal systems and spaces in which dissenting intellectuals can lead their lives freely and without encumbrance.

DISSENT ON THE BORDER

"Walking with the Comrades" marks a pivotal moment in Roy's writings: the representational quality of her arguments and activism, which she had long disavowed, becomes harder to disavow. In a 2001 interview, N. Ram, editor of the *Hindu*, asks Roy to respond to criticism that she often sentimentally romanticizes the *adivasis* and their lifestyles. In reply, Roy says that when she wrote "The Greater Common Good," she was "aware of two things: One, that I was not going to write on 'behalf' of anyone but myself because I think that's the most honest thing to do—in our society particularly, the politics of 'representation' is complicated and fraught with danger and dishonesty. Two, I was not writing an anthropological account of the lifestyles of people that I knew very little about."[98] At the very least, "Walking with the Comrades," written a decade later, which has pictures of the Maoists with whom Roy lived for a time and who are the subject of the essay, includes a picture in which Roy, a bandanna around her head, is sitting down with the Maoists surrounding her, her face looking up at theirs, and their heads bowed down toward her. With a pad and pen in her hands, Roy strikes a pensive pose; she possesses the symbols of modernity, the tools and technology of civilization, which those surrounding her do not have. She is the intellectual trying to understand the others and record their lives, describe their activities, explain their interests, and legitimize their demands by translating them into the official language of modern society.

If Roy were a non-Indian or someone who could be called Western or white, her situation could easily have been viewed as that of the typical colonial anthropologist writing treatises about the natives in order to bring enlightenment to all and sundry, a critical stance that often becomes a ritualized pose adopted by new initiates or true believers in the postcolonial discourse of orientalism. To the *adivasis*, Roy is playing the role of the writer, listener, sympathizer, translator, and interpreter of the ideas of civil society and the abjection of democracy. To be sure, despite all her vigorous protestations, Roy seeks to give voice to the voiceless, and she does so not by reading about her subjects but by going to their villages, staying with them, listening to them, learning about them, and writing about them— not only for them, but for others who are unlike them. She is the mediator. She is the translator. She is the medium who makes herself available as a conduit for representation. They speak to her, and she speaks to others who may listen or may be reluctant to listen. This does not mean that Roy becomes one with the *adivasis* or that she tries to pass herself off as one of them. That mode of representation is not the issue. What instead is constantly in play in Roy's dissents is representation as translation, as the finding of language to embody one kind of reality, one kind of experience, and render its pathos and humanity legitimate and central to the sustenance of a different embodiment of experience—of modernity, of a society increasingly saturated with new technologies, of democracy and self-governance. Roy is a border crosser: she stands between the culture of the middle and rich classes and that of the poor and tribal classes. They speak different languages, and she mediates between them, doing so by taking a position for one against the other.

Neera Chandhoke puts it well in "The Conceits of Representation" with reference to the antidam movement:

> For whereas it is undeniable that a powerful social movement has arisen in the area, it is equally undeniable that it has been led and continues to be led by those very social activists who are able to

represent the agony of the tribal in languages that are familiar to the inhabitants of civil society. The tribal in other words does not represent himself or herself historically for she does not possess the linguistic competence to do so. She has to rely on others who possess this competence. That means that between the tribal and civil society and the state, we find layers of mediation provided by activists who are conversant with the convoluted vocabularies, the intricacies and the rhetoric of modern languages.[99]

Whether the subaltern can or cannot speak is a key issue; the focus here is not on its propositional validity, but on the roles played by people like Roy, who willingly and knowingly translate tribal experiences into languages of Indian civil society, and who also translate the significance of the state to the tribals. "The success or failure of her story as an intellectual," argues Ranjan Ghosh, "depends heavily on how she moves between roles and prevents her biases from beclouding the vocation she is obligated to as a writer."[100] One of her biases, argues Jefferess, which she has uncritically adopted from the antidam movement, includes constructing the *adivasis* of the hills as the embodiment of state victimization, although Hindu Patidar farmers and *adivasis* in the plains have also been affected, with the result that "they are displaced by the dams and within Roy's narrative, as well."[101]

Despite her strenuous protestations, Roy is both translator and mediator. Rather than acknowledging the complex dynamics of her position vis-à-vis the *adivasis*, the state, and civil society, Roy disavows her deep entanglement with representational practices and relies instead on becoming a writer, as Baneth-Nouailhetas puts it, who "is not so much a creator as a medium, a tool for the translation of essential facts—facts whose essence is meaning—into language."[102] By repeating an already formed story through herself as a medium and tool, Roy is unable to use language to shape the content, form, purpose, sociohistorical contexts, and affective impulse of the story, but she can identify with and take a position on the ethical imperatives of its Manichaean drama. Baneth-Nouailhetas offers a sharp criticism: "The militant text is presented in the same vein as Romantic poetry, as practically unmediated, a truth guaranteed by the urgency of the situation."[103]

The unique challenges of this mode of representation, and Roy's own orientation to herself as a subject who exercises her agency to initiate such a representation, are just what Roy—as writer, activist, thinker, and citizen—must acknowledge and examine. What needs examination is not just her politics but also the conceptual apparatus that enables her to engage in particular kinds of public criticism and activism, develop particular political stances, and choose particular objects of critique. Roy and her audiences and readers should pay careful attention to the many roles she plays as a writer, activist, and public intellectual, as she and her work move across global circuits of information, knowledge, and exchange, so that we can develop a keener appreciation of the vicissitudes of history and a deeper understanding of the contradictions of globalization. And do so on the border.

Unlike Roy, who is famous for her critiques of America and globalization, the Iranian diasporic writer Azar Nafisi gained fame for a memoir, her best-selling *Reading Lolita in Tehran*—which has been severely castigated by critics for supposedly giving credence to American orientalist misconceptions about the Middle East. In the next chapter, while demonstrating the weakness of such arguments, I show that an understanding of non-American histories and experiences is pivotal for studying America in global contexts, and that we must necessarily translate empire as a "complicated [site] with multivalent social and moral meanings and outcomes, frustrating any effort to give them a singular interpretation,"[104] so that we can better critique American empire.

CHAPTER FOUR

Culture, Empire, and Representation

READING LOLITA IN TEHRAN

Azar Nafisi, author of the best-selling novel-cum-memoir *Reading Lolita in Tehran*, has been criticized for being a stooge of the Central Intelligence Agency, a powerful cultural apologist for the imperial policies of the Bush administration, and a dupe who has allowed herself personally and professionally to be turned into an instrument for cultural warfare. In this chapter, I argue that most of those who view Nafisi as a cultural propagandist in the service of American imperialism offer weak and uninformed arguments because they simplistically view contemporary globalization as either the triumphant Americanization of the world or as the eternal fight of the global South against the North, the Third World against the First World. Such critiques of American empire collapse world history into international American history and fail to examine the uneven dynamics of cultural globalization as American literature travels outside the borders of the United States and comes into contact with non-American readers, and new communities of readers respond to these texts and use them for a variety of purposes.

Reading Lolita in Tehran offers us a challenge: to delink the connection between Vladimir Nabokov's *Lolita* and America—that is, between a literary text and the national canon of American literature—and study how literary texts travel across international circuits of intellectual exchange, acquire new readers, and generate diverse interpretations that cannot be reduced to a slavish desire among non-Americans to imbibe American culture. Readers in Iran are not reading "our" American text but reading it as "global transit extends, triangulates, and transforms its meaning," to extend Wai Chee Dimock's insight, and as the memoir becomes a "new semantic template, a new form of the legible, each time it crosses a national border,"[1] we are compelled to grapple with *"Lolita* in Tehran, how *Lolita* gave a different color to Tehran and how *Tehran helped redefine Nabokov's novel, turning it into this Lolita, our Lolita."*[2] *Reading Lolita in Tehran* urges us to develop international perspectives; gain more knowledge about non-Western peoples, their histories, cultures, and traditions; and appreciate the role of migration, border crossing, and transnational exchange in shaping cross-cultural interaction in the contemporary world. However, to several critics, Azar Nafisi is nothing but a skillful apologist for imperial America because she uses her literary talent to obtain cultural legitimacy for American literature while denigrating all things Iranian. So what is all the fuss about *Reading Lolita in Tehran*?

The book charts the travails of seven women who meet in a professor's house in Tehran in the mid-1990s to read and share their ideas about American literature. Nabokov's novel *Lolita* seems to dramatize a mythic American concern: what does it mean to be an individual? In discussions about Humbert's artfully seductive yet perversely controlling narrative about his love and passion for Lolita, Jeffersonian ideas begin to resonate in the women's group: "What we have here is a first lesson in democracy: all individuals, no matter how contemptible, have a right to life, liberty, and the pursuit of happiness."[3]

Two approaches to this scene quickly present themselves to us: first, that American studies has become internationalized; and second, *Reading Lolita in Tehran* firmly consolidates American cultural hegemony, rather than reinventing American literature in a local space. What the female students read is a canon familiar in the United States—works by Nabokov, F. Scott Fitzgerald, Henry James, and Jane Austen—but they read it in another country, Iran. The women's obvious passion for these writers and deep engagement with their novels bespeak the global hunger for American literature and, by extension, the ability of American studies to travel across the sea and take a firm root in Iranian imaginations—which demonstrates, quite forcefully, the immense appeal of Americana in the rest of the world. America has traveled to Iran and has given rise to other meanings in new locations, perhaps because there is something inherently subversive about American writers, themes, and culture.

The first approach takes the United States as the universal symbol for freedom, individual rights, and human dignity, and finds internationalization in the scope and nature of the absorption of Americana in cultures and societies outside the United States. Turning this view on its head, the second approach argues that although Iranian women read and adapt Americana, the ideological threads that bind the works together as an Anglo-American canon are at least a bit frayed. Reaffirmed as the pantheon is the old, traditional canon of American and British writers, which is simply exported to Iran by an Iranian subject, who is herself a product of an elite education and the post 1960s U.S. counterculture. After meeting Bijan Naderi in Berkeley, California, marrying him, and returning with him to Iran after the overthrow of the shah in 1979, Nafisi becomes a professor in the English Department of the University of Tehran. Given her activism in the United States against the shah's government, it comes as no surprise to see Nafisi embarking on her professional career determined to revolutionize Tehran's academic community and Iranian society in general. Her choice of Nabokov, Fitzgerald, James, and Austen for her students can put her in the long line of international academics who study in the United States and then travel the world or return to their countries of origin, spreading the gospel of American culture. In this sense, both the approaches have a lot in common, although one is triumphant in its mission of globalizing America, and the other is disturbed by its success.

However, because neither approach recognizes any presence or experience that is not shaped by or related to the United States, neither can offer us a way to discriminate between the realms of culture and politics, or to understand how and why these realms may at times overlap or change their borders. Such approaches espouse what Winfried Fluck refers to as "cultural radicalism," in which "the central source of political domination is no longer attributed to the level of political institutions and economic structures but to culture." Power is viewed as having such a pervasive scope and influence that it suffuses not just literary texts and cultural artifacts, but the entire range of discourses within and against which they are foregrounded. The emphasis is on "the system's cunning ways of constituting 'subjects' or ascribing 'identities' through cultural forms." Examinations of culture and literature are predicated on "'patriarchy,' 'the West,' 'the ideological state apparatus,' 'discursive regime,' 'the symbolic order,' and so on leading to a 'constant pressure to outradicalize others.'"[4] Since culture is viewed "as an 'invisible' form of social control and domination," cultural radicalism conceives "of literary form as ideological mimesis."[5] Systemic coercion and epistemic control in culture and discourse are emphasized so much that form, nuance, context, uneven historical processes, and changes become redundant since power is assumed to be all-pervasive and thus capable of overriding them. This leads dissenters from American empire, specifically in the context of the criticism made against Nafisi and *Reading Lolita in Tehran*, to claim, variously, that the text is just another orientalist propaganda tract, that its writer hates Islam, that she has questionable qualifications to direct the Dialogue Project at Johns Hopkins University, and that all this is a nefarious neoconservative plan to provide cultural ammunition to the U.S. military confrontation with Iran.

Common to most of these dissents is the invocation of Edward Said's *Orientalism*, which serves as a conceptual framework for the development of a critique that can unmask in both Nafisi and her text a will to power encoded in a language of neoliberalism. This is not the place for an analysis of Said and his important work. What matters here are the frequent invocations to him and orientalism, invocations that function as appeals to a transcendent being or muse—in this instance, orientalism—as a discursive presence, whose premises and methodologies can be uncritically imposed wholesale on a range of contemporary literary texts written by Iranians in the diaspora. In what appear to be desperate attempts to make literature relevant to the real world, the conceptual rigor needed to read a book as both a literary text and something that textually performs many kinds of cultural work, and the knowledge gleaned from and across disciplines needed to examine the operations of power at multiple levels in society, the function of ideology, and the dynamic nature of hegemony are hard to come by. Instead, literature and culture are viewed as flip sides of power, ideology, and politics, and their modes of operation and their impact on society are assumed to be equivalent. Legitimate criticism of current U.S. foreign policies and the government's domestic performance, often formulated as dissent from empire, is couched in a discourse of internationalism and globalization. But this dissent often simultaneously re-centers America in world history and revives an American exceptionalism, albeit with a major difference—historically, that exceptionalism was a determined ignorance about the role of violence, possession, and control in American modernity; today, it is a central tenet of belief for America and Americans, obtained at the moment when internationalism becomes the ethical ground for critiquing American empire within a global frame.

CULTURE IN THE
SERVICE OF EMPIRE

Some critics have gone so far as to accuse Nafisi and others like Firoozeh Dumas (*Funny in Farsi*) and Marjane Satrapi (*The Complete Persepolis*) of contributing to the myopia of Western societies toward the East. Negar Mottahedeh points out that "it seems undeniable that *Reading Lol-*

ita in Tehran and its author have been promoted, at least in part, to fulfill the ends of total war," which aims not only to use military power to effect change but to modify cultural behavior itself so as to more completely consolidate imperial power. To Mottahedeh, Benador Associates' public promotion of Nafisi (who is now listed with the Steven Barclay Agency) is problematic since Richard Perle and James Woolsey, "who notoriously referred to the war on terror as 'World War IV,' are still clients of the agency." As an agent of this company, Eleana Benador's positive comments on her website about Afghani and Iraqi women's participation in 2004 Athens Olympics are, to Mottahedeh, "trac[ing] the cognitive links the neo-conservatives draw between the war and Middle Eastern women." Moreover, Nafisi's acknowledgment of Bernard Lewis, a distinguished historian from Princeton University, as someone who "opened the door" for her is yet another indication of her ties to a network of conservatives. As evidence, Mottahedeh cites former Deputy Secretary of Defense Paul Wolfowitz, who lauded Lewis as a historian of originality and brilliance. Indeed, Mottahedeh finds Juan Cole's disagreement with Lewis sufficient to make Nafisi's acknowledgment of Lewis irrefutable proof of her complicity in promoting American cultural imperialism.[6]

Clearly, the point here is to discredit Nafisi and her memoir on the basis of her academic and professional affiliations. Such evaluations of a writer's work do not require any close reading—or even any reading at all—of the writing. The dissent offered here is based primarily on positions and affiliations. There has been vociferous condemnation of the Bush doctrine—"either you are with us, or you are with the terrorists"—but a similar mind-set is evident in this dissent, where an us-them dichotomy is set up between liberals and conservatives. Indeed, not only does it make reading Nafisi's memoir superfluous, it makes reading Lewis's work unnecessary, since one can rely on book reviews and identify writers' institutional and professional affiliations in order to critique their work.

In "The War on Terror, Feminist Orientalism and Oriental Feminism," Roksana Bahramitash argues that Geraldine Brooks's *Nine Parts of Desire* and Azar Nafisi's *Reading Lolita in Tehran* gained popularity because they are "feminist," but they "reinforce popular stereotypes of Muslims as backward and primitive. Furthermore, they have helped to create and to maintain a widespread (albeit factually erroneous) notion that Muslim women are victims of an inherent misogynism in Islamic tradition."[7] The feminist concern about women's oppression, when it becomes a pretext or rationale for colonial ventures, is feminist orientalism, and creating and justifying certain policies toward the Middle East is orientalist feminism. And these texts, Bahramitash argues, embody both. She is especially critical of Nafisi because "Nafisi's selective and partial view of Iran is not innocent but seems to have a particular agenda, namely to contribute to the Islamophobia that already exists in North America. Nafisi's contempt for Islam as a religion pervades *Reading Lolita*, as demonstrated by such statements such as 'It is a truth universally acknowledged that a Muslim man, regardless of his fortune, must be in want of a nine-year-old virgin wife.'"[8]

The first argument, that *Reading Lolita in Tehran* draws on feminist orientalism and orientalist feminism, is a straw man: it mischaracterizes the book's focus, attributes certain motives to its writer, and then condemns both. The book does not focus on "Muslim women," as Bahramitash has it, and thus does not affirm stereotypes of their being "backward and primitive." From beginning to end, the book is about Iran, Nafisi's experiences there and in America, and her interaction with her students in Iran. To say that *Reading Lolita in Tehran* focuses on "Muslim women" is to invoke woman and Muslim as universal categories and make them into a straw man, in order to dismantle the argument that was mischaracterized in the first place—and all this is done to impute ideological motivations to Nafisi and her text.

The second argument, that Nafisi is contemptuous toward Islam and encourages Islamophobia through her text, relies on a decontextualized twist of interpretation.[9] As noted above, Bahramitash cites this line as evidence: "It is a truth universally acknowledged that a Muslim man, regardless of his fortune, must be in want of a nine-year-old virgin wife." But the line is actually spoken by one of the young women in the reading group, Yassi—who says it, notes Nafisi, "in that special tone of hers, deadpan and mildly ironic, which on rare occasions, and this was one of them, bordered on the burlesque." This is followed immediately by a comment from another woman, Manna, who paraphrases the same Jane Austen quote but in reference to a Muslim man desiring many wives, and who looks at Nafisi "conspiratorially, her black eyes brimming with humor."[10] Because Bahramitash does not pay any attention to the literary aspects of this scene—the facts that the lines were spoken by women who are also characters in the memoir; that the context was one of irony, which creates discrepancy between what is said and implied, and of humor tending toward the burlesque, which in this instance incorporates wit and satire—she treats a comment made by one individual in Nafisi's memoir as the author's anthropological proclamation about Muslim men and quickly charges the writer for having "contempt" for Islam.

Hamid Dabashi takes this to an extreme when he accuses Nafisi of being a "colonial agent" in an article that appeared in *Al-Ahram Weekly*. First, we should take note of a good argument that Dabashi offers about the use on the front of the jacket of Nafisi's memoir of a picture ostensibly showing two teenage women reading *Lolita* in Tehran. As Dabashi points out, there are several things about the picture that are neatly excised— the women with headscarves were reading news about Iranian parliamentary elections in 2000; the newspaper they were reading was *Mosharekat*, a publication known to sympathize with reform; and behind the women was a picture of President Khatami, who campaigned on a reformist platform.[11] In the mid-1990s, owing to public pressure and interest, the government was slowly but reluctantly attempting to make a few of its institutions more transparent and accountable to the people; it also started to ease up on the close surveillance of civil society by morality squads.[12] All these details are erased so that the photograph shows two young women with scarves covering their hair, their heads bowed, which invites the reader of Nafisi's memoir and the viewer of the photograph to imagine them engaging in subversive reading—that is, reading Nabokov's famously infamous *Lolita* in Tehran. Dabashi's analysis points to the techniques of representation used by major U.S. publishers to promote certain stereotypes about women in the East, especially the Middle East, that position them as passive victims thirsting for anything remotely American.

Indeed, to the publishers, there could be nothing so gratifying to the American reading public as seeing young women eagerly consuming—nay, doing something most Americans do not do regularly, actually reading— American literature with such utter disregard for their safety in a nation ruled by Islamic zealots. However, rather than extending such insightful critiques of cultural representation, Dabashi refers to Nafisi as a member of the class of "comprador intellectuals," who has written a book that "exude[s] so systematic a visceral hatred of everything Iranian" that "this book is partially responsible for cultivating the U.S. (and by extension the global) public opinion against Iran, having already done a great deal by being a key propaganda tool at the disposal of the Bush Administration (since 2001) and Iraq (since 2003)."[13] To Dabashi, the Islamic Republic of Iran is guilty of "murdering secular intellectuals, while systematically and legally creating a state of gender apartheid," but what Nafisi's memoir does is operate under the guise of critique while "facilitating the operation of a far more insidious global domination—effectively perpetuating (indeed aggravating) the domestic terror they purport to expose." In a move that Americanizes the oppression of Iranian peoples, Dabashi's axiology makes the murderous Iranian regime less a matter of concern than the American empire, and even claims that, in her role as a "native informer," Nafisi panders to imperial America's desire for knowledge about Iran that it could use to justify possible war, which makes the Iranian regime further oppress its peoples.

Using the logic of guilt by association, Dabashi faults Nafisi for her ties to Bernard Lewis: "The relationship between the author of *Reading Lolita in Tehran* and Professor Humbert Humbert of Orientalism is quite a warm and fuzzy one, mutually quite beneficial."[14] What galls Dabashi is that Nafisi becomes skeptical of Edward Said when, on returning to Iran, she questions her assumptions and finds Lewis's work helpful, which she did not while in the United States. Nafisi disagrees with Said—"But I do not think you can say that from Aeschylus to Balzac to Flaubert, everyone was an Orientalist"—and finds that in Iran his work was accepted uncritically: "In a country like Iran, many Islamists took his theories and jubilantly proclaimed what they believed he was saying."[15] For such statements and Nafisi's acknowledgment that Lewis "opened the door" for her in the United States, Dabashi contemptuously refers to the historian as "Humbert Lewis" and Nafisi as an informer offering knowledge about Iran that could be put "at the service of the US ideological psy-op, militarily stipulated in the US global warmongering."[16] The suggestion that Bernard Lewis is like Humbert Humbert in Nabokov's *Lolita*, a man with strong inclinations for sexual relations with pubescent girls like Lolita, is to smear people, not debate them. Dabashi piles up assertion after assertion, innuendo after innuendo, insult after insult without offering any examination of the memoir at all, except for a section on the use of pictures of the novel's front cover, which I already noted was a good point. In an interview with Foaad Khosmood, Dabashi cites a list of neoconservatives with whom Nafisi had been associating or who share her imperialist ideology: Martin Peretz, Amir Taheri, Bernard Lewis, Paul Wolfowitz, Eleana Benador, Fouad Ajami, Kanaan Makiyyah, Roya Hakakian, Ramin Ahmadi, Abbas Milani, Moshen Sazegara, and Elliot Abrams. Contrasting these people with another group he claims are seriously studying empire—namely, Michael Hardt, Antonio Negri, Niall Ferguson, Chalmers Johnson, Amy Kaplan, Judith Butler, and Zillah Eisenstein—Dabashi delivers his coup de grâce:

> To me there is no difference between Lynndie England and Azar Nafisi. But I am trying to see how these two complementary types operate in legitimizing and executing the banality of this empire. . . . I have said before and argued that here is an organic link between what Lynndie England did in Abu Ghraib and what Azar

Nafisi did in RLT—and what holds these two underlings in the service of George W. Bush's war on terror is no over-riding ideology, but a mere Kafkaesque careerism best described in Hannah Arendt's notion of "the banality of evil"—in other words, in and of themselves they are exceedingly pathetic people, and yet they are instrumental in a monumental barbarity.[17]

Readers will recognize Lynndie England as the U.S. Army private who was court-martialed for torturing prisoners at Abu Ghraib, in Iraq. Dabashi equates Nafisi with England because to him culture and politics are simply two sides of the same coin. What one does in culture—writing literature or memoirs—has the same effect in the social and political world. Both Private Lynndie England and Azar Nafisi end up playing the role of Adolf Eichmann; these two "pathetic people," Dabashi implies, espouse the Nazi mentality so disturbingly portrayed in Arendt's book. The assumption that the torture of prisoners works on the same level as the writing of a memoir, partially fictionalized, is taken as a self-evident truth; it needs no explanation, analysis, or demonstration. The truth-value of this assertion, to Dabashi, is best demonstrated by repeated denunciations, as if their sheer repetition provided evidence of their accuracy. Everything else in his dissent from American empire and Nafisi, besides the section on the use of cover pictures, degenerates into vicious name-calling, which one would be as reluctant to tolerate as if a critic of Edward Said called this eminent public intellectual "Edward bin Laden Said" on account of his stringent criticisms of U.S. foreign policy toward the Middle East. This is the kind of dissent that strains mightily—and fails—to pass for reasoned discussion.

Like Dabashi, rather than continuing the promising line of inquiry into how the figure of the alien is integral to the construction of national identity and Americanness, Ali Behdad dismisses Nafisi and Roya Hakakian as "native informants . . . and today's neo-Orientalists" who "have helped transform, for example, the trope of the veil and the figure of the despot into discursive sites upon which to stake ahistorical claims, readily appropriated by Western liberals and neo-conservatives alike, about the incommensurability of Islam with democracy, while cementing the connection in the popular imaginary between Moslem identity and the forces of fanaticism, oppression, and terror."[18] There is no analysis of Nafisi's text in Behdad's essay, only references to Wolfowitz and, of course, Bernard Lewis, orientalism, Edward Said, and Arjun Appadurai. The literary text is just plugged into a broad argument about minorities in the United States and the severe restrictions on cross-cultural interaction due to the strictures adopted by the Office of Foreign Assets Control in the U.S. Treasury Department, which prevented the circulation and translation of books from countries like Iran and Cuba.

AMERICAN EMPIRE AND
NETWORKS OF CONSPIRACY

The well-known Americanist John Carlos Rowe has critiqued Nafisi and her novel in his essay "Reading *Reading Lolita in Tehran* in Idaho." Agreeing with Dabashi's views on Nafisi, Rowe states that his purpose is to "try to work out the scholarly and historical terms that are often lacking in Dabashi's more strictly political analysis."[19] Characterizing Dabashi's meretricious comments as "political analysis" is inordinately generous on Rowe's part, and—more to the point—it suggests that politics is a matter of demagogic denunciations that do not require "scholarly and historical" engagement, which is just what makes them "strictly political." Rowe focuses on both extrinsic and intrinsic aspects of Nafisi's text in order to show that "Azar Nafisi's *Reading Lolita in Tehran* is an excellent example of how neoliberal rhetoric is now being deployed by neoconservatives and the importance they have placed on cultural issues," since they are able to use a text like this to "build the cultural and political case against diplomatic negotiations with the present government of Iran."[20]

The extrinsic factors that Rowe considers are the following: "Nafisi's political affiliations are indisputably neoconservative,"[21] since she is working at the Paul H. Nitze School for Advanced International Studies (SAIS) at Johns Hopkins University; she was supported by the Smith Richardson Foundation, which draws on the wealth of the Vicks VapoRub company, and also supports conservative organizations like the American Enterprise Institute; at Johns Hopkins, Nafisi is the director of the Dialogue Project, which focuses on issues affecting Muslims around the world. For someone with Nafisi's credentials (the holder of a doctorate in English from the University of Oklahoma; a professor of English at the University of Tehran, the Free Islamic University, and the University of Allameh Tabatabai; and a fellow of Oxford University), her position as research associate at SAIS, which includes training diplomats, "pose[s] a set of intriguing questions."[22] Given her extensive knowledge of Iran, Nafisi could serve as a consultant at SAIS, but her background hardly merits her appointment as a research associate, contends Rowe. However, there are other extrinsic factors that Dabashi's and Rowe's analyses do not consider—namely, Nafisi's public comments about American perceptions about Iran, Muslims, Islam, women, and the Third World. She finds in America a very "simplistic view of what we call 'Islam'" and counters that by noting the immense social and cultural variety one finds in Indonesia, Nigeria, Iran, Turkey, and Saudi Arabia. It is unhelpful to talk about "Islamic feminism," she argues, for the same reason that it is pointless to talk about "Christian feminism or Judaic feminism." The argument for respecting cultures, notes Nafisi, should not be taken to mean that women in Muslim countries like to be flogged or stoned, to have their bodies and minds constantly supervised, and to be made subservient to the interests of others. She cautions Americans not to view the September 11 hijackers as people who represent Islam or even a variety of Islam, and asks "Was Stalin representative of the Russian people?" The hijackers are part of a "political movement that has hijacked a great religion."[23] In an interview with Robert Birnbaum, Nafisi notes that the historical event of burning witches in Salem, Massachusetts, should not be taken to mean that "the culture of Massachusetts is burning witches," and she points out that modern Islamic fundamentalism is not some peculiar problem with Islam but should be viewed, like Stalinism and fascism, as a modern phenomenon.[24] Clearly, there is much more complexity and even contradiction to Nafisi and her writing than Dabashi, Behdad, and Rowe's analyses suggest.

The intrinsic factors that Rowe focuses on include the following: although Nafisi critiques the Islamic Republic of Iran, she is not critical enough of the repressive SAVAK, the secret police of the shah's regime, and the fact that the United States supported the Pahlavi dynasty for a long time. Nor does she address the violent aspects of modernization in Iran, and she tends to downplay the privileges of her social position in Iran (her father was mayor of Tehran, and her mother was a member of parliament). Furthermore, she fails to distinguish clearly between postmodern feminism and second-wave feminism. Rowe's analysis of how the idea of the political is deployed without irony in the novel is insightful: Nafisi constantly urges her students to avoid turning literature, especially Western literature, into political tracts—that is, to refrain from viewing literature as nothing but politics in disguise. But, as Rowe observes, her own reading of literature, with its primary emphasis on the aesthetic power of the artistic imagination, is itself a politicized interpretation of the role of art in society.[25]

This is what Nafisi tells her students about politics and literature:

What we search for in fiction is not so much reality but the epiphany of truth.[26]

We were, to borrow from Nabokov, to experience how the ordinary pebble of our ordinary life could be *transformed into a jewel through the magic eye of fiction.*[27]

I mentioned that one of the criteria for the books I had chosen was their authors' faith in the critical and *almost magical power of literature*, and reminded them of the nineteen-year old Nabokov, who, during the Russian Revolution, would not allow himself to be diverted by the sound of bullets.[28]

We condemn Humbert's acts of cruelty towards them even as we substantiate his judgment of their banality. What we have here is the first lesson in democracy: all individuals, no matter how contemptible, have a right to life, liberty, and the pursuit of happiness.[29]

In all these passages, literature is viewed as something that has magical qualities; it gives us epiphanies; it can embody democratic ideals like liberty and equality. In other words, literature is precious: it stores wisdom and knowledge. These ideas of literature do not relate well to what most professors of literature in the United States identify as more promising approaches—psychoanalytic, structuralist, poststructuralist, Marxist, new historicist, postcolonialist, feminist, and so on. Rowe even criticizes Nafisi on this count, since she does not account for how the writers she implicitly canonizes—Nabokov, Fitzgerald, James, and Austen—have all been studied in ways shaped by literary and cultural theory in the United States (like the approaches mentioned above): "there is very little mention of these professional studies in Nafisi's book."[30] In a similar vein, Bahramitash argues: "It is striking that in her teaching of English literature at university level she fails to teach her students about the most influential feminist literary criticism of the time, that of the post-colonial theorists."[31]

The problem with this argument is that it views contemporary theory and its impact on literature and cultural study as the standard by which literary writing produced by people in a diaspora can be evaluated. Just because contemporary theory is a uniquely American phenomenon that draws from specific European intellectual currents does not mean that it is necessarily the most updated and well-informed approach to the study of literature.[32] When viewed in transnational frames, this argument posits theory as understood and practiced in the United States as the yardstick by which people in other countries ought to evaluate their interpretations and experiences of reading literature. Indeed, to most of us teaching American literature in the United States, especially at the undergraduate or graduate levels, speaking and writing about literature in terms of its epiphanies and magical qualities seems anachronistic, given our hypersensitivity to the machinations of ideology, race, gender, class, and location. But it is just this kind of anachronism that cannot be invalidated by comparing its updatedness or lack thereof with what we in the United States take to be cutting-edge developments and methodologies. The publication of Nafisi's memoir in the United States does not gainsay the crucial fact that is it based on her experiences in Iran, rather than in the United States. It seems as if the value of literature in Iran is very different from the value of literature in America. How can we explain this? What is it that makes literature have such magical qualities for this group of female readers, especially when the texts that they are reading are the same texts that we read in the United States?

If we view Nafisi as a naive teacher of literature in Iran, as a scholar who studied in American universities and goes back to Iran and celebrates American literature in her classes and with her students and friends, it would be hard to explain why other people besides Nafisi continue to place such value on the act of reading American literature. This is because such a perspective neglects the real-life experiences of the people who are reading American literature. The reason why they view literature as having magical qualities has everything to do with their material social circumstances—they live in a society in which, as individuals, their ability to exercise freedom is severely limited. I am not referring to all Iranian women, but very specifically to those women who come to Nafisi's secret reading club. Nafisi does place a lot of emphasis on reading literature for aesthetic pleasure: "Literature in and of itself should be read for the pure sensual pleasure of reading, which is quite unique." But she makes that point in a particular context: "Books become even more important in repressive regimes. Under totalitarian conditions (as existed in Iran when I was living there), the emphasis was on confiscating individual freedoms, and books have the capacity to redeem some of that lost integrity and sense of individuality."[33] Thus to view the value the women place on literature as a quality that literature intrinsically possesses is to overlook how literary value is socially created, and how this created value is inscribed with the political tensions of this community of readers meeting underground. Nafisi writes: "For a long time I had dreamt of creating a special class, one that would give me the freedoms denied me in the classes I taught in the Islamic Republic. I wanted to teach a handful of selected students wholly committed to the study of literature, students who were not handpicked by the government, who had not chosen English literature simply because they had not been accepted in other fields or because they thought an English degree would be a good career move."[34] And again: "We were not looking for blue-prints, for an easy solution, but we did hope to find the link between the open spaces the novels provided and the closed ones we were confined to. I remember reading to my girls Nabokov's claim that 'readers were born free and ought to remain free.'"[35]

The government's intense scrutiny of teaching practices, selection of texts, and choice of students creates an atmosphere in which the act of reading is viewed as potentially disruptive. What teachers say and do in class is often monitored by the university administration, and teachers can face severe repercussions if they do anything that the university or the government considers inappropriate. To create an alternate space that does not have the same kind of pressure, Nafisi decides to hold classes in her home and invites students there.[36] In this communal space, when they read literature, they do not have to fit all their interpretations into already created templates. In this sense, the novel itself becomes a space of freedom. The value accorded to literature by the official arms of the government clash with the values accorded to literature by this group of readers. Let me stress again that this does not apply to all Iranian women, however much most American readers may want to believe that it does. It is in relation to the pressure to impose values on literature and on practices of reading that Nafisi and her students try to create a countervalue. It is imperative for us to understand this conflict of interests because only in this context can we appreciate how and why literature is viewed as having magical qualities, rather than immediately hearkening back to Jacques Derrida's deconstruction, Stephen Greenblatt's new historicism, Michel Foucault's power and discourse, Judith Butler's gender as performance, or Gayatri Spivak's notion of subalternity in order to show that Nafisi and her students are illiterate about how theory has transformed the reading and teaching of literature in the United States.

There is a troubling moment in Rowe's essay where he claims that Nafisi and her book are "part of a neoconservative conspiracy to co-opt neoliberal rhetoric for its own purposes" and are thus in the service of propagating a cultural defense of American imperialism.[37] He writes:

In developing this dialectical argument, I do not presume to know the appropriate terms for an effective criticism of the Islamic Republic of Iran. Indeed, I confess my ignorance of the internal workings of that state's political institutions and its social habitus, simply as a statement of fact that I am incapable of challenging Nafisi's account of the repressive conditions under which she and many others lived (and many died). . . . In my confession of ignorance, I also do not mean to turn a blind eye upon the conditions Nafisi describes in Iran. . . . My concern is with her proposed alternative: the cultural, economic, and political "modernization" offered by liberal Western democracies, especially as they are exemplified in the liberal idealism of what she judges our "best" literature.[38]

The focus of his essay, Rowe emphasizes, is not the representational nature of Nafisi's memoir, since he cannot "challenge" her memoir unless he knows something about Iran, which he does not—as his "confession" of ignorance makes clear. What he takes issue with is Nafisi's offering an "alternative" in the form of idealizing democracy, albeit Westernized, in what she takes to be its "best" literature. But we need to ask on what basis a critic can start to challenge Nafisi's alternative, if he or she has simply no knowledge at all about what exactly that alternative is supposed to supplant? How is it possible to challenge Nafisi's alternative unless one has at least some understanding of why she is proposing it, of what kinds of experiences she has had that have shaped her ideas about the nature of the alternative she proposes, however invalid a close scrutiny may reveal them to be? What is happening here is that an elaborate critique of Nafisi has been made with nary a reference to Iran or its cultures, peoples, and histories. Rowe's critique is very much centered in America and around America, especially around how neoconservatives in America are using neoliberal critique, the extent to which Paul Berman is reviving a presumed authentic liberalism in Nafisi's memoir,[39] and Nafisi's institutional affiliations and professional friendships in the United States. It is all about the United States, America, the grand fight between liberals and conservatives, and smart neoconservatives who are happily and effectively co-opting neo-Marxism, postcolonial theory, and deconstruction.

But Rowe's argument does not stop here; he goes on to make a sweeping claim in a passage at the end of the essay, where he writes about spending time in Idaho, which is where he read Nafisi's book—hence the title of his essay, "Reading *Reading Lolita in Tehran* in Idaho." The people of this region, on the borders of Idaho, Montana, and Wyoming, often refer to it as "God's country." They are highly skeptical about the Bureau of Land Management, National Forest Service, National Park Service, and other branches of the central government. They pay in cash for purchases, drive pick-up trucks, and are resourceful in doing things for themselves, like hunting for food and building things; they are the people of the great American frontier "who tend to be profoundly religious, openly racist, and incurably sexist."[40] Rowe goes on to say:

> To be sure Idaho is hardly a match for the repressive regime of the Islamic Republic of Iran, but "God's country" is certainly as fanatically political and ideological in its fantastic commitment to its version of "liberal individualism." Reading *Reading Lolita in Tehran* in Idaho is an object lesson to the attentive cultural critic that the danger of totalitarianism in the United States, equivalent to what Nafisi finds in the Islamic Republic of Tehran, is far closer to Code Red on the great frontier of the American West and in the White House itself than from those postmodern slackers in the halls of academe or on the back shelves of the Library of Congress.[41]

The inhabitants of the American West, the specific place that Rowe often visits, are caricatured as having a propensity to be "incurably sexist," implying that they have a disease—sexism—that cannot be cured. These people are beyond redemption, at least the kind of redemption that enlightened critics can offer, since they are so naive that they do not even recognize a fundamental economic reality: their economies are sustained by the dollars that flow in from tourists, which makes them even more pathetic since their frontierlike self-reliance and their talents and skills of creating and doing things on their own are totally useless. There is no mention of the ethnic and racial make-up of these people. Given demographic statistics, it is probable that they are white Americans. But we need to note the parallels that Rowe draws here: these people are just as fanatical as those in the Islamic Republic of Iran. Furthermore, such fanatics can be found in the White House, which is the important lesson for critics—"the danger of totalitarianism in the United States, equivalent to what Nafisi finds in the Islamic Republic of Tehran," is very much alive and well in Idaho and in the halls of power in Washington. There is one major problem here: Rowe has already confessed ignorance about the Islamic Republic of Iran, as noted above: "I confess my ignorance of the internal workings of that state's political institutions and its social habitus."

How can a critic say that he knows nothing about the Iranian state and yet claim that he finds "totalitarianism in the United States" to be "equivalent" to what Nafisi experienced in Iran? As I noted earlier, Rowe's essay is focused on America, yet it includes sweeping generalizations about totalitarianism in both America and Iran. At this point, we need to ask how he defines totalitarianism. Is he taking Nafisi's word for its existence in Iran? If so, why is he relying on Nafisi who, he claims, is actively working to promote American imperialism, who is part of a vast neoconservative conspiracy to use culture to thwart peaceful negotiations with Iran? All this ought to make her knowledge and her work deeply suspect, yet without reference to the work of any other writer who is knowledgeable about Iran, Rowe's only basis for equating totalitarianism in Iran and in America is *Reading Lolita in Tehran*! In other words, there is a lot to be gained by reading this book, a lot to be learned about Iran, the brutality of the Islamic Republic, and the travails of its female citizens. In this passage, Nafisi's information about Iran turns into reliable knowledge only insofar as the case can be made for Iran and America both being totalitarian, Rowe's main argument. Anything else in the book is the result of a neoconservative conspiracy.

DIASPORA AND THE BURDEN OF REPRESENTATION

Critics have also taken another tack in criticizing Nafisi and her work: she has cashed in—quite literally, given the memoir's status as a bestseller—on the current climate of fear among Americans given the attacks of September 11 and the U.S. invasion of Iraq. A good example of this criticism is *Jasmine and Stars* by Fatemeh Keshavarz, who offers her book—part memoir, part criticism—as a specific rebuttal to Nafisi and *Reading Lolita in Tehran*. To Keshavarz, *Reading Lolita in Tehran* espouses a New Orientalism that essentializes men's relation to religion and women's relations to men; it relies less on Europeans writing about the non-West and more on native writers and intellectuals writing about their own experiences, albeit in ways that exoticize the East; and although there is a higher degree of self-consciousness in these narratives, they "do not hide [their] clear preference for a western political and cultural takeover"[42] as they "amplify fear and mistrust by ignoring similarity and highlighting difference."[43] However, Keshavarz's discussion of *Reading Lolita in Tehran* too quickly condemns the book as New Orientalism, as the following two examples demonstrate. In *Reading Lolita in Tehran*, there is an extended account of an episode when Sanaz and her friends, on a short vacation to the

Caspian Sea, find themselves accosted by the Revolutionary Guards. Although finding nothing criminal in the girls' activities they nonetheless put them in prison for two days, subject them to virginity tests—twice, the second time to confirm the first's test's results—force them to sign a confession, and summarily sentence them to twenty-five lashes each. About this episode, Keshavarz observes: "Sanaz has been subjected to flogging for no reason. We are then told: 'In some perverse way, the physical punishment was a source of satisfaction to her. A compensation for having yielded to those other humiliations.'"[44] What we need to pay attention to here is Keshavarz's conclusion about the episode: "The women, in other words, are turned masochistic by the punishment."[45] To interpret this episode as Nafisi's New Orientalist account showing that Iranian women have masochistic tendencies requires a simplistic reading of the text. What we find in this passage is a woman who experiences so much guilt for signing a false confession that as her body is lashed by the jailers, she "punishes" herself by viewing her predicament of being subjected to lashing as a result of her confession. In light of all the humiliations that she and her friends were subjected to, what is worth noting in this passage is the extent to which Sanaz expects so much more from herself than from her jailers; what bothers her is that she, as a woman—both an individual and as a member of a group of people in Iran who are sometimes victimized in such ways—had to make compromises like offering a confession in order to save herself. When Nafisi writes that in dealing with the outlandish demands made by a state intent on subjecting its female citizens to greater control, "we had to poke fun at our own misery in order to survive,"[46] it does not mean that Nafisi is turning women's oppression into a big joke, or that Iranian women have a great sense of humor. Pondering the kind of mental tension that women subjected to such treatment experience, Nafisi acknowledges the power of such episodes to generate psychic disorders: "There, we spoke as if the events did not belong to us; like schizophrenic patients, we tried to keep ourselves away from that other self, at once intimate and alien."[47] Women facing such arbitrary pressures and force from the *komiteh* (revolutionary groups that enforced morality) on a constant basis sometimes developed an almost pathological fear about being subjected to searches, threats, physical harm, and other kinds of harassment. Shirin Ebadi emphasizes: "For women, public space—from the produce stand to the park to the bus stop—became fraught with uncertainty. You simply did not know where, at what hour, and under what pretext you might be harassed, and often the confrontations with the *komiteh* turned alarming."[48] The tremendous mental strain on women in such con-

ditions of severe social surveillance and control is being addressed in Nafisi's memoir; it's not some carelessly chosen idea or practice in Iran that she
focuses on—driven, perhaps unwittingly, by the power of New Orientalism to paint Iranian women as masochistic. *Reading Lolita in Tehran* and
its author offer more in the form of exploring these issues than Keshavarz's
discussion acknowledges.

Another frequent criticism leveled against *Reading Lolita in Tehran* is
that it is too narrow in its representation of Iranian society. Paying attention to the location of a critic, such as Keshavarz, sheds light on how experiences of travel, relocation, and knowledge about American higher education shape such critiques. Speaking about Nafisi's comment about Manna's
lack of exposure to romance in novels and songs, Keshavarz writes, "I
could not read such comments and think: not me! I never felt alien to this
worldly love."[49] But is this a reasonable criticism? Why should a reader expect a literary text to reflect her own unique experiences? *Reading Lolita
in Tehran* does not claim that everything in the novel applies wholesale to
all the women in Iran, much less to Iranian American women. Such statements would be easy to disprove, and Nafisi is hardly the kind of writer
and intellectual to make such claims. On the contrary, these are just the
kinds of sweeping claims that she speaks sharply against. What is it, then,
that animates *Jasmine and Star*'s critique of *Reading Lolita in Tehran*? Two
things stand out: the stark differences between Nafisi's and Keshavarz's
migration to America, and Keshavarz's greater sensitivity to issues of cultural representations based on her experience as a professor in the United
States. She writes: "Living in the West, faced with demeaning stereotypical
representations of myself as an Iranian Muslim woman, I needed women
who stood out in memory, who made me feel empowered."[50] There are several comments in her book about what American readers may think about
Iran: "Throwing this kind of charged comment at a reader who has a limited context comes very close to misinformation";[51] "the white, middle-
class, Western reader, normally barred from entering this world, finally
has a chance to slip under the veil";[52] "the American reader has the right
to know that items displayed in that tent reflected a broader global per-
ception of what is known as America's use of might against those who disagree with its views and interests"; and "the American reader is protected
against harsh facts."[53] As an Iranian American Muslim woman and a professor in an American university, Keshavarz's awareness of public reactions to September 11 attacks and to the Middle East in general create a
powerful desire in her to see positive Iranian characters and portrayals of

Iran in literature. All of the passages quoted above point to the emphasis that she places, based on her experience with America, on Americans' lack of knowledge about the world.

The question is, does this context of American ignorance make it reasonable for Keshavarz to evaluate *Reading Lolita in Tehran* based on whether or not the book is portraying positive Iranian characters? It would be very hard to answer in the affirmative because doing so would compel us to dismiss authors such as James Welch, Maxine Hong Kingston, and Roberta Fernández as part of a massive conspiracy (a new conservative one, too!) to misinform the American public and serve the case of empire. Welch's *Winter in the Blood* is about a nameless Native American narrator who drinks and moves aimlessly between his reservation and the outside world. Its tone and imagery are extremely bleak. But does this mean that Welch is guilty of New Orientalist tactics in denigrating all Indians on reservations as drunks and bums? Kingston's *The Woman Warrior* tells the story of an aunt who is left nameless since she transgresses social strictures, but does this mean that Kingston is portraying all Chinese women as passive, senseless victims? Fernández's *Intaglio: A Novel in Six Stories* has a narrative about rape and recovery along the U.S.-Mexico border, but does this mean she is representing Mexican American men as potential rapists? For a Native Indian, Chinese American, or Mexican American reader to dismiss these novels as Orientalist narratives because they do not represent his or her experiences would be pointless. But the connection Keshavarz makes between her personal experiences—saying how they are fundamental in determining her reading of contemporary Iranian literature—and her searching for, hoping for, even yearning for positive individuals, characters, and stories about Iran is an important point in her book. And it is an extremely weak basis for an outright dismissal of *Reading Lolita in Tehran* as a New Orientalist narrative.

Another weak argument concerns what Keshavarz views as *Reading Lolita in Tehran*'s "contempt" toward Iranians when Nafisi highlights the irony of a large group of Iranians' showing up for a viewing of films by Andrei Tarkovsky without knowing how to spell his name. Keshavarz points out: "In a European city such a turnout would likely be seen as an indication of cultured behavior. *Reading Lolita in Tehran*, however, does not extend such a positive judgment to the Iranian crowd. Instead, it expresses surprise at the interest of the audience, 'most of whom would not have known how to spell Tarkovsky's name.' How is this fact determined? We do not find out."[54] In the novel, Nafisi is very far from regarding these filmgoers as uncultured people who yearn for things they do not understand. In fact, she refers to the large gathering of people as the "most amazing feature of the day" because although the films were heavily censored and missiles were being lobbed at Tehran by Iraq in the days prior to the event, thus creating a tense social atmosphere, many people thronged the cinema halls to watch Tarkovsky's films. This was not a rally, protest march, political group meeting, or secret gathering. This large attendance showed, to Nafisi, how "thirsty" the Iranians were "for some form of beauty" as they "experienced collectively the kind of awful beauty that can only be grasped through extreme anguish and expressed through art."[55] This is not an elitist disdain of the masses, as Keshavarz makes it out to be. It is a recognition of the people's deep interest in art and things of the imagination, especially in daunting social and political conditions. Arguing that such examples show that *Reading Lolita in Tehran* and its writer are agents of the New Orientalism is to make a claim based on a highly selective, decontextualized reading of the memoir.

In the first chapter of *Jasmine and Stars*, Keshavarz gives some biographical details: she has been working in the United States since 1987; she was never "employed officially in an Iranian university since the 1979 revolution and the ascendancy of the Islamic Republic"; and she believes "in principle" that people should exercise sartorial choices, although she understands that some Iranian women feel obliged to "wear the head scarf that is now mandated by the constitution."[56] Nafisi's personal history is almost the exact opposite: although Keshavarz never had any experience teaching in Iran after 1979, the bulk of Nafisi's professional career was spent in Iran after the revolution; her refusal to wear the veil leads to a major confrontation between her and the university administration, including her expulsion and resignation; in the mid-1990s, she conducts a secret reading club with students, on which her memoir focuses; and she moves to the United States with her family in 1997. Evidently, the major cultural conflicts that ensued after the revolution directly affected Nafisi's and Keshavarz's personal and professional lives differently. It would be a mistake to view this as granting Nafisi a more authentic narrative voice, and, indeed, it is vital that we scrutinize her writing for its accuracy. But the issue here is not authenticity; rather, it is understanding the specific experiences that shaped both writers. Faulting Nafisi for focusing too much on challenges that women faced in Iran and criticizing her for not portraying positive characters, as Keshavarz does, is to impose a literary straitjacket on writers and their choice of subjects based on the reader's personal experiences—in this case, as an Iranian American in the United States. It would be just as reductive to criticize Kesharvaz for putting too much emphasis on jasmine, stars, and poetry and not enough on the daily challenges of the women who, although fully sensitive to the beauty of Persian culture and literature, struggle to affirm their sense of identity and independence.[57] Keshavarz tends to place undue emphasis on specific events and passages in the text, while missing the larger contexts in which Nafisi and the young women reflect on their experiences. And this emphasis, as we have seen, is determined to a large extent by the critic's personal desires for positive representations of Iran in Nafisi's memoir.

Nafisi's *Things I've Been Silent About* faces such criticism head-on: unlike *Reading Lolita in Tehran*, this text is written in the more traditional format of a memoir, with detailed historical contexts; names of peoples, persons, and events; photographs of people missing or presumed killed by the government. More to the point, Nafisi's account of her childhood and adolescence in Iran, pursuit of higher education in England and the United States, marriage, divorce, exile, and migration is situated in a cultural ethos in which the work of Persian writers, filmmakers, poets, and activists, ancient and contemporary—Ferdowsi (*Shanemeh*), Rumi (*Masnavi*), Saadi (*Golestan, Boostan*, and *Kelileh va Demneh*), Forough Farrokhzad (*Another Birth*), Alam Taj, Simin Behbahani, Houshang Golshiri, Shahrnoosh Parsipur, Bahram Beyzaii—shape her identity and worldview. Nafisi views literature "not as a pastime but as a way of perceiving and interpreting the world—in short, as a way of being in the world."[58] This book directly contradicts her critics' accusations that she privileges Western literature in reorienting young women to their social conditions. Although critics of her *Reading Lolita in Tehran* obviously had not read this new memoir, it does not validate their claims that *Reading Lolita in Tehran* was conservative cultural imperialism disguised as liberalism. What needs to be accounted for is the cultural moment—more precisely, the phenomenon—marked by the intersection of several events and trends in which *Reading Lolita in Tehran* and its author's public statements in interviews and lectures became enmeshed: the invasion of Iraq, the growth in Americans' interest in Middle Eastern peoples and cultures, and the need for authentic representation of cultural difference. The challenge is to critique the tendency among American readers to draw on orientalist stereotypes to engage with cultural difference, and to indulge in self-congratulation for having an Anglo-American canon embodying liberal tenets that Third World peoples find irresistible, without dismissing the entire memoir and its writer as agents of empire and cultural imperialism. Perhaps a contra-puntal reading of Nafisi and *Reading Lolita in Tehran* with another writer and text can help us move beyond such an impasse.

GENDER, RELIGION, AND REVOLUTION

Iran Awakening, by Shirin Ebadi, winner of the 2003 Nobel Peace Prize, of-fers a contrast to *Reading Lolita in Tehran*. However, as I shall soon show, both texts focus on women and religion although they do so in different ways—some of which emphasize the revolution's fundamental impact on women. As an Iranian in exile, Nafisi seems to stand in contrast to Ebadi who, unlike the millions of Iranians who fled the country after 1979, de-cides to stay and continue her work as an activist and attorney. Even as her decision to stay in Iran exacts a price in terms of close friendships and re-lationships and results in her demotion from judge to clerk, Ebadi contin-ues her work and, eventually, when she is allowed to practice law again, she earnestly pursues it as her vocation. Nafisi writes a book in America; inter-estingly, Ebadi also publishes her book not in Iran but in America, which the biographical section on the book jacket's flap notes is "her first book for a Western audience," a significant point in light of her being awarded the Nobel Prize in 2003. Ebadi also notes that "the censorship that prevails in the Islamic Republic has made it impossible to publish an honest account of my life here."[59] Interestingly enough, she faced a different kind of cen-sorship in the United States, where she could not publish her memoir due to the prohibitions on trade with countries blacklisted by the Office of For-eign Assets Control (OFAC) of the Treasury Department. In fact, the law-suit filed by Ebadi and her literary agency, the Strothman Agency, against the OFAC was preceded by another suit (both were filed in 2004) against the OFAC, brought by the Association of American Publishers Professional and Scholarly Publishing Division, the Association of American Univer-sity Presses, PEN American Center, and Arcade Publishing to suspend the rule requiring authors and publishers to obtain a license from the OFAC. In 2005, the OFAC granted Ebadi permission to publish her memoir in the United States.[60] Her memoir is different from Nafisi's in many ways: there are no pedagogical situations involving professors and students; Ameri-can culture and literature are not the primary focuses; there is more his-torical continuity because Ebadi has remained in Iran, while Nafisi left the country in 1997; and Ebadi's Islamic beliefs and convictions stand in clear contrast to Nafisi's, insofar as these matters are discussed in the two texts.

Iran Awakening directly contradicts moments of cultural radicalism in the critiques of Mottahedeh, Dabashi, Rowe, and Keshavarz in that it does not conflate culture with politics, cultural critique with political participation, or cultural change with political change. Ebadi's memoir shows that even if Iranian women—unlike Nafisi's students, who were keenly interested in American literature—were fully steeped in the literature, songs, and films of Sa'di, Hafez, Rumi, Simin Behbahani, Mohammad Reza Shafi-Kadkani, Abdulkarim Soroush, Abbas Kiarostami, Tahmineh Milani, Rakshan Bani Itemad, Forough Farrokhzad, and others, the theocratic state would still afford them a particular status, as women. Why is this so? The transition from Iran to the Islamic Republic of Iran required a wholesale transformation in social relations and attitudes: "The imposition of Islamic penal code, inspired by Islamic law, is a momentous overhaul in how society is governed. It would fundamentally transform the very basis of governance, the relationship of citizens to laws, the organizing principles and social contracts to laws along which society is conducted."[61]

Ebadi's entire experience as a lawyer after she obtained a license to practice in 1992 involved arguing in both lower and higher courts against laws that made a woman's testimonies worth only half as much as a man's, women's lives to be worth half of men's lives, and women's consent to divorce almost unnecessary. In the case of Leila Fathi, an eleven-year-old girl from a village near Sanandaj who was raped and murdered, and whose body was dumped in the hills in 1996, Ebadi argues against the court's ruling that although two men were found guilty and sentenced to death, Fathi's impoverished family had to come up with the money for the state to carry out the sentence. This ruling had to do with an interpretation of Islamic law in which the so-called blood money that victims could appeal for in compensation for a crime was reduced to half its value on account of Fathi's gender.[62] Seeking to "advocate for female equality in an Islamic framework," Ebadi publishes an article in *Iran-e Farda* drawing attention to women's unequal status in society and argues against the law's evaluation of blood money that gives the same compensatory value to damage to a man's testicle that it does to the ending of a woman's life.[63] The women in *Reading Lolita in Tehran* would have known about such discrimination through personal experience or public information.

There is one important difference between the two texts that we should note: their historical timelines. By identifying the historical span of each text, we can get a better sense of why this temporal difference, when not clearly taken into account by reviewers, critics, and readers, can lead to charges of false representation or misrepresentation against *Reading Lol-*

ita in Tehran and Nafisi. Unlike the several million Iranians who fled their country over the four decades after the revolution, Ebadi stays in Iran with her family, which gives her a degree of experiential authority to speak for and of Iranian women, and a sense of historical continuity that cannot easily be obtained by Iranian writers in exile or abroad. Nafisi leaves Iran in 1997, and *Reading Lolita in Tehran*'s recollection of the past stops at that year. But it was during the mid-1990s, before her departure, that large-scale movements for reform and change emerged in Iran, one good indication of which was the election of Mohammad Khatami, who was president from 1997 to 2005. Over the last decade or so, changes in Iranian society that Nafisi has not experienced or witnessed firsthand have become evident: almost 65 percent of university students now are women, as are 43 percent of Iranians in the workforce. The unprecedented growth of information technology over the last few years has also made it difficult for the government to impose censorship and tightly control the flow of information.[64] Fourteen women have also become members of parliament. The police force created to maintain public morality "went from omnipresent invaders to a periodic nuisance," and Ebadi notes that at the polling place where she went to cast her vote in the 1997 election that brought Khatami to power, she and her daughter, Negar, "didn't see a single woman wearing chador."[65] This offers a striking contrast to *Reading Lolita in Tehran*, in which a professor and seven female students must meet secretly in her house to discuss literature. Because Nafisi emigrated to American in 1997, any change after that date simply cannot be part of *Reading Lolita in Tehran*. Nonetheless, her novel is often interpreted to represent contemporary Iran, which makes it easy to point out major discrepancies. This should not be taken to mean that the memoir's account of Iran prior to 1997 is beyond dispute. But in our reading of *Reading Lolita in Tehran*, we need to take into account this historical context, since it would be illogical to critique the novel in light of all the changes since 1997.

What both authors take into account, as they approach it from different historical, legal, cultural, and literary perspectives is this: "the legal system was underpinned by Islamic law; and every facet of a woman's place in society—from access to birth control to divorce rights to compulsory veiling—was determined by interpretations of the Koran."[66] As Dabashi observes, Ayatollah Khomeini's rise to power was a "purgatorial passage, a vindictive kingdom ruled with terrorizing vengeance and unsurpassed tyranny. The shah's tyranny seemed pathetic in comparison to the violence Khomeini inflicted on the nation."[67] Three issues need further comment here: Islamism's ambivalence toward modernity vis-à-vis the state; the patriarchal underpinnings of traditionalism, whose engagement with modernity renders women invisible; and the production of America discourse in Iran.

ISLAMISM AND THE
PRODUCTION OF AMERICA

Janet Afary and Kevin Anderson's *Foucault and the Iranian Revolution* is relevant to this discussion not only because it shows the failure of Foucauldian ideas of power, sexuality, and regimes of control to adequately account for the Islamicization of the Iranian Revolution, for which the book presents a persuasive argument, but also because it recognizes the highly textured nature of the forces that coalesced to foment dissent against the monarchy. It is a dissent that could not, for many reasons, prevent the powerful clerical faction from assuming control of the state apparatuses and turning the nation into the Islamic Republic of Iran. The refreshing thing about Afary and Anderson's approach is that they take religion seriously as a category of analysis and examine how the Islamicization of social and political power, although legitimately criticizing the forced programs of modernization pursued by both shahs during the better part of the twentieth century, established an alternative regime of truth by investing Iranian Shi'ite symbols, rituals, and observances with symbolic meanings in order to grant legitimacy to a new, repressive mode of political organization.[68] These symbols and rituals "were present throughout Iranian culture, not just in the specific religious practices of believing Muslims,"[69] which shows that Islamism did not introduce new religious practices so much as manipulate them and twist their significance to suit its political agenda. This Islamism was "a carefully staged and crafted version of Shi'ism that had been first developed in the 1960s and 1970s as a response to the authoritarian modernization of Muhammad Reza Shah's government."[70] Sanam Vakil points out: "Mixing together Islamic imagery and populist discourse, the government implemented a thorough Islamicization of Iranian society where changes to the school syllabi, street names, dress codes, and the new legal system all reflected the return to Islamic norms."[71] In *Social Origins of the Iranian Revolution*, while analyzing the numerous factors and forces—including the *bazaaris*, mosques, landed elites, industrial workers, rural communities, urban populations, intellectuals, artists, activists, the Tudeh Party, and the mujahedin—that influenced the revolution, Misagh Parsa details the dynamics underpinning the "level of state intervention in capital allo-

cation and accumulation" and the multifarious connections that such interventions strengthened "between economic and political structures."[72]
However, the focus of my discussion is not an analysis of the revolution
but the identification and contextualization of a specific modality of what
Parsa calls "variables."[73] One of these was the pivotal shift in Shi'ite jurisprudence advocated by Khomeini that involved radically altering the constitution, which was ratified in December 1979. Parsa observes: "While the
new constitution was being debated, hostages were taken at the American
Embassy. The hostage crisis was *effectively used to rally popular support for
the government and promote unity.* Much of the controversy *was deflected
away* from the constitution and *directed instead toward the United States,*
thus facilitating the ratification of the constitution."[74]

At this crucial juncture, the production of America discourse becomes central to displacing attention from the new constitution toward
a different other so that "support" and "unity" could be achieved. What I
am doing here is drawing attention to certain rhetorical ploys, theological
debates, historiographic tensions, and gender politics that were central to
this "staged and crafted version" of Islamism as it is represented in *Reading
Lolita in Tehran* and *Iran Awakening.* Questions arise: What is the nature
of theocratic power? How and where does it derive its legitimacy? What is
its relation to what Dabashi points out is Iran's history of negotiating colonial modernity? In what ways are the bodies of women and the idea of
woman—as material beings and discursive subjects—central to reimagining Iran in an Islamicized historic time? And how is all this related to
the production of America discourse in the sense that dwelling in American configures it: as a mode of grappling with the pressure of modernity
(in this instance, colonial modernity) and the specific actions of the U.S.
nation-state?

We can begin by revising what Frank Lechner identifies as traditional
notions of fundamentalism, which view it as a "fringe" social phenomenon that is "subjectively meaningful and open to objective interpretation,"
an "archaic form of religiosity," or a sign of a "grand ideological struggle
between modernity and tradition."[75] Far from imposing an old order on
the present, by "selecting elements of tradition and modernity" and by revitalizing "religious identity . . . as the exclusive and absolute basis for a
re-created political and social order that is oriented to the future rather
than the past," fundamentalisms attempt to "remake the world in the service of a dual commitment to the unfolding eschatological drama (by returning all things in submission to the divine) and to self-preservation (by

neutralizing the threatening 'Other')."[76] By accepting the primacy of religion in ordering social life, such future-oriented tendencies of fundamentalisms undermine the model that contrasts the modern and the premodern. It might be better to use the term "Islamism" in this context rather than "fundamentalism," since Afary and Anderson point out that like fundamentalism, Islamism insists on literal interpretations of holy texts, but unlike fundamentalism, it draws extensively on modern and alternate sources to shore up its authority.[77]

In relating these ideas to the Iran of *Reading Lolita in Tehran*, we need to avoid the focus on Islam, the religion, as the primary site for reform and liberalism because it is not Islam as a body of beliefs, cultural practices, and theological doctrines[78] that is the basis of Iranian society. Rather, it is the Islamicization of the nation-state that legitimizes a specific form of fundamentalism—Shia hierocracy—that often uses woman as a symbolic register in which the female in the domestic economy sanctioned by Islamism can also be Americanized as the threatening other. In entwining woman and America in very specific instances, as *Reading Lolita in Tehran* shows, the theocratic state can produce a subject whose material and discursive management produces an allegory of the nation's struggle with modernity in which Islam is marginally positioned in relation to a predatory America. This America is less about the U.S. nation-state and more about modernity—gender equality, free expression, individualism, reason, and secularism—which stands in opposition to religious authority, hierocracy, and tradition.

As Ann Elizabeth Mayer notes, the revolution against the shah's regime should be not be viewed primarily as a movement devoted to restoring a premonarchic nation but as a popular indictment of the regime's selective programs of modernization that consolidated the monarchy, stifled opposition to elite power, created a secret police—the SAVAK—that suppressed dissent, and sought to impose modernity from the top down, as evidenced by the 1936 banning of the veil that most Iranian women ignored. While it should be acknowledged that the 1963 reform acts granted women suffrage, and the 1967 Iranian Family Protection Act gave women greater freedom in divorce proceedings and settlements, the rise of a "Westernized elite" who were "estranged from Iranian traditions" and had "little in common with the values and outlooks of less affluent Iranians"[79] led to a popular uprising in which, as Nahid Yeganeh notes, women viewed themselves "as members of different political and social forces" and even wore veils not to celebrate the coming of an Islamic state but as a "sign of oppo-

sition to the Shah."[80] As Nafisi observes in an interview, "the problem with
the Shah was not that his modernism destroyed his regime; it was that
he still carried vestiges of totalitarianism and tyranny."[81] Iranian women,
notes Azar Tabari, viewed the revolution as an opposition to the shah's
"barbarism, oppression, and exploitation."[82] With the shah's exile, "there
was a fundamentalist takeover of a revolution that was fought primarily
for secular political and economic goals."[83] After 1979, Islamism became a
dominant force, as it sought to create a theocracy whose strategies of narrating Iranian history created a people who could imagine themselves as
national subjects in and through the body and sign of woman, domesti-
cated and veiled, which allowed two variable gendered positionings. First,
as a marker of Islamic purity within a complex of international relations,
Islamism's woman affords a space in which the nation is feminized in relation to a masculine America, reflecting the fear of American penetration
into Islamic cultures. And second, to create a new nation, Islamism ratio-
nalizes the marginalization of women in order to sustain its patriarchal
ideology.

As noted above, Nafisi's memoir recounts the imprisonment of vaca-
tioning students by Revolutionary Guards, who imprison the women, flog
them, and perform virginity tests to confirm their purity. In another in-
cident, a student voicing his opposition to reading *The Great Gatsby* be-
moans America's "sinister assault on the very roots of our culture. What
our Imam calls cultural aggression. This I would call a rape of our culture," which becomes "the hallmark of the Islamic Republic's critique of
the West."[84] In this instance, the category of woman in the discourse of
Islamism is inflected with contradictory meanings, facilitating a certain
flexibility of subject positions as both men and women are compelled to
occupy a feminized national space vis-à-vis Iran's interactions with the
West. Put differently, the feminization of internationalization—that ongoing process of cultural rape in Iran that the student wants to resist—simultaneously authorizes the consolidation of patriarchal power within the nation, as women are "caught in the ongoing struggle for power between the
clergy and the secular state."[85] Nima Naghibi puts it well: "The more powerful the imperialist presence, the weaker the position of the third-world
subject, and the more this subject position becomes associated with effem-
inate and weak female identities."[86] In an address to women at the Feyzieh
School of Theology in 1979, Khomeini lauds women for their indispensable
role in the revolution while also imploring them to reconstruct the nation:
"If nations are deprived of brave and human-making women they will be
defeated and ruined. . . . Women must involve [sic] in the fundamental as-

pects of the country. . . . God willing, you must reconstruct the country. *In early Islam women would participate in wars alongside men. . . .* We want women to reach the high position of humanity. Woman must have a say in her fate."[87] Women's active roles in this "urban protest movement" embody the "paradox of fundamentalism's promotion of the political mobilization of women" that "recreate[s] a patriarchal segregation of the sexes" in order to secure the nation and reinstate, in a fundamentalist vision of salvation-ist history, its own "radical patriarchalism."[88]

The idea that the new nation, which was soon to be theocratized, needs the labor of women, the bodies of women, and the contributions of women to reconstruct a country is an idea that surely comes across clearly. But in evoking an Islamic time of gender equality in the public sphere of war, the private realm of individual choice is made to overlap neatly with the obligations to Islam and the nation. In this matrix, because there is no tension between agency, positionality, and ideology, for women to oppose Khomeini's program of national reconstruction would be tantamount to refusing the freedom afforded by the new nation and denying early Islamic history as significant. But there is more to this deployment of woman in Islamist discourse: it needs an other against and through which the legiti-macy of the Islamic nation can be thrown into sharp relief. It is here that we see the production of America discourse as a form of othering America, but in both senses of the term: the United States as America, and America as a symbol of modernity.

The clerics and left-leaning organizations promote the view of the American embassy as the habitation of spies and demonstrators, and even those with little knowledge of America—who "didn't even know where America was, and sometimes thought they were actually being taken to America"—are bused to Tehran from neighboring cities and towns to en-gage in protest; in return for shouting "Death to America" and "every now and then [burning] the American flag," they would be "given food and money" and "could stay and joke and picnic with their families in front of the nest of spies."[89] To Nafisi, this marks the mythification of America, the manufacturing of protest that produces a discourse about America as the great Satan, as the distinct other from which the Iranian nation should be saved. When she notes that America was "turned into a never-never land by the Islamic Revolution" and that as "the myth of America started to take hold of Iran . . . America had become the land of Satan and Paradise Lost,"[90] her distinctions between protests against U.S. influence over the shahs and against the Westernization of Iran begin to blur. To be sure, re-sentment toward the United States for its involvement in Iranian politics during the twentieth century, especially its support of the shah's regime, is absolutely pivotal to understanding the massive uprisings of the late 1970s that culminated in the overthrow of the regime, a point that Stephen Kinzer's *All the Shah's Men* makes by detailing British and American involvement in the coup that successfully deposed Prime Minister Mohammed Mosaddeq in 1953 and restored the shah to the Peacock Throne.

However, the subtitle of his book, *An American Coup and the Roots of Middle East Terror*, is misleading because although Kinzer attempts to historicize anti-Americanism in Iran by providing brief accounts of pre-Islamic Iran, Shi'ism, the rise of the Pahlavi dynasty in the twentieth century, and the Islamic revolution of 1979, this history serves as a backdrop against which two major players emerge in the international theater—the United States as America and Iran as the Eastern other—with the coup of 1953 as the event that led to Iranian antipathy toward all things American and eventually to the spread of global Islamic anti-Americanism. In other words, absent British and American interventions in Iran, this nation would have, in all probability, blossomed into a democracy—an idea Kinzer does not state directly but hints at throughout his book. The problem with Kinzer's argument is that it needlessly conceptualizes Iranian history primarily in terms of the country's response to America, a move that validates a certain period in history—namely, 1953—as marking both the emergence and suppression of democracy in Iran. Having performed such a feat, Kinzer is compelled to follow his own logic further: American interference explains Iranian anti-Americanism.[91]

And there can be no doubt that once again, for all our efforts to historicize 1953, America is *the* major player in world history. All roads used to lead to Rome. Today, all roads lead to America. *Reading in Lolita in Tehran* and *Iran Awakening* dwell in American in the sense that they rupture Kinzer's cartography, which continues to recenter the United States in global discourse and world history. Nafisi's and Ebadi's memoirs make visible the Islamicization of discourses of dissent and movements of protest, with high investments in shoring up clerical power, theocratizing the nation-state, consolidating patriarchal systems of privilege, and producing woman as the primary site of these struggles, all of which point to the central tension in fundamentalist movements: how to recreate the social order by using religion and tradition and the modern apparatuses of the nation and the state in order to negotiate the challenges of modernity. The singular focus on the United States as America or modernity as America effectively forecloses any inquiry into the complex workings of Islamism and its effective consolidation of the nation-state.

HISTORY AND THEOCRACY

In *Pious Passion*, Martin Riesebrodt points to a major tension: the celebration of the 2,500th anniversary of the monarchy in 1971 fundamentally
challenges Islamic periodization by anchoring monarchical power in pre-
Islamic Zoroastrian history, and the replacement of the Islamic calendar
with the Achaemenian calendar in 1976 and the brutal crackdown on dissent over several decades leads to the crisis in 1979 that results in the shah's
flight and Khomeini's triumphant return from Paris as a populist leader of
the revolution.[92] 1976 is not simply another period in Iranian history; it is not
another way of periodizing the *telos* of modernity but, following Dabashi,
is "an ideological shift by the Pahlavi regime to a deliberately pre-Islamic,
Persian, and monarchic claim to legitimacy."[93] Because, as Prasenjit Duara
astutely observes, periodization is also about the "epistemology that produces the meaningful world,"[94] the shah's restoration of the Achaemenian
calendar in 1976 threatens to decenter Islamic periodization.[95] Since 1971
and 1976 inscribe themselves as alternative periodizations, they can end up
"conferring [new] meaning on individual identity."[96] Therefore, the history
of the Iranian nation and its subject-producing power are at stake.

However, it would be a mistake to miss the material aspect of these
celebrations, and why such a conflict on the terrain of ideology and historical consciousness acquired meanings in the public realm that went far
beyond the terms of the conflict itself. These celebrations and the conflict
were inscribed in a set of material processes that demonstrated yet again
the power and wealth of the monarchy, and its blatant sympathy with the
West and its culture. In the middle of the twentieth century, about 50 percent of Iran's thirty-five million people lived in rural regions, and 80 percent of the country's economy was linked to oil. With the deposition of
Mossadeq and the reinstallation of the monarchy, international companies were involved in the control of oil production and shared the resulting profit, leading to an exacerbation of differences between the political,
secular, middle classes and the rural, agriculture- and service-based, more
religiously oriented populace. The business classes viewed their country's
growing integration into the international economy as a threat.[97] For the
1971 celebration of Persian Achaemenid history, the shah spent $300 mil-
lion to provide luxurious amenities—including air transportation from
abroad—for thousands of guests and others.[98] Clerical communities—
with their intimate links to and influence over the economy and culture
of the bazaar, mosques, Hosseiniyehs (places to observe rituals), shrines,
religious schools, commemorative sites for the dead, and Saqqa Khaneh

(places where water could be obtained)—could justifiably accuse the regime of financial corruption and despotism. In a strongly worded declaration given in Najaf, Khomeini lambastes the shah for spending 80 million *tumans* to adorn Tehran for the festivities and asks why poor people—especially those interested in pursuing religious studies, a noble vocation indeed in Khomeini's eyes—should celebrate the monarchy when a center of learning, Fayzia Madrasa, and its students have been harassed by the regime's henchmen. But to Khomeini, the aggrandizement of the regime is not simply one instance of the abuse of royal prerogatives. The core issues are the legitimacy of political authority and the nature of governance. Since Islam's historical emergence, the monarchy has always been at odds with the clerics and scholars who were authorized by Mohammed to govern Muslims. Iranian history, contends Khomeini, shows that royalists were always keen on transgressing the Prophet's mandate as they usurped the authority of the clergy. This celebration of Persian history[99] in the twentieth century was yet another attempt to create social legitimacy for the monarchy, which also means that this was another major battle in which Muslims were presented with an opportunity to reaffirm the true principles of Islam by opposing the monarchy and thus paving the way for the fulfillment of the Prophet's plan for governance.[100] Indeed, to appease the increasing number of protestors against the monarchy, Prime Minister Sharif Emami, at the shah's urging, officially ordered that Iranian calendars follow Islamic periodization rather than the Persianized one that had been promulgated earlier.[101] All this shows that what was happening was not just a great metaphysical battle between Islam and monarchy, religion and secularism, or premodernity and modernity. Far from being a massive resurgence of irrational religious fervor, the revolution undermined the monarchy at the level of political economy by grounding its dissent in the unequal and often unjustified violence of the material conditions in which large segments of the populace had to live.[102]

To the sociologist Said Amir Arjomand, the "Second Islamic Revolution" in 1979 embodies not only the renewal of hierocracy but the successful appropriation of the state by the clergy, which marks the realization of Khomeini's twofold plan: the reestablishment of theocracy and the "complete eradication of Occidentalism," or Western orientations and attitudes, in Iran. By mobilizing anti-Americanism, a move that seemed more effective than using the Kurds and liberal intellectuals as the demonic other, Khomeini began to reframe revolutionary dissent as a "phantasmagorical struggle with the imperialist Satan."[103] However, using an exclusive focus on anti-Americanism to examine the revolution obscures the profound

transformation in Shiite theology and history in Iran—namely, the legitimation of the imamate in the person of Khomeini. Arjomand views this as
a pivotal moment in Iranian history because "never since the majority of
Iranians had become Shi'ite in the sixteenth century had they called *any
living person* Imam."[104] Khomeini's program of theocratizing Iran goes beyond restoring clerical authority in the "Mandate of the Clergy" because
he limits the powers of the mandate by making it derive its own legitimacy from the office of the imamate, which he, as imam, would occupy.[105]
In another sense, Khomeini drives another wedge in hierocratic authority: his achievement lies in wresting juridical power away from both the
monarchy and the clergy and institutionalizing it in the *velayat-e faqih*
(supremacy or guardianship of the jurist), which crystallizes supreme
power in the mandate of the jurist and not in the Council of Guardians.
This marks a radical shift from pluralist jurisprudence to Mahdistic centrality, as Khomeini astutely manipulates public sentiment about himself
as representing the twelfth imam, the Mahdi; being the Mahdi himself;
or playing the role of a "forerunner of the Mahdi."[106] Although American
and Western interference, colonialist ventures in Iran, and the shah's resolute pro-Westernization no doubt formed the central axes around which
the revolution defined itself, the premeditated and carefully orchestrated
Islamicization of dissent, which cast both the United States as America
and modernity as America in the role of emissaries of Satan and thus the
embodiment of evil, was primarily geared toward undermining the legitimacy of the monarchy, including the long-held distinction in social authority represented by the separation of powers in the monarchy and the
hierocracy, and establishing a religious genealogy that linked the twelfth
imam of the ninth century to the new imam of the twentieth century. The
production of anti-Americanist discourse becomes central to overcoming
Iranian opposition to Khomeini's Mahdistic millenarianism, so that resistance to *velayat-e faqih* can be construed not as a polemical shift in Shiite
jurisprudence but as a failure to combat the great Satan that is America,
and its anti-Islamic emissaries of Western Europe.

Ashura—an important day of observance for Shias, when they commemorate the death of Hussein at Karbala, Iraq, at the hands of Yazid,
son of a rival caliph, Mu'awiyah, on October 10, 680[107]—is cleverly imbued
with a contemporary political relevance by Khomeini, who casts the shah
of Iran as the murderous Yazid, intent on destroying the true Iran, albeit
an Iran thoroughly Islamicized by Khomeini's specific interpretations of
the faith. Dabashi's emphasis on colonial modernity—a modernity whose
double edges were the promise of Enlightenment and the effects of colo-

nial violence—in *Iran* demonstrates the impact of European colonialism
in the region (the British, French, and Russian empires battled for control
of Persia in the nineteenth century, as did the United States and the Soviet
Union in the twentieth), and his perceptive readings of Iranian intellectuals, activists, and reformers and their cultural work shows how they struggled to articulate ideas of freedom, equality, and rationality and concretize
them in political institutions.[108]

However, in Khomeini's anticolonial revolution, colonialism and modernity implicated the shah, the West, the United States as America and
America as modernity, and all those who dissented from the imam's interpretations of Islam. Undoubtedly, modernity was imposed during the
Pahlavi dynasty, but the revolution against the shah was, in its modes of
cultural representation and historical sensibility, more expansive in the
sense that it sought to produce social and political legitimacy by actively
marginalizing those it deemed as threats to its existence and ideology.
The many antishah groups and movements—including the Tudeh Party,
Cherik-ha-ye Fada'ie Khalq, Mojahedin-e Khalq, and Mossadeq's program
of nationalization[109]—did not find it easy to win allies among clerics eager
for political power. The shah's opponents were in fact subtly and at times
directly opposed or co-opted by Khomeini, who "imbued the old passion
plays with a passionate hatred of the shah, of Israel, the United States, and
the West, of Iran's non-Muslims, especially Bahai'is and Jews (the latter
tracing their heritage in Iran back to 500 BCE), and of women's rights advocates."[110] Urging people to go to their rooftops in the night and "scream
Allaho akbar, God is greatest . . . revealed how effectively the ayatollah was
able to play on the religious emotionalism of the masses in his campaigns
against the shah," reminisces Ebadi, admitting that even she, as a young
woman, followed this advice.[111] Overthrowing the shah was only the first
item on an agenda that included subjugating those who violently opposed
the clerical takeover, controlling the Kurds who sought to separate from
Iran, preventing another intervention like the U.S.-British one of 1953,
and putting into place a new constitution that would give Khomeini total
power, and Dabashi adds that even the American hostage crisis, although
not directly initiated by the clerics, was serendipitous because it furthered
the Islamicization of the nation. It was only after most of these plans were
firmly in place or set in motion that the hostages were released. When
Saddam Hussein attacked Iran in 1980 and began a decade-long war, his
action proved to be invaluable for the new Islamic Republic: its sense of
national unity was strengthened by the presence of a foreign enemy, which
made it more difficult for dissident groups to destabilize the theocracy.[112]

The downing of an Iranian civil airplane in 1988 by the USS *Vincennes*, resulting in the deaths of 290 passengers and official commendations, in the United States, for the plane's crew, reinforced Iranians' fears of subjection to a new phase of U.S. intervention in their country,[113] which gave credence to previous Islamist denunciations of the United States as an imperial power. In such a context, our critiques of U.S. imperialism, European colonialism, American exceptionalism, and the United States as America should also take account of the complex interweaving of multiple economies that generate a complex array of overdetermined discourses, symbols, ideas, philosophies, and sociocultural practices implicating the United States as America and America as modernity and imbricating fundamentalist theologies, monarchic modernity, traditional patriarchalism, and the Islamicization of the nation-state.

However, this focus on Iranian sociopolitical contexts should not obscure the crucial fact that *Reading Lolita in Tehran* was published in English in the United States by Nafisi, who had settled there in the mid-1990s after leaving Iran with her family, and that it became a bestseller in the United States at the same time that the country started its military occupation of Iraq. Nafisi had previously lived outside of Iran for considerable periods of time, especially in the United States in the 1970s, where she finished her graduate studies before returning to Iran on the heels of the revolution. This back-and-forth movement, this experience of migration and settlement, shapes Nafisi's personal sensibilities even as it profoundly influences the historical canvas and contexts in Iran that are prominent in her memoir, and her emphasis on the social function of literature as it relates to the nexus of gender, religion, and theocracy. With its ambiguities and tensions of constructing home in foreign locations, and its undermining of stable points of reference in the movement of travel, the diaspora is a promising framework for an examination of the memoir's exploration of place, time, and nation in shaping individual identity and collective memory.

THE PORTABLE WORLDS OF
DWELLING IN AMERICAN

The anguish of the diasporic subject is surely one of the forces shaping the narrative voice and structure of Nafisi's memoir. Her stay abroad nourishes an exilic passion for recreating home in other locations: "During my first years abroad—when I was in school in England and Switzerland, and later, when I lived in America, I attempted to *shape other places according to my concept of Iran*."[114] Positioned outside Iran, Nafisi begins to "Persianize" the foreign landscape because it evokes the memory of home.[115] Even her involvement with student protests in the United States is influenced by her "yearning for home," since she is able to use an "ideological framework within which to justify this *unbridled, unreflective passion*."[116] When she begins her career at the University of Tehran after returning to Iran, she feels like "an emissary from a land that did not exist, with a stock of dreams, coming to reclaim this land as my home."[117] In her essay "The Stuff That Dreams Are Made Of," Nafisi reiterates this point: "The idea of return, of home, of Iran became a constant obsession that colored almost all of my waking hours."[118]

Nafisi is keenly aware of and articulate about the diasporic quality of her life, but there is insufficient reflection in her memoir about how writing in the diaspora is intimately connected to practices and politics of representation. She tells her magician friend that her students have "creat[ed] this uncritical, glowing picture of that other world, of the west," to which he replies that she may have "been helping them create a parallel fantasy"[119] since "all that is good in their eyes comes from America or Europe, from chocolates and chewing gum to Austen and the Declaration of Independence."[120] The magician suggests that rather than creating a parallel world, Nafisi can "give them the best of what that other world can offer: give them pure fiction—give them back their imagination!"[121] But this emphasis on the imagination and fiction that is not burdened with politics still does not address what Nafisi herself points to—the "uncritical" attitudes toward the West and American culture. In light of the fact that Nafisi left Iran in 1997, now teaches in an American university, and published the book about Iran in the United States, what seems most prominent to her is Iran, even given all her travel in Europe and education in America. Searching for the lost homeland and writing about it in places outside the homeland is certainly driven by a diasporic desire for regaining what was lost in travel and movement. But in the diaspora, the home assumed to have been lost and the culture assumed to be far away lose their primacy as fixed frames of reference because the very movement that travel embodies generates multiple angles of vision that alter these frames. These shifts are not fully explored in Nafisi's memoir, in spite of the urgent necessity to scrutinize what she only acknowledges: an "uncritical, glowing picture" of other peoples, nations, cultures. This is one reason why, observes Mitra Rastegar, ambiguities emerge when authorial intention, readers' and reviewers' expectations, enduring stereotypical representations, and general disinterest among Americans in worldly affairs intersect in the publication and reception of the memoir and its writer in the United States. Between speaking of and speaking for the young women, argues Rastegar, Nafisi often ends up lending undue weight to her personal observations in the text, which makes it "susceptible to being read as representing an entire community of people, rather than just the author's life."[122]

Matters get more complicated because, as Keshavarz perceptively points out, most of the men in the memoir are one-dimensional, almost threatening figures, whereas the women are presented as distinct individuals.[123] At pivotal moments in the book, when Nafisi discusses or observes a scene, event, idea, text, or person, she constantly refers to Western writers—Nabokov, Saul Bellow, James, Austen—rather than Arabic and Persian writers. This is not just an argument for inclusion. It's a more challenging perspective because it demonstrates that a certain kind of subjectivity is produced—a notion of the self and its relation to the world—that is inextricably linked to texts and writers from the Western canon. The memoir "perpetuates the highly problematic position that Iranian self-identity comes through an embrace of Western cultural forms and representations."[124] Rarely do we find moments in the book where a fundamental orienting of the self, a refashioning or affirming of collective or individual identity, is made in relation to elaborate discussions of Persian, Arabic, or Muslim cultures, writers, and texts, something that Keshavarz does remarkably well in *Jasmine and Stars*. Speaking of the episode in the memoir where the women come to Nafisi's house and remove their veils and robes—revealing the vivid colors of their dresses and accessories, which contrast with the bland, homogeneous colors of the veils and robes—Simon Hay says that it is not enough to affirm, as Nafisi does, that these women are able to lay claim to their irreducible individuality. The memoir does not move beyond this notion of individualism, where homogeneous colors clash with diverse hues and each woman is recognized for her uniqueness. The links among literary reading and empathy, self-reflection, abstraction, contingency of one's beliefs—all of which are crucial for liberal democratic societies in their emphasis on consent, shared governance, rule of law, individual rights, and so on—become naturalized and are not subjected to further examination. In this sense, the memoir keeps undermining what it also keeps insisting: the power of literature to open up alternative possibilities that can help readers gain insight into their personal lives and social histories, as well as reflecting on their experiences by subjecting to critical scrutiny their own responses to literary texts. This is why, as Hay notes pointedly, the book's "ideology is insidious, never bluntly articulated as ideological, and it argues by persuasion and finesse, *never by engaging with any alterity*."[125]

To counter the highly politicized, Islamicized ethos that imputes anti-Islamic prejudice to American literature and the West, Nafisi deploys a seemingly apolitical aesthetics to affirm the magical, epiphanic power of imaginative writing, which should not be viewed as a simplistic celebration of literature as an ahistorical entity completely unrelated to worldly activity. One reason why *Reading Lolita in Tehran* is compelling reading is because the women's reading of American literature enables them to create parallel worlds that reflect and refract their daily experiences. There is hardly anything apolitical about this, given that each time they meet secretly to read American literature, they are both recognizing and subverting the social structures that prohibit them from doing so. But Nafisi views their counter stance as driven by an aesthetics that strives not to succumb to the dictates of Islamism; she locates the subversive potential of this aesthetic in the work of art and in reading: "We do not read in order to turn great works of fiction into simplistic replicas of our own realities, we read for the pure, sensual, and unadulterated pleasure of reading."[126] But Rowe insightfully suggests that even the most critical discussion of freedom, women's rights, and Western classics often tends to be circumscribed by Nafisi's worldview: "There is a rhetorical slippage between her suggestion that these students are simply bad students for not doing their homework or they are not reading *according to Nafisi's hermeneutic protocols*."[127] These protocols seek to derive a transgressive energy in depoliticizing literature, but the very process by which this is achieved is itself deeply political—a central tension that is not adequately explored in *Reading Lolita in Tehran* and is in fact disavowed by its author. What comes across in the memoir is that Nafisi is a powerful presence in the group; the young women look up to her and greatly respect her expertise and knowledge. Let me elaborate on this crucial point: Nafisi, as a writer, does not reflect critically enough about her potential to become a guiding force for the group of students, so that even women who may, for instance, actually like to wear the veil but not for political reasons, and who want to offer perspectives that counter the kind of individual freedom associated with characters in Western classics could end up finding Nafisi's very progressive views a challenge to negotiate.

But the danger in critiquing this absence in the memoir is to assume an equivalence between the politics of Islamism and the politics of aesthetics of these students. Islamism's notion of power and its exercise of that power are deeply enmeshed in social relations, which fundamentally changes the social status of women—making them dependent, derivative, supplementary, redundant, passive, and reactive. The same cannot be argued for the aesthetics that, with its emphasis on deflecting social power, comes close to according a depoliticized value to literature. But this attempt to depoliticize can be explained as a strategy of resistance. What cannot be explained thus is the normative value accorded to art and the imagination: they are given a universal, a priori value that trumps every other social desire, presence, and pressure on the practices of writing and reading, except what are specifically employed by the readers of *Lolita* in Tehran and by Nafisi, the memoirist. One such disavowal is the absence of social class and its socializing nature in the quotidian reality of Nafisi's home.

Although it might seem like the seven women who are part of the secret reading club come from various social classes and backgrounds in Iran, most of them are fluent in English and have the interpretative skills to engage in the kind of detailed discussions that the memoir recounts, which sets them apart as a group. Bahramitash offers a compelling argument about the differences in class consciousness when she identifies the difference between the physical presence of the nanny, Tahereh Khanoom, in Nafisi's house, and her narrative presence. When Revolutionary Guards barge into the house, attempting to gain access to their neighbor's tenant's apartment, the nanny is asked to go upstairs where the satellite dish is located. Presumably, Khanoom is the one who is better able to deal with the guards since she "knew their language better."[128] Bahramitash suggests that the nanny's perspectives about her own experience, not included in the memoir, could counter those of the students and Nafisi.[129]

There is another instance where I think class consciousness is clearly registered but not explored: "Satellite dishes were becoming the rage all over Iran. It was not merely people like me, or the educated classes, who craved them. Tahereh Khanoom informed us that in the poor, more religious sections of Tehran, the family with a dish would rent out certain programs to their neighbors."[130]

Nafisi acknowledges class differences in the comment "people like me, or the educated classes." What this passage also suggests, besides class difference, is the social relationship between the educated and the religious poor. Unfortunately, however, this relationship is one of distance, not intimacy. It is the nanny who provides ethnographic knowledge about the poor to someone like Nafisi, who does not hesitate to mark her own class status. There is no indication here, and little indication elsewhere in the memoir, that this knowledge could be obtained not by relying on nannies but by actual, sustained involvement with the uneducated poor.[131]

The last lines of the memoir raise troubling questions about the pervasive influence of American culture and literature on Nafisi's attempt to engender a space for female creativity: "I went about my way rejoicing, thinking how wonderful it is to be a woman and a writer at the end of the twentieth century."[132] Passages like this produce a narrative of female empowerment in which America awakens a slumbering consciousness and welcomes it into the hallowed realms of modernity. What is not adequately emphasized is the location of the writer—in the First World, the United States, where she is a professor at a prestigious university—which becomes the enabling condition for experiencing freedom as a writer and as a woman. The memoir cannot address the question of whether it is or ever was possible for women living in Iran—who never left the country, who may not have had the kind of institutional exposure to American literature that Nafisi's Iranian students did, or the informal experience of participating in reading clubs where American popular culture is discussed—to experience even a modicum of such freedom. Who are the women in Iran who are rejoicing about having what kinds of freedom? This is a question that cannot be asked of the memoir because its focus on Nafisi, the writer, is not critically reflective about how its narrative construction of memory, displacement, and relocation offers scant recognition of the power of Muslim, Arabic, or Persian cultural traditions to offer women spaces for creativity and self-expression.

Viewed in the broader context of Nafisi's interest in the traditional canons of British and American literature, these passages point to the circumstances of a privileged upbringing and the experience of exile, and they raise perplexing questions about the politics of creating an "Iranian homeland" in diaspora—what Salman Rushdie calls "imaginary homelands"[133]— and its asymmetrical correspondence with another Iran, the culture and society of those without the privilege of class and cultural mobility, who inhabit a topography that is circumscribed by the Iranian state. We may even come to agree with critics like the ones discussed above and become skeptical of the writer's extensive use of American ideas and Western culture to make sense of Iranian society. But such skepticism can be freighted with our own motivations as readers positioned outside of Iran and desperately searching for an Iran available to us outside of Nafisi's Westernized exilic perspective. But Westernized and Western are not stable ideas; they are social creations as well. If we do not examine the political dynamics of such creations and the individual and collective interests and motivations that animate them, we could end up trapping ourselves within our own First World desire for Third World authenticity, a desire that betrays our own colonially inspired longing for the other that pits the diasporic subject against the native subject, as if assuming that the position the latter occupies naturally affords pure knowledge.

In the epilogue, Nafisi writes: "And I know now that my world, like Pnin's, will be forever a 'portable world.'"[134] And she tells how she and her husband "spent long hours talking about our feelings, our ideas of home—for *me* portable, for *him* more traditional and rooted."[135] This is not simply a matter of different individual preferences but of how the experiences of women in postrevolutionary Iran are incommensurable with the experiences of men. This does not mean that women's and men's concerns do not overlap, as an emphasis on social class, tribe, religious sect, and education can easily demonstrate. The focus here is on how religiously justified and informed ideas of gender orient men and women differently to both a secularized and theocratized nation and to their experiences of exile, home, and nostalgia in the diaspora. This is why when a "nomadic"[136] subject like Nafisi affirms the ideals of the Declaration of Independence in postrevolutionary Iran—"all individuals, no matter how contemptible, have a right to life, liberty, and the pursuit of happiness"[137]—in discussing American and British writers and texts in other places, we cannot easily assume that American studies and America imperialistically cannibalize the minds, cultures, values, and traditions of the Iranian people. We cannot pit the global against the local and assume that globalization is nothing but the Westernization or Americanization of the world. Nor can we stop dislodging the binaries of globalization by combining the local and the global into glocalization. *Reading Lolita in Tehran* dwells in American in the sense that it moves the Declaration of Independence out of its national frames and borders, lifting America out of its local contexts and compelling it to confront other space-time coordinates authorized by modern and Islamist nationalisms. Using America, Nafisi's students create different, fictional worlds, other parallel and portable worlds whose boundaries overlap neatly or predictably with neither the United States as America nor with the America of Islamic Iran. Dwelling in American, they produce an "incomplete signification" by "turning boundaries and limits into the in-between spaces through which the meanings of cultural and political authority are negotiated."[138] Dwelling in American, these "incomplete" women slip in between the woman authorized by the Islamic state and the woman of the East imagined by the West. As *Reading Lolita in Tehran* begins to internationalize American literature, the woman affirmed by Islamism becomes a grotesque figure who continually frustrates patriarchy's desperate search for the ideal woman and undermines the strenuous attempt of the United States as America to bestow on Eastern women the gifts of freedom and democracy by exporting American culture and American studies to Iran.

Nafisi and her female students in Tehran are not reading "our" American text, our American *Lolita*, however much the memoir sometimes, despite itself, seems to suggest this at certain levels of cultural representation. For American readers to celebrate this text with self-congratulatory enthusiasm and take pride in a great national American literature that appeals to people all over the world, they would have to ignore Iran, Iranians, and their rich and ancient history. One alternative is this: We need to become dispossessed readers and dislocated subjects because it is not the New England of Lolita that we are asked to use as the first and final measure of the text's ability to translate itself in a foreign register; we are forced to enter the portable worlds of "*Lolita* in Tehran, how *Lolita* gave a different color to Tehran and how Tehran helped redefine Nabokov's novel, turning it into this *Lolita*, our *Lolita*."[139] As "global transit extends, triangulates, and transforms its meaning," *Reading Lolita in Tehran* becomes a "new semantic template, a new form of the legible, each time it crosses a national border."[140] In other words, rather than trying to settle down in America in order to become an American text, *Reading Lolita in Tehran* becomes a portable America as it unsettles the weight of ideology, nation, gender, and religion by uprooting the settlement of America in America discourse and American studies.

In the next chapter, I shift the focus to examine the connections between culture and literature in the globalization of information technology (IT) in Thomas Friedman's *The World Is Flat*. I examine how Friedman reorients world history as American history by deploying a New World mythology to develop an account of the contemporary world. This mythology harnesses the discourse of American exceptionalism to Americanize IT globalization and conflates the rise of new transnational classes having links to India and the United States with broad national development across many classes within India. The deployment of culture as a category of analysis in Friedman's text belies its use as a powerful agent for social legitimation in order to normalize IT development in India as the exemplary local manifestation of a newly reconfigured global order.

‎⚡ CHAPTER FIVE ⚡‎

Empire and the New World Mythology of Information Technology Globalization

THE WORLD IS FLAT

How do culture and literature influence the globalization of information technology, and what role do they play in legitimizing American cultural imperialism? In what way does empire, in its cultural dimensions, exert its force? As new technologies emerge and gain worldwide use, what social and economic imbalances are reinforced? What does it mean to speak about empire in the twenty-first century, in a world that is fundamentally interconnected and interdependent? In answering these questions with reference to Thomas Friedman's bestselling *The World Is Flat*, I make two main arguments: first, his text embeds IT globalization in a narrative of European modernity that firmly positions Euro-America as the most privileged site from which to conceptualize the phenomenon of outsourcing; and second, the U.S.-Indian IT economy is creating a new transnational class whose cultural production is inscribed by a class consciousness that mobilizes a racialized national identity in the United States. I examine *The World Is Flat* by taking a literary and cultural studies perspective and study the use of metaphor, myth, and discourse in its account of contemporary IT globalization. This account is embedded in the field of meanings offered by the myth of Columbus as discover of the New World, which legitimizes the mapping of the world according to the ideological, political, and economic forces seeking to consolidate a neoliberal vision of IT globalization. *The World Is Flat* is based on a profoundly Eurocentric vision of world history. This chapter focuses on the manner in which literary language and mythic discourse function as modes of cognition, as meaning-making apparatuses in Friedman's book. As I shall soon argue, he does not relegate culture to the marginal status of icing on the cake of objective sociological and journalistic analyses of contemporary global phenomena. On the contrary, culture becomes a site of social, political, and economic struggle in which the legitimation of the very logic of IT globalization is at stake. It's in the nexus of culture, mythology, and journalism that Friedman's worldview and ideas about contemporary empire are articulated and legitimized.

INFORMATION TECHNOLOGY GLOBALIZATION

With the boom in the IT sector of the economy in the late 1990s—including the surge in startup software companies, the development of bandwidth technology or DSL (which integrates telephone and Internet services at a low cost and offers extremely fast rates of access and downloads), extensive use of satellites, and the significant migration of IT workers from other parts of the world to the United States— American businesses realized a crucial fact: India and China, especially, had a vast pool of talented computer engineers and programmers with good English-language skills who were willing to work for a fraction of the cost charged by U.S. workers. This resulted in a massive outsourcing of jobs from the United States as companies like EDS, IBM, 3Com, Autodesk, Siemens, Hewlett-Packard, Bank of America, Capital One, Microsoft, Intel, i2 Technologies, Novell, Oracle, Philips, SAP, Sun Microsystems, and Texas Instruments began outsourcing work to India and China.[1] According to the National Association of Software and Service Companies, total revenue for the Indian IT industry was expected to exceed $88.1 billion in the 2011 fiscal year, with the number of IT jobs in India increasing to 2.5 million in that year and leading to 8.3 million new jobs in related sectors.[2] Among the "top 25" global software companies are Indian companies like Tata Consulting Services, Wipro, Infosys Technologies, and Satyam Computers—but only one company each from Germany (SAP) and France (Atos Origin). Although the rest are U.S. companies, the significance of Indian companies in the global IT marketplace is also clear.[3] During the next decade, close to four million jobs, paying $150 billion in wages, could leave the United States, replaced by jobs in India. IT outsourcing affects lawyers, doctors, accountants, data entry and computer operators, paralegals, diagnostic service providers, medical transcribers, editors, publishers, architects, and call-center workers, among others.[4] Michael Corbett in *The Outsourcing Revolution* emphasizes that outsourcing covers the entire range of business operations since it "will be used not only to drive down costs, but also to increase the speed, flexibility, and level of innovation taking place within organizations of all kinds."[5] Outsourcing is not just a specific international business practice. It is a business paradigm for the twenty-first century. The entry of India into this new economy, according to Ashutosh Sheshabalaya, marks a "Great Displacement": "India's focus is a full sweep of high-value white-collar services rather than blue-collar manufacturing." He observes: "It is therefore clearly no longer a question of IT services, or low-cost coding. India not only has matured as an offshore supplier of skills; these skills now encompass a huge, *growing and near-comprehensive sweep* of white-collar competencies and jobs."[6]

But a central problem is that these developments, in both India and the United States, have often been conceptualized primarily in economic and political terms: Is the IT industry good or bad for these countries? Does India need to modernize rapidly to become a key player in the global economy? How can developing countries liberalize their economies and take their rightful place in the new world order of globalization? These are the kinds of questions that preoccupy Friedman in *The World Is Flat*, which seeks to map the globalization of IT.

FLAT WORLD MYTHOLOGY

Let us begin by laying out Friedman's key arguments. When he says that the "world is flat," Friedman means that "countries like India are now able to compete for global knowledge work as never before—and that America had better get ready for this."[7] There are ten forces that converged over the last fifteen to twenty years that have led us to our present situation: the crumbling of the Berlin Wall in 1989, which led to the end of the Cold War; the emergence of the browser Netscape, and its impact on the Internet when it went public in 1995; the impact of languages and protocols like XML and SOAP, which made it possible for different applications and programs to interact and offered users tremendous flexibility in managing digitized data; the use of open sourcing that provided source codes online and enabled people anywhere in the world to collaborate online and develop, change, or improve codes, applications, and programs; the Y2K bug in the late 1990s, the importing of IT professionals from India and other countries to the West, and the linking of the United States and India through fiber-optic cables; offshoring manufacturing and service-sector work to countries like China and India; the use of supply chaining—the coordination of production, packaging, delivery, storing, inventory, stocking, reordering, and so forth—which, when done well, helps Wal-Mart, for instance, move "2.3 billion merchandise cartons a year down its supply chain into its stores";[8] insourcing, as done by UPS, when it changed its operations from focusing only on providing delivery services to becoming a "dynamic supply chain manager";[9] in-forming—the ways in which Google, Yahoo, and MSN Web Search help users to "build and deploy [their] own personal supply chain—a chain of information, knowledge, and entertainment";[10] and finally, increasing digitization, which makes what is digitized mobile and accessible. When these forces, or flatteners, are consolidated into systems and practices, when their "convergence" impacts workers, CEOs, managers, educators, and politicians, increasing numbers of people will be able to benefit from and participate in the IT economy. Here is Friedman's main idea:

> The convergence of the ten flatteners had created a whole new platform. It is a global, Web-enabled platform for multiple forms of collaboration. This platform enables individuals, groups, companies, and universities anywhere in the world to collaborate—for the purpose of innovation, production, education, research, entertainment, and alas, war-making. . . . No, not everyone has access yet to this new platform, this new playing field. No, when I say the world is being flattened, I don't mean we are all becoming equal. What I do mean is that more people in more places now have the power to access the flat world platform—to connect, compete, collaborate, and, unfortunately, destroy—than ever before.[11]

He makes a similar point elsewhere: "When I say the world is flat what I mean is that we have created this platform. We have created a totally new platform for multiple forms of sharing knowledge and work irrespective of time, distance, geography, and, increasingly, even language that more people than ever can plug and play on."[12] This is where culture comes in, and there are two ideas of culture that become relevant in *The World Is Flat*. First, culture is a meaning-making mode of apprehending large-scale historical processes; culture connotes civilizations, broad and very general patterns of thinking and behaving that set one group of people apart from another group. Culture here is about "connecting the dots . . . across the spectrum, and kind of put[ting] it all together."[13] It is culture as myth, as a narrative that gives form and meaning to disparate events and processes and to intercontinental forms of commercial exchange and cross-cultural interaction. Second, culture refers to everyday practices, sets of daily behaviors, and those values, perspectives, and biases that shape our sense of the routine, the normal, and the commonsensical and—in the words of A. L. Kroeber and Clyde Kluckhohn—how they constitute "continuous methods of handling problems and social situations," or comprise "a scheme of living by which a number of interacting persons favor certain motivations more than others and favor certain ways rather than others for satisfying these motivations."[14] This is culture as a strategy for adaptation, a technique for coping.

Let's begin with the first use of culture—as myth. Myth emphasizes the idea of beginnings, starting points of reference that enable a community to develop an understanding about the cosmos and supernatural beings. As Mircea Eliade observes, myth focuses on the "fabled time of the 'beginnings.'" In this sense, myth offers an account of how things came about, how the world and life itself were created. But although myth often focuses on the "dramatic breakthroughs of the sacred"—the entry of the transcendental into the realm of the human—myths also serve as "exemplary models for all human rites and all significant human activities." To the modern mind, the focus on history or historiography—"*the endeavor to preserve the memory of contemporary events and the desire to know the past of humanity as accurately as possible*"[15]—is of paramount concern. To Bruce Lincoln, myth can be "ideology in narrative form" and can seek to shape notions of what is true, what is real.[16] Three things stand out— myths offer initial reference points that provide ways of looking at the past, present, and future; myths affirm specific subject positions toward whatever they seek to explain, in that they show us how to relate to that reality, how to orient ourselves as social and individual beings in that reality; and myths provide the cultural framework to support and legitimate particular ideological beliefs and historical narratives.

A clear indication of the use of myth is the full title of Friedman's book: *The World Is Flat: A Brief History of the Twenty-First Century*. "History" and "twenty-first century" immediately tell us that this is not just about the present but also about how the future is going to unfold, which means that to understand the future, the book is also going to talk about how we came to the present moment through the past. This is why the first few pages recount one of the most popular myths of America—the coming of Christopher Columbus to the New World. The first chapter is prefaced with an excerpt from Columbus's journal about his mission for Spain to go to India by a "Westerly route, in which we have hitherto no certain evidence that anyone has gone."[17] This dramatic moment gets replayed in the twenty-first century as Friedman, fashioning himself after the Admiral of the Ocean Sea, notes that he was going to the fabled land of the East to report on his findings but, unlike his predecessor, he was taking a Lufthansa flight and, rather than flying West, he was going East:

> I had come to Bangalore, India's Silicon Valley, on my own Columbus-like journey of exploration. Columbus sailed with the *Niña*, the *Pinta*, and the *Santa Maria* in an effort to discover a shorter, more direct route to India by heading west. . . . I too encountered Indians. I too was searching for the source of India's riches. Columbus was searching for the hardware—precious metals, silk, and spices—the source of wealth in his day. I was searching for software, brainpower, complex algorithms, knowledge workers, call centers, transmission protocols, breakthroughs in optical engineering—the sources of wealth in our day. Columbus was happy to make the Indians he met his slaves, a pool of free manual labor. I just wanted to understand why the Indians I met were taking our work, why they had become such an important pool for the outsourcing of service and information technology work from America and other industrialized countries.[18]

Although reaffirming the hegemonic myth of the discovery of America, this passage distinguishes between Columbus's intention to bring glory to the Spanish empire through exploration and conquest and Friedman's intention to "just understand" what makes India tick in the twenty-first century. But it is worth asking two questions of Columbus that do not get asked in *The World Is Flat*: what ideologies and cultural ideas enabled Columbus to set off in search of India, and how did they justify the enslavement of Indians?

Ironically, the answer can be found in the section from Columbus's logbook that Friedman uses to preface his first chapter:

> Your Highnesses, as Catholic Christians, and princes who love and promote the holy Christian faith, and are *enemies of the doctrine of Mahomet*, and of all idolatry and heresy, determined to send me, Christopher Columbus, to the above-mentioned countries of India, *to see the said princes, people, and territories, and to learn of their disposition and the proper method of converting*

THE WORLD IS FLAT

them to our holy faith; and furthermore directed that I should not
proceed by land to the East as is customary, but by a Westerly
route, in which direction we have hitherto no certain evidence
that anyone has gone.[19]

As the world is divided neatly into the Christian and the Islamic, what
justifies the exploration of the world is the possibility not only of adding
new territories to the Spanish empire but also of making new subjects for
empire. The intimate connection between the act of exploration and the
mind-set of colonial thinking is self-evident. Columbus makes no apolo-
gies; in fact, he specifically makes this link very clear. Learning about India and going to India are not two separate things that are occasionally interrelated. Learning is possible *because* of the imperial policies of empire;
and empire sustains itself by funding enterprises that can generate knowledge about the world to be used in the service of extending empire. This
means that the enslavement of Indians was not an aberration in the mission of Columbus's transoceanic enterprises in the fifteenth and sixteenth
centuries. Slavery enacted the fundamental logic of New World modernity. In this context, culture as myth allows us to understand the implica-
tions of Columbus's explorations for empire, the position of Spain in relation to other competing empires, and how and why Spain and voyagers
like Columbus embarked on such expeditions. When Friedman distances
himself from Columbus's enslavement of Indians, he does so by asserting
that he is interested only in understanding India and Indians. But what
comes across clearly in the passage from Columbus that Friedman cites
is that the discourse of learning was deeply implicated in the activity of
colonizing. This is why Friedman clarifies that his intent is not to make
slaves of Indians. What we cannot be confident about is the answers to
this question: what are the logical consequences of subscribing to Friedman's model of globalization as seen through the myth of Columbus?

Columbus's letters regarding his four voyages to the New World shed
light on points that conflict with Friedman's ahistorical and conceptually
flawed adaptation of the discovery myth. In the letter Columbus wrote
about his first voyage, the New World is depicted as a land of dreams, a
place where all that the European mind had only imagined for centuries
was at last laid bare before Columbus. With its "many harbors" and "many
rivers" and "very many sierras and lofty mountains," "trees of a thousand
kinds and tall" that "touch the sky," and "large tracts of cultivable land"
where there is "honey, and there are birds of many kinds, and fruits in
great diversity," the New World is a place of beauty and riches, and not

of "human monstrosities." As Columbus says, "Española [the island where the modern countries of Haiti and the Dominican Republic are located] is a marvel."[20] In the narrative about his third voyage, as the realities of the New World fail to conform to this image of paradise, the focus shifts from finding gold, metals, and spices to the nature of the world itself—is the world round or flat? Columbus revises the idea that the world is round, an idea held by Ptolemy and "other wise men who have written of this world." Instead, it is shaped like a pear, he notes, "which is everywhere very round, or that it is like a very round ball, and on one part of it is placed something like a woman's nipple, and that this part, where this protuberance is found, is the highest and nearest to the sky. . . . I call that 'the end of the East,' where end all the lands and islands." At this point, where fresh and salt water meet, may be found the "earthly paradise" where "a fountain" forms the four major rivers of the world—the Ganges, Tigris, Euphrates, and Nile. Columbus now is no longer an ordinary seaman; he is an exceptional discoverer in the tradition of Aristotle, Seneca, and Pliny. Spain is also not an insignificant empire in Europe but one that, like the Greco-Roman empires, "spent money and men and employed great diligence in learning the secrets of the world and in making them known to mankind."[21] Indeed, at this point, Columbus becomes a divine messenger whose utterances the people can disregard at their own peril: "Of the new heaven and the new earth, which our Lord made, as St. John writes in the Apocalypse, after He has spoken of it by the mouth of Isaiah, *He made me the messenger and He showed me where to go.*"[22]

In the fourth voyage, this sense of divine mission is further accentuated by heavenly visitations in which Columbus is assured of his election as God's messenger to the world. "The Indies, which are so rich a part of the world," Columbus is made to understand, was "given thee for thine own; thou hast divided them as it pleased thee, and He enabled thee to do this. Of the barriers of the Ocean sea, which were closed with such mighty chains, He gave thee the keys; and thou wast obeyed in many lands and among Christians thou hast gained an honorable fame." At the time of this writing, Columbus was a prisoner in Jamaica. Mistreated and shunned by his contemporaries, this letter ends on a note of lamentation: "Weep for me, whoever has charity, truth, and justice."[23] Columbus's articulation of wondrous joy on the first voyage has given way to a note of despair and utter historical confusion by the time of the fourth voyage, as he ransacks historical archives and religious traditions to render the New World intelligible and in so doing accords to himself the role of a prophet whose sole objective was to lay bare to humanity the secrets of the world. In-

deed, right up to his death, Columbus believed that he had found a westerly route to India, the Americas were parts of the Far East, and the inhabitants of these regions were Indians. World history has demonstrated
the validity of knowledges that conflict with Columbus's prophetic knowledge: the territories west of the Atlantic formed a separate landmass; the
inhabitants of these regions were very different from the peoples of the
East; and his "India" would eventually come to be known as the Americas.
Since mythification serves particular ideological and political purposes,
Friedman's use of the Columbus myth as a lens through which to examine current forms of IT globalization systematically downplays the ways
in which history, fantasy, and religious belief get interwoven with the economic and sociopolitical imperatives of the transoceanic missions around
1500. Where Columbus saw himself as a divine messenger unearthing the
earth's secrets for all humanity, Friedman five hundred years later seeks
to explain the global IT world for all Americans but ends up validating a
historical perspective to make sense of globalization in ways that leave the
United States and American culture at the center of postmodern global
configurations of power. Friedman the historian morphs into a chronicler,
to use Walter Benjamin's distinction: while the historian seeks to explain
the "happenings with which he deals" and provide "an accurate concat-
enation of definite events," the chronicler advances "models of the course
of the world." He is more concerned with fitting world events into a predetermined, divinely mandated paradigm and therefore finds "the burden
of demonstrable explanation" unnecessary. Benjamin further notes that
history thus becomes "inscrutable," something that cannot be adequately
explained outside of the chronicle's narrative.[24] But as we have seen, this
inscrutability has to be discursively produced, and the deployment of culture in chronicling globalization is pivotal to rendering inscrutable current forms of globalization as facts of nature, incontrovertible evidence of
a cosmic ordering of the world—thus heralding, as the hyperglobalizers
see it, "the emergence of a single global market and the principle of global
competition as the harbingers of human progress."[25] No wonder that by
the time we come to the end of *The World Is Flat*, the fantasy of new little
Americas and Europes popping up all over the world has become a marvelous dream.

One monstrous manifestation of this marvelous dream is particularly
clear in Friedman's response to a question about Google and China from
Nayan Chanda in an interview. A few years earlier, Google had agreed to
allow the Chinese government to filter the results of Google searches in
China. Not surprisingly, websites about Fulan Gong and the protests in

Tiananmen Square were among the first to be blocked by the Chinese government. According to Andrew McLaughlin, a policy counsel for Google, the decision to develop Google.cn in response to the government's strictures was a "hard compromise," as Google tried to avoid an "all or nothing" bargain. In the nitty-gritty decision-making process of multinational corporations that must weigh countless options and bargains, this seemed to make "business sense"—"how can we provide the greatest access to information to the greatest number of people?"[26] Friedman's response to this imbroglio is telling: "Let's take the high road. Let's keep our eye on the prize. Yes, in China, you cannot Google search for Tiannaman [sic] Square or Fulang [sic] Gong. *You can still search for Thomas Jefferson, you can still search for Ben Franklin. Isn't that what's really important?* If 95 percent of my searches go through, isn't that what's really important."[27] This privileging of the traditional pantheon of Jefferson and Franklin to make sense of profound social and cultural disruptions in China ends up Americanizing IT globalization. This inscription of American exceptionalism recenters American symbols and cultures in the new, IT-enhanced network of nations and economies. Such a recentering allows China to be imagined or conceived of as a nation, community, or geographic location in what Anne McClintock refers to as "prepositional time": "The world's multitudinous cultures are marked, not positively by what distinguishes them, but by a *subordinate, retrospective relation* to linear, European time."[28] If, indeed, another Tiananmen Square happened, according to Friedman's reasoning, it would be the direct result of the ability of Chinese Internet users to access websites on the American founding fathers. Like Columbus, Jefferson and Franklin need not be argued for, only posited as axiomatic touchstones for the spread of global markets and democracy. They now become symbolic commodities, characterized by a fetishism that constantly disguises the social and political contradictions that form the matrix of their emergence and continued purchase. Their value resides not so much in an understanding of the historical contexts in which they lived, or in the disjunctive modalities of U.S.-China economic and social relations, the uneven forms of cross-cultural give-and-take between China and other nations and between U.S. and Chinese cultures. Rather, it is in how they can be invested with symbolic cachet in a discourse of globalism seeking to legitimize the growth of IT globalization. This legitimating function, which is one of the most pervasive and resilient uses of culture in *The World Is Flat*, recenters U.S. history and culture in mapping IT, which is exactly why Friedman is now able to use Jefferson and Franklin as the primary referents to develop an account of China's late-twentieth-century economic and political history.

Another aspect of the itinerary of culture in *The World Is Flat* is evident in its author's stated intentions: "I just wanted to understand why the Indians I met were taking our work." Like Columbus, Friedman also interacts with non-Western peoples; talks to them; examines their lives, histories, and cultures; and reports back to his audience at home. To assume that this kind of representational work is done simply for its own sake is to miss one of the essential purposes of the book—to make us, Americans, aware of where and why "our" jobs are moving offshore and the strategies we can use to compete successfully in this new global economy. This knowledge about India and the competitive nations of the Third World can be put to good use, can be acted on by Americans. This is the connection between knowledge and praxis, learning and human labor. Here, again, culture becomes very important, perhaps absolutely important since it is culture, used in the second sense of the term given above, that helps us come to grips with these new challenges. The "dirty little secrets" of American education include the decline in the number of science graduates from U.S. universities compared to the sharp increase in that number in Asia and Europe. Citing the National Science Board, Friedman notes that between the mid-1980s and 1998, the number of U.S. science graduates declined 12 percent.[29] The fact that Microsoft's third research center is located in Beijing (Microsoft Research Asia) and produces top-notch scientists does not augur well for American education, given the decrease in federal funding (a 37 percent decline from 1970 to 2004) for science and mathematics.[30] To deal with these crises, Friedman offers "compassionate flatism, which is a policy blend built around five broad categories of action for the age of flat: leadership, muscle building, cushioning, social activism, and parenting,"[31] which he goes on to elaborate in separate sections.

Compassionate flatism recognizes America's strengths: its sheer openness, in which people have a great deal of freedom to pursue creative, professional, or personal projects and dreams; its protection of private property; its emphasis on the rule of law; and its multiracial and multicultural history. Developing the ability to obtain and use skills in different areas can help us navigate the fluctuations of the job market.[32] This is why Friedman stresses leadership in the political arena: "There is more to political leadership than a competition for who can offer the most lavish safety nets. Yes, we must address people's fears, but we must also *nurse their imaginations*. Politicians can make us more fearful and thereby be disablers, or they can *inspire us* and thereby be enablers."[33] Because multinational companies are now able to exert their power over large groups of people and even nations, "one new area that is going to need sorting out is the relationship between global corporations and *their own moral conscience*."[34]

Parenting becomes especially important since children learn how to live in the world from their parents: "In short, we need a new generation of parents ready to administer *'tough love.'* . . . Education, whether it comes from parents or schools, has to be about more than just cognitive skills. It also has to *include character building.*"[35] In all these passages, what come across as important are character, inspiration, the role of the imagination, morality, social conscience, parenting, and love. We are now dealing with culture in the second sense in which I am using the term here: culture as ways of acting, patterns of behaving, values worth cherishing, and the entire spectrum of activities, ideas, and beliefs out of which people derive strategies for adapting to life's challenges.

In the section titled "Culture Matters: Glocalization," Friedman further emphasizes the importance of culture as he underscores the "outward" and "inward" dimensions of culture worth valuing. By accepting and absorbing different influences and ideas from the outside, a society can learn to adapt and change rather than insist on its essentialized identities and histories. When a country's leaders and people learn to develop "a sense of national solidarity and a focus on development," it can create an environment that fosters growth and creativity. The overlapping of outward and inward aspects of culture is what Friedman refers to as "glocalizing": "The more you have a culture that naturally glocalizes—that is, the more your culture easily absorbs foreign ideas and global best practices and melds those with its own traditions—the greater the advantage you will have in a flat world."[36]

All this sounds good. Few would disagree with the importance that Friedman gives to leadership, creativity, social conscience, adaptability, and glocalization. He is certainly putting culture to good use. But there is more going on here. Culture, as it is deployed in *The World Is Flat*, consolidates a profoundly Euro-America-centric view of the world. What is at stake here is history itself, global history in fact, and thus how we develop our historical consciousness. Ironically, Friedman's use of *The Communist Manifesto* dramatizes this point. Since IT globalization effects societal changes worldwide, Friedman refers to Karl Marx and Friedrich Engels' analysis of the tremendous power of capitalism to overcome the barriers of nation, religion, caste, tradition, and creed and to spread globally. His quotation from *The Communist Manifesto* reads in part:

> All fixed, fast, frozen relations, with their train of ancient and venerable prejudices and opinions, are swept away, all new-formed ones become antiquated before they can ossify. All that is solid

melts into air, all that is holy is profaned, and man is at last compelled to face with sober senses his real conditions of life and his
relations with his kind. . . . The bourgeoisie, by the rapid improve-
ment of all instruments of production, by the immensely facilitated means of communication, draws all, even the most barbar-
ian nations into civilization. . . . It compels all nations, on pain of
extinction, to adopt the bourgeois mode of production; it compels
them to introduce what it calls civilization into their midst, i.e., to
become bourgeois themselves. In one word, it creates a world after its own image.[37]

As IT-driven globalization threatens to transform "all that is solid"
into "air," a pervasive sense of disruption becomes evident, which is what
Friedman means by the "great sorting out"[38] in the early decades of the
twenty-first century. But what he neglects to address in quoting this passage from Marx and Engels reemerges as the driving force of the entire
book itself: the rise of a new bourgeoisie in the twenty-first century, and
its intent to fashion the world after its own image. Pointing to the struggles against AIDS and other diseases in China and India, Friedman notes
the limited participation in the flat world by people in these countries. The
challenge is to have more and more people become actively connected and
involved with the flattening processes:

> Let's stop here for a moment and imagine how beneficial it would
> be for the world, and for America, if rural China, India, and Af-
> rica were *to grow into little Americas or European Unions in eco-
> nomic and opportunity terms*. But the chances of their getting into
> such a virtuous cycle is tiny without a real humanitarian push by
> flat-world businesses, philanthropies, and governments to devote
> more resources to their problems. The only way out is through
> new ways of collaboration between the flat and unflat parts of the
> world.[39]

Notice that culture is absent here. But that does not matter, because
although it is absent as a separate category, it is what grants legitimacy to
the idea. Here, culture is functioning in its role as myth, as a sense-making
apparatus that can collect the disparate histories and disorderly economies and polities of the world and organize them into a seamless single
history that begins with Columbus's epic journey to the New World and
brings us to the present moment, when the entire world is laid out be-

fore Americans like a tabula rasa on which we can inscribe our grand visions for the future. Here, as Lincoln puts it, myth becomes "ideology in narrative form," an "assertive discourse of power and authority that represents itself as something to be believed and obeyed."[40] If Friedman had put it this way—if only "they," meaning India or the Third World, can become like "us," meaning Euro-America or the First World—the meaning of the passage would not change one bit. Indeed, Friedman embraces exactly what Marx and Engels were most wary of—that is, the rise of a new class of people, the bourgeoisie, and its quest to shape the world according to its desires. Here is that passage from the *Manifesto* again—"It compels all nations, on pain of extinction, to adopt the bourgeois mode of production; it compels them to introduce what it calls civilization into their midst, i.e., to become bourgeois themselves. In one word, *it creates a world after its own image.*"[41] It is, as Roberto Gonzalez notes, about "sell[ing] a way of life—a world view glorifying corporate capitalism and mass consumption as the only paths to progress."[42] The messiness of world histories cannot be accommodated in the vision of global history affirmed by the new bourgeoisie of the twenty-first century. "Every major global issue Friedman tackles," David Hazony observes, "seems to wind up either eclipsed or radically reinterpreted by the workflow revolution."[43] The non-West's value in the world of IT lies in its potential to become like America. When we read a text like *The World Is Flat* and uncritically view the world through its myths and paradigms, we run the risk of legitimizing a vision of the world in which a specific class of people can speak for all the peoples of the world, where the interests of the bourgeoisie become the interests of the many, and where the hegemony of the bourgeoisie can be reproduced without challenge. Indeed, attending to contemporary geopolitical changes would show that the flattening of the world has less to do with the emergence of a global platform for opportunity, creativity, and progress than it does with the rise of global cities in the non-West and their integration into an already existing city-based world economy.

GLOBAL CITIES AND THE IT ECONOMY

The phenomenon of flattening is directly related to an expanding economy in which several cities across the world are becoming integrated into a global network. This integration is resulting in cities (not necessarily nations) in the non-West emerging as world cities—or, more to the point, global cities. In his introduction to *World Cities beyond the West*, Josef

Gugler offers a useful scenario of tiers and core regions: the primary tier of world cities includes New York, London, and Tokyo, and the core regions of the world system are the United States, Canada, Japan, Australia, New Zealand, and Western Europe. Newer cities that are becoming integrated into the primary tier are Mexico City, São Paulo, Johannesburg, Cairo, Moscow, Bombay, Bangkok, Jakarta, Singapore, Shanghai, Hong Kong, and Seoul, among others. However, integration does not result in a major change in the dynamics between core regions and elsewhere that structures the global economy, because these new global cities tend to draw from, supplement, or function as adjuncts to other cities and core regions. These new cities function as pivotal hubs in a global network; they are "global service centers" that have firms specializing in investment, banking, finance, accountancy, advertising, and law.[44] A review of the top hundred global corporations shows that many of their subsidiaries are in these new cities. All these cities have either direct air connections to other world cities or to core regions. Moscow, for instance, has more direct flights to New York than to other cities in the United States. Most of the cities outside the core are manufacturing centers—which makes the core cities and their nations dependent on them. Moscow and Cairo have long histories as world cities, but the important shift is that they are now global centers not for manufacturing, but for services.[45] Gugler notes that as core cities began to invest heavily in these emerging world cities, the social and economic divisions there began to deepen as the benefits of becoming a world city are enjoyed by a few, while the rest are confined to second-class status in these places.[46]

What *The World Is Flat* celebrates as a paradigm-shifting convergence of technology, innovation, and creativity is actually symptomatic of the kinds of shifts that Gugler identifies. Geographically localized in this way, what Friedman presents as a worldwide phenomenon of growth and opportunity for millions of people becomes a specific trajectory of global integration, a particular conjuncture of processes leading to certain modes of city-based economic, cultural, and social integration across the world. The fact that his book begins with Friedman in Bangalore, India, interacting with CEOs of major Indian companies with transnational ties should not be construed as serendipity. Far from it. There is a clear logic at play here—the logic of a new global economy, in which non-Western cities play an increasingly important role as favored sites for IT-enhanced services.

Often viewed as the new Silicon Valley of Asia, Bangalore has become a potent symbol of the new IT economy. To get "Bangalored" is to be caught up with or in the rising tide of outsourcing. As the city becomes

a major technology center with an international reputation, urban planning and infrastructure become absolutely central to its future. Its new
planning boards, which include members representing different parts of
the IT sector, work in tandem with the state government to devise and
implement new roads, routes, residential enclaves, technology parks, and
other public infrastructure. What is troubling, points out Janaki Nair in
The Promise of the Metropolis, is that the state is gradually abandoning its
role as arbiter of public goods—its supervisory function to ensure redistribution, equity, and accountability in public projects—as these new boards
and organizations are given increasing power or have gained enough clout
to influence urban planning on a scale hitherto unknown: "At no previous
stage in the economic history of the city has industry aspired to redefine
the image of the city, manage its services, and streamline its finances with
as much confidence as the captains of the new economy, represented by
the BATF [Bangalore Agenda Task Force] and its subsidiary Janaagraha."[47]

An important displacement becomes apparent: the consumer is re-
placing the citizen, as indigenous and transnational companies and organizations are able to exert inordinate influence by circumventing, in some
instances, established procedures and processes, subverting or tweaking
them in order to remake the entire city into a global technopolis. To the
Karnataka State and to India, the image and idea of Silicon Valley served
as a guiding template for the urban transformation of Bangalore. In *Network City*, James Heitzman pungently writes: "Silicon Valley was thus a
mantra, a pious chant that channeled intellectual thought and public per-
ception, rather than an analysis of extant socio-economic phenomena."[48]

There is no doubt that dependent market and economic sectors like
travel, tourism, transportation, and hotels have benefited considerably
from the growth of the IT industry. However, the rapid transformation of
Bangalore into an urban technopolis has exacerbated class divisions and
further sharpened the differences among social groups as residential enclaves, business parks, offices, institutions, buildings, training centers,
roads, and laboratories, all geared to serve the needs of the telematics (the
integration of computers, information, and communications technologies)
and biotechnology industries, have transformed the urban landscape. In
his conclusion, Heitzman makes a pointed observation: "Perhaps it is here,
in the grotesque distancing of the gated urban enclave from the barefoot
boys cleaning dishes behind the tea stalls, that we see the mark of the
global, the resemblance of Bangalore to other world cities."[49]

Furthermore, in the IT economy new classes tend to form across national and international borders, while generating types of cultural con-

sciousness. The formation of these classes and their ability to harness the power of culture to make their own specific experiences, ideas, and attitudes attain inordinate influence in public discourse—and, at times, function as the central archive for constructing models and theories of IT globalization—is a development that needs scrutiny. In this context, Marx and Engels' caveat about the desire of the bourgeoisie to remake the world in its own image gains contemporary urgency.

TRANSNATIONAL CLASSES AND CULTURES

The growth and global dissemination of IT has created digital divides that could be analyzed at four levels, observes Kenneth Keniston in his introduction to *IT Experience in India*: at the national level, the already stratified classes of rich and poor respond to and use technology in ways that often reflect their class positioning; at the cultural level, the hegemony of English as a global computer language serves to disadvantage those without fluency in this tongue; at the international level, the dynamics of development or underdevelopment get inextricably linked to the interaction among so-called developing and First World nations; and at the class level, a new group of skilled knowledge workers begins to establish transnational ties and cultivate a cosmopolitan, urban, technology-suffused culture.[50] Keniston calls this group "digerati" because they are the "beneficiaries of the enormous successful information technology (IT) industry and other knowledge-based sectors of the economy such as biotechnology and pharmacology."[51] The growth of coffee shops, educational institutions, institutes, malls, pubs, and international airports, for instance, is directly related to the rise of the digerati—who have, personally or via their jobs, constant exposure to and contact with other digerati in places like the United States, Taiwan, Ireland, and Israel. It is likely that the digerati could end up living in "an increasingly separate, cosmopolitan, knowledge-based enclave."[52] In *The New Argonauts*, AnnaLee Saxenian calls these classes the "new Argonauts" after the Greek adventurers who traveled with Jason in search of the Golden Fleece. International mobility is paramount to the new Argonauts, as they move back and forth between the countries where they live and their countries of origin or affiliation. And as they travel and relocate and become mobile again, they transfer critical skills, knowledge bases, labor, capital, and other vital elements of the IT industry, transforming the earlier phenomenon of brain drain (the migration of skilled labor from all over the world to the United States) into brain circulation (the circulation of skilled labor in the world, with the United States as a central hub).[53] It is significant that in a book on Taiwan, China, and India, Saxenian titles the chapter on India "IT Enclaves in India," which is of a piece with Keniston's note of caution about the danger that the digerati will create enclaves or specially designed and constructed urban landscapes in which these new classes conduct their daily lives. Saxenian notes: "Bangalore and its smaller counterparts are fast-growing, wealthy enclaves in a very poor, mostly rural, economy with a national per capita income of less than $1.50 per day."[54] Heitzman's "gated urban enclave" and Saxenian's "wealthy enclaves" signal a shift in emphasis from community to enclave. What is possible in enclaves is the cultivation not of community but of lifestyle, and the difference between the two proposed by Robert Bellah and his coauthors in *Habits of the Heart* is helpful in this context: "Whereas a community attempts to be an inclusive whole, celebrating the interdependency of public and private life and of the different callings of all, lifestyle is fundamentally segmental and celebrates the narcissism of similarity."[55]

The American context of Bellah and coauthors' analysis points to a split between leisure and work, private and public, that does not have the same relevance in the Indian context. However, the point here is that the enclave-like growth spurred by the IT economy is being shaped by a cultural ethos shared and, more to the point, shaped primarily by the beneficiaries of this economy. Work and leisure, professional interests and private desires, coalesce to the point where urban growth is both structured by and reflects their close interdependence. It is for this reason that enclave becomes more important than community, that lifestyles of work and leisure of IT institutions, employees, businesses, subsidiaries, and tangentially connected economies gain precedence over the commonweal. These developments, argues Chakravarthi Ram-Prasad, are more likely to create among IT professionals (part of a burgeoning middle class) a heightened indifference toward politics, class divisions, and the well-being of the community. The tendency is to encourage private personal or professional philanthropy, since the state is viewed less as an institution set up to address the needs of the people[56] than, to extend Ram-Prasad's point in this context, as a bureaucratic instrument to meet requirements, follow procedures, obtain licensures, and politically legitimize or protect the needs of the IT industry.

At the national and state levels, higher education's heavy investment in engineering, business management, and computer science is intended primarily to address the need for new workers and professionals for the burgeoning IT industry. But the irony is that although prestigious Indian institutions produce brilliant students who can compete with their peers around the world, the national rate of literacy is 58 percent (just 46.4 percent for women), which is well below the UN average for countries with low income rates.[57] In addition, the Indian IT industry is so heavily export-oriented that it repeats the enclave-like patterns of urban growth and renewal in the economic sphere: over the last six years, the general economy of India grew at 5 percent while IT exports grew 20 percent, making up 62 percent of all export sales.[58]

Those plugged into this new IT economy of the twenty-first century form, as Carol Upadhya insightfully notes, a "transnational class." In the 1980s the Indian government encouraged foreign companies like Texas Instruments to set up operations in India. It also set up software technology parks in the early 1990s to further attract indigenous and foreign attention. It is in the 1990s that we see a new kind of economy begin to grow quickly and quite independently of the old economies of the public and national sectors, while simultaneously integrating itself in the global economy.[59] Since, as Arvind Singhal and Everett Rogers observe, "Indians in Silicon Valley have also begun to 'give back' to their homeland, making the earlier debate about the 'brain drain' passé,"[60] NRI (nonresident Indian)[61] IT professionals have played a pivotal role in spurring the growth of software companies and their subsidiaries in both the United States and India. In 1993 the Indian Venture Capital Association was formed and, by the late 1990s, close to 80 percent of venture capital in India came from abroad. Also in 1993, the Indus Entrepreneurs was established, with the sole purpose of promoting investments in the software industry in India and the United States but geared toward Indians or Americans of Indian descent.[62] With 50,000 IT professionals in the United States by 2000 and almost 10 percent of U.S. IT start-ups between 1995 and 2000 managed by Indian Americans, the IT industry soon began to acquire an ethnic face. This segment of the economy became associated with India, Indians, and Indian Americans in popular culture and scholarly discourse around the world. As Upadhya points out, "the entry of foreign VC [venture capital] funds into India represents not only the interest of international capital in the Indian software industry, but also efforts of the NRI business community to extend their business interests into India. NRIs have invested in the industry directly as promoters of firms, as well as through venture capital funding and private equity funds."[63] Soon "cross-border" firms conceptualized, funded, or managed by Indians and Indian Americans in India and the United States began to emerge, offering highly specialized services rather than low-end, back-office services. According to the *India Reporter*, in 2005, of the $20.35 billion of venture capital raised in the United States, companies owned or run by South Asians accounted for 6.55 percent of the total, or close to $1.45 billion, an increase of twelve percentage points over 2004.[64] These firms make it a priority to establish their presence in the United States while setting up operations in India, but interestingly "ownership and control are increasingly concentrated outside of India although the original entrepreneurs are usually Indians based in India, and the actual work, or production of value, takes place in India," and this is why the "older discourse of economic nationalism predicated on clear national boundaries is inadequate to comprehend this kind of structure."[65] Even as brief a historical sketch as this clearly suggests that a new economic class has emerged, one with significant access to capital and labor but whose operations are networked in cross-border, transnational forms.

Given the fluid and hybrid structures and networks of the IT industry, this new class, contends Upadhya, tends to have a "different ideological orientation" toward globalization and, as it gets increasingly iconized in both India and the diasporic Indian communities in the United States, this class has gained tremendous visibility as a fine example of socioeconomic progress.[66] Iconization tends to spotlight a few individuals' tremendous success and makes their lives the standard according to which the success of others in IT can be measured. Although this is hardly a new phenomenon, we should at least examine specific instances of such ionization and the signs and symbols through which class identity and consciousness get coded. Singhal and Rogers' *India's Communication Revolution* includes numerous short biographical and informative sections profiling successful individuals in IT in the United States and India. They include Narayana Murthy of Infosys Technologies; Azim Premji of Wipro; Arjun Malhotra, cofounder of Hindustan Computer and CEO of Techspan, a software company; Subhash Chandra, chairman of Zee-TV; Sam Pitroda, who once led the Center for Development of Telematics and was appointed head of the Department of Telecommunications in India under Prime Minister Rajiv Gandhi; Chandrababu Naidu, a former chief minister of the state of Andhra Pradesh, who gained an international reputation for turning a nascent IT industry in South India into a global IT center within a decade; Gururaj Deshpande, cofounder of numerous start-ups in Boston; Atin Malavia, also from Boston, whose Redstone Communications was acquired by a German company in 1999 for millions of dollars; Sabeer Bhatia, cofounder of Hotmail; Vinod Khosla, cofounder of Sun Microsystems; Love Goel, the CEO of the online branch of Federated Department Stores; and women like Vani Kola, CEO of Right Works; Anu Shukla, CEO of RubricSoft; and Lata Krishnan, an entrepreneur in Silicon Valley. It is in the seemingly innocuous details in the biographical sketches of these people that the language of class—which has a powerful ideological impact—is effectively deployed. For example, after noting that Hotmail was sold in 1997, Singhal and Rogers report that Sabeer Bhatia started a company called Arzoo and that he "lives in a skyscraper apartment in San Francisco with smashing views of the entire San Francisco Bay area."[67] The passage about Atin Malaviya, whose Redstone Communications was bought by Seimens for $500 million, sheds interesting light on the role of culture:

> How has Malaviya's lifestyle changed? He and his wife have bought *a new home in an affluent Boston suburb*, and Malaviya has replaced his 10-year old GEO with a new Audi sports car, *which blends with the BMW and Mercedez Benz cars* in the parking lot at Unisphere. Malaviya spends more time at home on weekends and has *resumed his art classes*. When asked by one of the present authors if he was considering retirement at the ripe age of 33, Malaviya responded: "This isn't enough. There is more to go."[68]

In such passages, class markers are clearly evident in the commodities and interests that individuals possess and pursue. Here, they include a suburban home, an Audi sports car, and art classes. The pressure to conform to a class in this context is evidenced by the phrase "which blends with the BMW and Mercedes Benz cars." It raises the question, what if one's car didn't blend? And would there be consequences? Ascertaining such consequences would be extremely difficult, but it is undeniable that there is some kind of pressure to conform and that this desire to blend in is related to specific commodities like cars. Art, which generally falls within the purview of culture, is also viewed as a leisure activity, one that can be pursued only after gaining economic success, and compelling art to follow the laws of economics. In the earlier example of Bhatia, the comment on his living in an apartment having "smashing views" of the Bay Area speaks to issues of lifestyle again. These passages demonstrate how practices of consumption and the ideology of consumerism form a nexus in which the iconization of an emerging class within the global IT economy is granted sociocultural legitimacy.

In U.S. media representations of outsourcing, the intersection of class with gender and nation raises pertinent issues. In examining how American nationalism gets intertwined with economic globalizations so that a white, middle-class subjectivity can articulate its angst when faced with the consequences of free market globalization, Mobina Hashmi argues that the category "American worker" is effectively deployed in anti-IT globalization discourse since it enables the erasure of stark class differences. She contends that "the most vocal constituency opposing offshore outsourcing—unemployed American IT professionals—belong to the professional elite that, historically, has an antagonistic relationship to the working class. However, this same group claims kinship with blue-collar workers under the umbrella of 'American worker' and grounds its claims to capitalist exploitation by selectively drawing on the history of agricultural workers and blue-collar manufacturing workers."[69]

What the struggling poor and blue-collar workers have often been told to do during times of economic upheavals and job losses—learn new skills, maintain focus, become competitive, develop a global worldview and compete globally—somehow, to the newly unemployed American IT workers, seems less commonsensical than it once did, because they consider their job losses to be the direct result of greedy corporations' collusion with corrupt governments eager to further their own interests at the expense of the "American worker." In the "stakes of globalization," as Hashmi perceptively points out, class formation and anxieties exert a powerful force on how the nation is imagined in the perplexing time of IT globalization.[70] Interestingly enough, that message of social uplift most often directed at the poor—which reminds them to better themselves, develop the habits of culture and custom to become responsible citizens of the nation, and contribute to society as productive workers—gets recast as an American saga in which David, the American worker, is battling for survival against Goliath, the overweening global corporation. But this American drama makes sense only if it can resuscitate a capacious national identity that can gloss over the classed and raced structures of American society.

Although this chapter critiqued the exceptionalist discourse within which the flattening of the world gains cultural and socioeconomic legitimacy in *The World Is Flat*, the contrapuntal dynamic of dwelling in American requires examining other aspects of IT globalization. This would mean weaving my own analysis of *The World Is Flat* and the impact of IT on India and America together with the threads that entangle it in broader, more textured, and finely grained cultural contexts and social settings. To enact the contrapuntal logics of dwelling in American, in the next chapter I examine a fascinating development in India—the phenomenal growth of call centers—and consider their function as pivotal hubs in the global networks of affective labor, and the role of culture in transnational businesses.

—҈ CHAPTER SIX ҈—

The Transnationalization
of Affective Labor

CALL CENTER CULTURES

How can dwelling in American—as a mode of critical analysis, a method of reading and understanding—be used to examine information technology (IT) globalization? How can we conceive of resistance and opposition to this new dispensation of empire? What would it mean to view non-Americans as social actors with major stakes for themselves, their societies, and their imagined nations in this dispensation of empire? What kinds of insides and outsides of the networked flow of power, information, and technology become available for resistance and opposition? What negotiations of individual and social needs, public policies, and business practices take place in the virtual and material spaces of call centers? As the previous chapter shows, *The World Is Flat* promulgates a profoundly Euro-America-centric view of the flat world, but is this all there is to IT globalization? How can we move outside the borders of America and the West to understand the manner in which our cultures and economies are deeply entangled with other cultures and economies, with major consequences for both our ways of life and theirs? These are the questions that gain significance when we turn our attention to call centers and extend the hermeneutic imperative of dwelling in American to reenvision—contrapuntally—the global networking of culture and information.

Call centers, cellphones, visual media, and new information technologies are central to the plot of the 2008 Oscar-winning movie *Slumdog Millionaire*. The plot revolves around two brothers, Jamal and Salim Malik, and a girl, Latika, who grow up in the slums of Mumbai (formerly known as Bombay) and, as young adults, attempt to eke out a living in the city by dint of sheer luck, bravado, and street smarts. Salim ends up working for an underworld don, Latika is pressured into becoming a mistress, and Jamal finds himself, owing to a series of serendipitous events, on the game show *Kaun Banega Crorepati?* (the Indian version of *Who Wants to be a Millionaire?*), tantalizingly close to answering the final question and winning the grand prize. The plot unfolds in a series of flashbacks and juxtapositions of the past and the present that show how Jamal's life experiences, rather than any formal education, enable him to answer questions on the game show. Working as a *chai wallah* (tea server) in a call center, Jamal is asked by an employee to sit in for him for a few moments and respond to calls. Using the call center's database, Jamal finds Salim's phone number, dials it, and connects with him; Jamal's brief conversation with another employee about dialing procedures to become a contestant on the game show implies that Jamal followed his own advice successfully to become a contestant. His main reason is to reestablish contact with Latika, hoping that—given the show's immense popularity in India—she would be watching the show when he was on. In fact, he is able to chat briefly with her when, using the game show's dial-a-friend option, he dials Salim's number and Latika answers the phone. The movie ends on a note of social promise and romantic reunion as Jamal correctly answers the final question to win the game and finally meets Latika at the Mumbai train station, their rendezvous. Although call centers, cellphones, and visual media are crucial to the development of the plot, as a cultural artifact, the movie exemplifies the hopes, aspirations, and problems of a significant segment of the Indian populace that is affected by the nation's integration into the new information-driven, computer-mediated, knowledge economy of the contemporary economic, social, and cultural global order. Call centers are at the center of India's emergence as a key player in the new global economy, and they have also become part of Indo-American popular culture in movies, videos, dramas, and novels—including *A Terrible Beauty Is Born* (2003), a play by Arjun Raina; *American Daylight* (2004), a film by Roger Christian; *Nalini by Day, Nancy by Night* (2005), a documentary by Sonali Gulati; *30 Days: Outsourcing* (2006), a reality show created by Morgan Spurlock; *Outsourced* (2007), a film by John Jeffcoat; *Hello* (2008), a film made in Hindi, a major Indian language, by Atul Agnihotri, and based on Chetan Bhagat's best-selling novel, *One Night @ the Call Center* (2005); *Call Center* (2008), a film made in Telugu, a South Indian language, by Kanmani Raja; and other videos produced by individuals and groups—some of them nonprofessionals, which are available on YouTube and Google video.

In this chapter, I will develop these central arguments: in managing affective labor, call centers have a high investment in creating and managing particular cultural ideas and practices; call center cultures do not emerge and thrive in social isolation but directly feed into social and cultural processes in order to perpetuate themselves, and they are driven by a certain logic of biopolitical reproduction; and it would be a mistake to view these cultures only as extensions of a global consumer culture in an Indian setting or as a clear indication of successful American cultural imperialism. I make these arguments in analyzing how, in the documentary *Diverted to Delhi*—which focuses on setting up and managing call centers—a particular itinerary of culture gets deployed, used, and adopted for various purposes by several players who have some stake in the globalization of the IT industry. I show that the transnationalization of what Michael Hardt calls "affective labor"[1]—the affects required and codified for the management of information, knowledge, symbols, services—involves setting up a system of intellectual and social surveillance in which ideas and notions of cultural difference are deployed and managed. Such cross-cultural encounters and forms of learning rationalize the biopolitical dynamics of the IT industry: the creation of new social classes, whose value to business process outsourcing depends on their ability to both generate and virtually embody specific affects of tone, accent, language, culture, and identity. But this is not all there is to call centers and affective labor. My central argument is that the biopolitical logic of such transnational cultural flows cannot be adequately examined by using traditional models of globalization as Westernization, hybridization, or even a combination of both. Call center outsourcing is deeply embedded in global cultural and economic flows whose dynamics are at odds and in some ways work contradictorily despite efforts and institutionalized structures designed to manage them to meet predetermined ends. This is why they cannot be viewed as a unidirectional, West-to-East manifestation of cultural imperialism and biopower. The range and scope of affective labor in these sectors cannot be reduced to U.S.-driven biopolitical reproduction. Rather, we should examine the pulse points of this transnational economy, where divergent, contradictory desires and possibilities, appropriations, and manipulations emerge and are negotiated by various actors. The ensuing discussion examines specific pedagogical practices of call centers as represented in *Diverted to Delhi*, and then, by drawing on cultural studies and sociology, explains how a focus on the gendered dimension of call center work reveals that the transnationalization of affective labor embodies what Arjun Appadurai aptly refers to as a "globally variable synaesthesia," where identities are manipulated and effects are dislocated.[2] But first, two points need to be described in greater detail: the social and economic context of the rise of call centers in India, and an explanation of key terms—immaterial labor, affective labor—used in the discussion.

CALL CENTERS AND AFFECTIVE LABOR

The debate about call centers is not only economic but cultural. In Indian call centers, especially those whose client firms and customers are from England, the United States, and Australia, creating friendly customer service includes demonstrating fluency in the English language and familiarity with customers' cultures, which often means Americanizing one's speech and immersing oneself in British, American, or Australian culture. Call center representatives (CCRs) are supposed to make customers feel and think that they are interacting with someone familiar, perhaps someone in their region, state, or nation—and not a person hundreds or thousands of miles away, born and working in a different country. Language classes for CCRs stress the development of accents and speech patterns, especially conversational ones that people might engage in with strangers they meet in unfamiliar or professional settings. Acquisition of cultural knowledge has also meant, in some instances, viewing several episodes of shows like *Friends* or *Baywatch*, and popular films. The goal is to create a customer service atmosphere by an adroit manipulation of affects—tone, accent, language, and cultural knowledge—to create a state of well-being, familiarity, and pleasantness. These affects are, of course, virtually mediated given the fact that thousands of miles separate customers from the CCRs who work in their call center cubicles, booths, or offices, using computers with audio and visual connections, and who can connect themselves or customers in a matter of seconds to other technicians or service providers located in various parts of the world, thanks to the phenomenal speeds of connectivity afforded by bandwidth technology and satellites.[3]

Call centers are part of the new postmodern economy, which has three important elements, point out Michael Hardt and Antonio Negri: the rapid increase and thorough infusion of computer-mediated communication in industrial settings; the interpretation of symbols and communication; and the production and management of affects that could be actual or virtual.[4] Hardt notes that the term "affective labor" brings together two major scholarly focuses: the feminist focus on the body and the gendering of work, largely in the United States, and the emphasis—mostly by French and Italian scholars—on the cognitive and knowledge-oriented nature of the new economy. As he explains, "the term affective labor is meant to bring together elements from these two different streams and grasp simultaneously the corporeal and intellectual aspects of the new forms of production, recognizing that such labor engages at once with rational intelligence and with the passions or feeling."[5] Further, "the challenge of the perspective of the affects resides primarily in the synthesis it requires. This is, in the first place, because affects refer equally to the body and the mind; and, in the second, because they involve both reason and the passions."[6]

But as Rosalind Gill and Andy Pratt rightly point out, the term is nebulous: "Designed to improve upon and narrow down 'immaterial labor', it lacks conceptual coherence and ends up collapsing entirely different kinds of work and experience. If *all* work has affective dimensions then what does it mean to say that any *particular* job involves affective labor?"[7] Hardt and Negri refer to immaterial labor as "labor that produces an immaterial good, such as a service, a cultural product, knowledge, or communication."[8] This still leaves unclear the extent to which affects are part of immaterial labor, especially when affective labor is used to reference another dimension of immaterial labor: "This labor is immaterial, even if it is corporeal and affective, in the sense that its products are intangible, a feeling of ease, well-being, satisfaction, excitement, or passions."[9] How exactly the "cultural product" of immaterial labor is different from these aspects of affective labor is not clear at all, but perhaps one way to sharpen the meanings of these terms is to stress the role of the computer and the highly mediated nature of information and communication in the production of immaterial labor and the stress on the affective aspects—feeling, satisfaction, and so forth—as immanent to productive practices.

As noted earlier, Hardt elaborates on affective labor as a term that integrates the focus on gender and the body, and on the new information and knowledge economy of the present, by bringing together the body and the mind, combining reason with the passions in order to "grasp simultaneously the corporeal and intellectual aspects of the new forms of production."[10] Affective labor is more expansive in its use and integration of affects than is immaterial labor, which might have affective dimensions but may not necessarily form its constitutive elements.[11] In discussing call center cultures, I think the term "affective labor" is more helpful than "immaterial labor" because, first, it captures a wide range of affects as constitutive of the management of work in call centers, and, second, it blurs the boundaries between work and home, official time and leisure time, in the sense that the management of affects in call center cultures has a significant impact on social and personal spheres outside the workplace. As

Winifred R. Poster points out, "ethnicity and citizenship have become crucial elements of the labor process in globalized services,"[12] and in call centers, national and ethnic identity are constantly negotiated and manipulated in the process of providing services mediated through electronic and
telematic technology. It is in this context that we can examine the crucial
link between culture and affective labor in the daily operations and practices of call centers as represented in the documentary *Diverted to Delhi*.[13]

TRANSNATIONALIZATION OF AFFECTIVE LABOR

A documentary about customer service jobs being "diverted" from Australia and the United States to India, this media text presents a general
overview of the kinds of language and culture coaching classes offered to
people seeking jobs at call centers, and the psychosocial pressures they
have to negotiate as they learn to put on Australian and American identities like names, accents, conversational styles, and cultural "hooks" to
make customers feel less anxious about interacting with people outside of
the United States and Australia. In the film, there is little doubt that Indian graduates exhibit a high degree of enthusiasm for learning about Australian and U.S. topography, locale, regional cultural differences, accents,
public sports, and movie and music cultures. Being exposed to and having
to learn about peoples and cultures beyond India is a major factor in sustaining their interest in pursuing call center jobs. It is unclear if they had
similar opportunities to study such international cross-cultural issues at
their universities. The film implies, in its presentation of students convers-
ing, that to be involved in some way with the IT economy enables them to
do things they could not do otherwise, especially learng about the world
outside India in a semi-institutionalized setting. No doubt most urban
youth are heavily exposed to Hollywood, MTV, and other cultural forms
and artifacts from America and other non-Indian countries. But there is a
difference between the kinds of insights one can generally obtain from a
wholesale exposure to American or non-Indian culture and the kinds of
insights one gets in a setting in which cross-cultural interests are a matter of systematized learning. This second type of exposure is what appeals
to these students. But important questions arise: What kind of knowledge
about cultures, cross-cultural interactions, and global awareness do such
institutes offer? In what way does a company's interests regulate knowledge and learning about culture? Do the institutes offer students an intel-

lectual space in which they can reflect critically on what they are exposed to, asked to learn about, and the entire gamut of pedagogical situations they find themselves in?

For instance, after going through intensive coaching sessions, students participate in a "naming ceremony," in which they choose non-Indian names. In a relaxed setting, they are asked to come to the front of the class, announce their names, and then say their adopted names boldly and confidently. The script they follow runs something like this: "Hello, my name is Rajesh. And my new call center name is Russell," or "my new call center name is Carol Lopez." There is one segment that is especially significant because it underscores how the logic of multinational businesses harnesses the ideological power of American exceptionalism in order to further not the interests of the American nation, but to cater to the satisfaction of American customers. Students are asked what seem to be open-ended questions, like "What do you think about America?" and "What perspectives do you have about America?" Here are some of the responses: "The man I am talking about is Columbus. He discovered America. And the spirit of Americans is 'I can,'" "They are very calorie conscious," and "America is a glamorous country. Be it the way they play, be it the way they work, be it the way they dress, be it the way they fight." One student who responds, "You will see the American flag everywhere" but not "Indian flags," clarifies—when asked by a classmate what he would like India to be—that he wants India "to be like America," presumably everywhere. This segment is punctuated by cuts to the comments of a chief trainer, who notes: "It picks up on whether people have negative attitudes to[ward] the U.S. Because if they do, we have to *get rid of it quickly*" (emphasis added).

CULTURE AND BIOPOLITICAL REPRODUCTION

This particular pedagogical exercise demonstrates the "high-tech and virtualized disciplining of the 'worker' in Indian call centers from far away geographies in the West,"[14] and the overt and not-so-overt ways in which largely stereotypical ideas of America, India, and globalization in general are reified in order to ensure higher profits and customer satisfaction. Almost all of the comments here echo hegemonic narratives of America—Columbus as the great adventurer who epitomizes the classic "I can do it" character of America; the ease with which the glamour of work and play is extended to violence, which can often justify violence simply because it would be glamorously American; and the desire to globalize India like

America. The fact that a class session like this is devoted to testing whether students have negative ideas of America and screening out those who express anything remotely negative evidences the kind of intellectual policing that is required to purge students of their ability to engage in any kind of critical reflection about their work and social lives. It is, indeed, a form of brainwashing with all the trappings of the glamour of globalization, American style. The more robotic the students are in their learning, the greater the chance that they will do the bidding of their employers without questioning, pausing, or analyzing. The disturbing thing about pedagogy such as this is that the goal is the complete submission of the student's intellect to the logic of global capitalism, which validates customer satisfaction as the ultimate horizon of social existence. This can be viewed as an instantiation of the cultural politics of biopower—the creation of multinational businesses in which the success of work and the profitability of labor are judged by the extent to which cultural learning can reproduce entire groups of people with certain ideas, tastes, accents, identities, and worldviews—in short, to extend Hardt's point, to create a condition of sociality that leads to a new society itself. This is biopower, because the flow of power facilitates the recreation and sustenance of groups of people not at the level of specific operations, forms, and patterns of work or labor, but at the level of social and cultural behavior, at the level of managing forms of life: "what affective labor produces are social networks, forms of community, biopower."[15] What we are looking at here are not direct flows of power, or even uneven flows of power between nations and economies. Michel Foucault's point about the discriminatory procedures that are put into place to manage life is what is at issue:

> But a power whose task is to take charge of life needs continuous regulatory and corrective mechanisms. It is no longer a matter of bringing death into play in the field of sovereignty, but of *distributing the living in the domain of value and utility.* Such a power has to qualify, measure, appraise, hierarchize, rather than display itself in its murderous splendor; it does not have to draw the line that separates the enemies of the sovereign from his obedient subjects; *it effects distributions around the norm.*[16]

Of concern here are the ways in which various social and cultural behaviors are brought into the "domain of value and utility" and how, in that very process, the norms are established—pro-business, pro-American, self-effacing, and self-altering—by systematically marginalizing critical, humanistic inquiry. Indeed, what began as a desire to acquire cultural intelligence in order for businesses to succeed results in a form of learning in which the culture of consumers located in the West is the only thing that future CCRs unexaminedly absorb and regurgitate appropriately in the digitized and telematic spaces that call centers set up and manage. Culture as idea, difference, and value is structurally interwoven into the entire field of worker and management relations, business arrangements, and call center infrastructure. Multinational and transnational industries are fully involved in transnationalizing affective labor by creating home-like atmospheres for their clientele—familiar accents, names, and locations. As A. R. Vasavi insightfully argues, cultural reproduction is directly linked to the production of new subjectivities on the individual and social level, as these employees become "subjects who both objectively and subjectively subscribe to the logics of the industry" that "combine[s] education, employment, and entertainment" and "*integrates the youth* into a world of goods, altered life-styles and personalities."[17] And this is possible only if "the transformation of Indian urban labor into a global proletariat"[18] can be achieved as affective labor becomes—to draw on James Ferguson and Akhil Gupta's notion of "transnational governmentality"— a central component of "a transnational apparatus of governmentality."[19] It is governmental not in the sense of embodying state power, but in the sense of organizing social power through various processes of managing society, and—in this specific instance—culture, cultural intelligence, and cross-cultural engagement become central to the productive economy of transnational circuits of affective labor in the IT industry. Raka Shome puts it well:

> Transnational governmentality constitutes transnational mechanisms and organizations through which the conduct (of the third world subject) is regulated and disciplined from macro levels (for example, regime changes, environmental planning) to micro levels of personal behavior and social identity (for example, cultivating a taste for Coke or McDonald's) in order to maximize profit and efficiency in the global economy.[20]

In *Diverted to India*, the purging of negative ideas or perspectives about America is a clear instance of regulating and disciplining the call center employees so that they can simulate the consumer's culture and simultaneously get socialized into a lifestyle whose products and habits of consumption are of a piece with consumer culture. Arguably, the location of consumers in the West is not the only manifestation of the structural imbalance of this global economy. The more relevant point is that this biopolitical reproduction of affective labor is driven by one overarching aim—consumer satisfaction. This is why, to Divya McMillen, it is a form of neocolonialism:

> Call centers then stand as strong symbols of a neocolonialist environment, where labourers need to enter into the cultural contexts of their employers and clientele based in the US, UK, Germany or the Netherlands, as the case may be, and using their knowledge of the range of customer services available to the client, converse fluently, *stripping away as much as possible indicators of their local Indian contexts.* . . . What then differentiates a neocolonialist environment from a colonialist environment is the context of globalization where *the focus is not on overt force and imposition but on interconnectivity.*[21]

This "interconnectivity" gives rise to hybrid cultures in emerging world cities like Bangalore, where people employed at call centers and other IT-enhanced businesses become active consumers at Pizza Hut, Kentucky Fried Chicken, Thomas Cook, American Express, Domino's, and so on.[22] Hybridity in and of itself is neither progressive nor regressive, and it does not simply exist or come into being as a natural condition of human existence, independent of the convergence of other forces and activities. Rather, the conditions in which a culture becomes labeled as hybrid, and the sociocultural processes that grant legitimacy to such a culture, need more examination. The fact that these young Indian university graduates look forward to the day when they are eventually hired as CCRs adds more irony to the situation. Vasavi's point about the formation of new subjectivities and the integration of youth into consumer culture, Shome's analysis of the regulatory mechanisms of the affective aspects of call center work, and McMillen's critique of the production of cosmopolitan hybrid culture can be read in tandem with Poster's argument that not only do call center cultures manifest the surveillance of affects but that such a form of globalized labor "transforms from management of emotions to management of citizenship."[23] This kind of "national identity management," to use Poster's phrase, ensures that the culture of consumers located in the West—or, in more general terms, the culture of customers per se—gains social and professional legitimacy at the expense of the CCRs' national, ethnic, or local culture. Poster goes further, noting that such "national identity management allows these firms to hide the exercise of power on the consuming public. Ultimately, they are managing the consumers' reality as much as that of the workers."[24] The greater the success of national identity management, the higher the possibility of obscuring, from the consuming public, the material fact of outsourcing: consumers assume that the workers are American and are working in their own country, and that it is business as usual.

The social and political significance of such identity management cannot be understated. For instance, during the 2004 U.S. presidential election campaign, the Maine Democratic Party released a flier that had, in a bold red block across the top, the words "George W. Bush Has Failed Maine Workers," and, in a dark blue block across the bottom, the promise that "John Kerry Will Protect American Jobs." In between was information substantiating the declarations: thousands of jobs were being "shipped overseas," and businesses engaging in outsourcing were getting tax breaks. In campaign speeches, Kerry urged Americans to work for "a prosperity where we create jobs here at home and where we shut down every loophole, every incentive, every reward that goes to some Benedict Arnold CEO or company that take[s] the jobs overseas and stick[s] Americans with the bill."[25] Given such public sentiment against outsourcing, companies engaged in the practice had good reason to provide their consumers with a familiar, comfortable interaction with company representatives, an interaction that erased traces of foreignness or otherness. To be sure, call centers were pivotal business processing centers in which the transnationalization of affective labor could be managed to comply with such consumer needs and demands. But as Poster perceptively notes, "many actors play a role in the national identity management process, whether directly or indirectly. Their actions represent various forms of agency in the process—by setting the rules, innovating the strategies, and carrying them out."[26] For some workers, altering their identities temporarily for professional reasons and cultivating cultural familiarity with their customers' societies comes at a cost.

THE SOCIAL EFFECTS OF HYBRID CULTURES

The transnationalization of affective labor is not without its psychosocial affects, as CCRs begin to grapple with the reality of juggling two different cultural identities, which are often in conflict. The CCRs begin to lead double lives—having and working with one kind of cultural identity on

the job, and going back to their original Indian identity and culture outside of work. S. Mitra Kalita says that "the emerging subculture of call-
center workers reveals that the United States has exported more than jobs
and products to India—it has exported values, as well. Call centers have
brought new wealth to India, but they are also fostering a cultural back-
lash, as the country's young, hip BPO [business process outsourcing] workers run up against the traditions of the older generations."[27] In the film, the
economist Jayati Ghosh's comments on the sense of alienation and despair
that such cultural clashes engender are worth quoting in full:

> I would see the call center phenomenon as a sort of a clear ex-
> pression of a much wider tendency in urban India, among urban
> youth in particular. And it is really the exploitation of that com-
> bination of part education, part aspiration, which is quite wide-
> spread. It's the exploitation of that combination to suit the needs
> of cost-cutting multinational companies. We have a younger gen-
> eration that is mesmerized by this so-called American Dream,
> which doesn't even exist in America. And whose expectations are
> molded along those lines—you know the kind of typical notion
> of life in, you know, in American suburbia where you have all the
> goodies. It really wants to be part of this global elite. So they will
> be copying the lifestyles insofar as they can; they will be consum-
> ing the same products; they will be going to the shops that have
> Nike and Benetton. I have seen examples where it creates another
> peculiar kind of conflict. The same young woman who works in a
> call center, pretends that her name is Karen, and lives in Arkan-
> sas, etc., etc., the same woman will actively become excessively
> religious. I have seen some young students observe the most re-
> gressive kinds of social practices as a reaction to the fact that in
> other aspects of their life they are succumbing completely to a
> sort of modern Western notion of existence.

The urbanization of Indian youth in the context of the growing integration of the Indian economy with the global IT economy is slowly creating new classes of people whose cultural tastes have a lot in common with
those who live in America. What links such classes of people together are
common desires and patterns of consumption—of music, food, popular
culture, and so forth. It is around such practices that a global consciousness emerges; in other words, being a participant in a global world is intimately linked to how well one can demonstrate, through one's practices of

consuming global goods, that one has the required cultural wherewithal to be a part of the global elite. Here "elite" connotes not education, wealth, power, knowledge, or access to capital or other kinds of fungible assets. It is specifically about becoming active consumers, while being positioned at particular nodal points in the global circuits of commerce and exchange that enable one to develop and sustain patterns of consumption.

Ghosh's point that "regressive" social tendencies emerge as these Indian graduates struggle to cope with the demands of juggling two identities and cultures is telling. Becoming overly religious or subscribing to increasingly nondemocratic ideas and practices in other spheres of life leads to another paradox of globalization: becoming active participants within a specific and localized conjuncture of the flows of globalization, without a simultaneous or concomitant engagement with any kind of humanist discourse or mode of inquiry that can enable one to draw on personal experience and develop the tools to critically examine the conditions of one's own locatedness in a global world, which leads to a profound loss of personal and social worth. Although they function as alternate sectors of employment in newly emerging IT-focused economies and earn a cultural cachet for their high salaries, technological modernization, and symbolic association with Western culture, call centers develop, train, and employ new knowledge workers under conditions of control and surveillance where the celebration and learning of cultural difference is predicated on the intellectual docility required for effective participation in the new economy.

To clarify the point: it is not the fact that these graduates are living double lives that is the concern—I do not assume that they all possessed some kind of happy, monolithic cultural identity prior to their integration into this new IT network. Rather, the problem is that the entire process of becoming part of the IT sector via the call center—the process of learning in and acculturating to the ethos of call centers—requires, evaluates, and measures as a precondition of employment the creation of a mental tabula rasa on which can be inscribed singularly pro-business, pro-American, pro-globalization, and pro-Western ideas and attitudes. The business of call centers, especially in their outsourced manifestation, is not business as usual; it is more than that. Although call centers constantly encourage and police the acquisition of a cultural persona deemed acceptable and even necessary for profitable business, they also become "site[s] where a simultaneous construction of the two interlocking figures of producer and consumer is taking place."[28]

In the documentary, a few students—in spite of going through an intense coaching course for call center jobs—fail to be selected. The film ends with scenes of a different India, one that is outside of the IT economy—people paddling a boat, and a large tract of land being plowed—with the narrator suggesting that people who are unable to find work in the IT sector have little else to fall back on. There are two problems with this framing of scenes: first, rural and urban Indias are contrasted as mutually exclusive social spheres, and the fateful choices presented are of being mired in a traditional, rural India or plugged into a fast-paced, competitive international Indian economy; and second, such a representation of contending Indias simplifies the systematized forms of cultural manipulation and socioeconomic marginalization within the IT call center industry. Over the last decade, it has become clear that rural India is just as affected by globalization as urban India—albeit with, in some instances, deadly consequences. Rural India is far from an idyllic place, with a stable agricultural economy grounded in ancient indigenous practices. Over the last decade, more than 25,000 farmers have taken their own lives, unable to face the challenges of pervasive drought, corrupt moneylending practices, inept state bureaucracies, callous police personnel, a lumbering judiciary, and shoddy policy planning and implementation by local, state, and national governments. It is noteworthy that the highest rates of suicides were in the same states that were seeing phenomenal urban growth as a direct result of IT globalization: Andhra Pradesh, Karnataka, Maharashtra, and Kerala.[29]

According to Vandana Shiva, farmer suicides coincided with the national government's implementation of liberal trade policies. Seed saving by natural pollination was replaced by hybrid pollination, and farmers had to purchase hybrid seeds produced by multinational companies. Coupled with drought, excessive rains, and so forth, this soon drove farmers into debt. In contrast, saving natural seed annually through natural means helps the seed retain its vital elements; there is a significantly higher chance for seed variation to occur in this process, although it is hard to create more yield and control growth. Hybrid seed offers more yield and is standardized for growth, but it needs fertilizers and pesticides, which the farmers have to buy. Hybrid seeds also do not remain the same when saved—that is, they do not contain the same essential traits for them to be used in a second cycle. Pressured to buy such seeds, dependent largely on seasonal rains, lacking access to bank loans—so they had to borrow money at exorbitantly high interest rates—and with high rates of illiteracy, farmers faced formidable challenges.[30] All these factors clearly show that *Diverted to Delhi's* juxtaposition of rural and urban Indias, with the latter advancing rapidly toward high growth rates and the former mired in timelessness and a stable agricultural economy, skews the profoundly uneven impact of various practices of globalization on individuals, societies, and businesses. The rapid growth of call centers in India is but one facet of IT, which is itself a specific but integral dimension of a whole range of global practices. For a documentary, *Diverted to Delhi* tends to have a very narrow focus on call centers and is not able to examine their growth in India as it relates to other forces and practices of economic liberalization that are having a disproportionate impact on various societies and regions across the country.

On the other hand, the urban, high-growth sectors of the information economy, like call centers and their biopolitical reproductive practices, engender new hybrid cultures of identity management and lifestyle changes, but they also offer limited professional advancement opportunities for call center employees, resulting in a very high rate of turnover. It is possible to get perplexingly mired within the new technopolis and become part of a labor force that has little control over its work conditions and can be easily coopted into hierarchical systems in the industry. The initial glamour of working in fast-paced environments—imposing buildings; new architectures; sophisticated, state-of-the-art computers and other electronic machines; clean, well-maintained office spaces; exposure to peoples and cultures beyond the local and nation; markedly high salaries compared to those paid in other sectors in the state or region—soon reveals the fact that the new division of labor and its social hierarchies is just a veneer. As the IT industry expands, call centers are doing most of the low-end, back-office work of the industry like data entry, accounts payable, customer service, survey collection and management, and medical billing and coding, even as the industry is taking on more-specialized, high-end work including research and development, pharmaceutical manufacturing and patenting, complex software programming, medical testing, tax filing, and application processing, all of which involve huge financial investments, infrastructure, complex skills, and high salaries.[31] For this reason, Carol Upadhya contends that "software services outsourcing appears to be just another chapter of an old story, in which the international division of labor is being redrawn to accommodate the interest of dominant economic actors."[32]

Babu Ramesh goes to the extent of calling call center workers "cyber coolies" because, he notes, "the technology-induced efficiency at work requires the agents to submit to a highly controlled work regime. . . . Work is monitored on the spot and after the working hours, with the help of specially designed software, computer networks and closed circuit cameras. The degree of surveillance required at work is even comparable with the situations of 19th century prisons or Roman slave ships."[33] Although Ramesh needlessly adds hyperbole to an otherwise reasonable critique, he emphasizes the degree to which companies seek to create workplaces in which every minute and hour can and should be accounted for and documented, referring to the fact that national holidays are not observed—except, of course, American holidays—since the majority of clients are U.S. companies, and the practice of forty-eight hour work weeks. Issues of privacy, control over one's work, flexibility, and transparency of management are difficult to address given the pressure to develop a highly competitive orientation toward work. Ramesh further observes: "It is widely internalized among the call centre agents that salary is a personal matter, which should not be shared with peers in the workplace. The firms in their code of conduct highlight that *discussing salary and related matters with fellow-workers would invite warning and disciplinary action.*"[34] Worker's rights, unionization, pay equity, and checks and balances to handle capricious management behavior and policies become increasingly difficult to observe or institute. The inflexible, closely surveilled work environment and interaction reflects the kind of cultural policing discussed earlier—the inculcation of cultural knowledge about others; the intellectual purging of any perspective counter to what is being inculcated; and the altering of names and performing of new identities simply for the benefit of customers and company interests.

ENTANGLEMENT AND APPROPRIATION

However, viewing call centers as just another form of global economic domination where profits, goods, and services flow along predictable channels from East to West presents a partial picture of the impact of this IT sector on Indian society. Countering such a view by positing and examining hybridization as central to IT globalization would be equally reductive. Globalization cannot be reduced to a fundamental dialectic between homogenization and fragmentation, uniformity and diversity, or foreign and native, because the texture of daily human activity resists such a dialectic or compartmentalization. Vasavi underscores this point well, noting that such a transnational economy embodies "multiple logics . . . of entanglement and appropriation" in which, even as IT businesses closely police the acquisition and use of cultural knowledge and identity, the youth actively appropriate certain benefits from this economy and engage in subtle subversions of surveillance procedures in the workplace.[35] Donald Winiecki refers to such acts of subversion in call centers as "shadowboxing with data," an activity in which "contained secondary adjustments are made" that do not necessarily undermine systems of monitoring and performance, but that manipulate them for personal benefit or to serve other interests.[36]

For instance, the high rates of turnover at call centers, which are commonly acknowledged, have a lot to do with the marketing and operational practices of these businesses.[37] Companies market call center employment as providing a space in which young people can, while earning significantly more than in other employment sectors for similar skills, have fun, mingle with future-oriented startups, and be part of a new economy that is taking India into the twenty-first century. This latter point is almost redundant, given the government's conspicuous and massive investments in this sector, of which potential employees are very well aware. But the very things that seem the most promising aspects of call centers—easy employability, high salaries, the glamour of working in multinational business offices— also encourages workers to become more mobile and less attached to a specific company, which results in high rates of turnover. Other factors— such as the stress of working long night shifts, altering sleep patterns, acquiring professional personae, and familial and societal opposition—help drive the turnover.[38] Rather than assuming the existence of a global plan to subjugate employees at call centers and turn them into Western subjects, or viewing these workers as lacking any kind of agency or desire and thus mindlessly succumbing to the power of hybrid, global consumer cultures, Mathangi Krishnamurthy points out that it would be more helpful to examine them as "agentive moments" that are "staccato bursts of reconfiguration and reorientation—mechanisms of habit-change or adjustment that often have very little to do with the public discourse of benefit and obstacle, acquiescence and rebellion."[39] Proceeding from an analysis of the complexly intertwined layers of social and cultural impact, and the different ways in which people position themselves and are positioned by the structures they inhabit, yields a richer picture of the variegated processes in which all kinds of compromises and resistances come into play at work, at home, and in the larger social arena.

Another example that demonstrates the "multiple logics of entanglement and appropriation" is the attempt to consciously manipulate the acquired cultural persona to deflect workplace criticism and stress. In many instances, the inculcation of Western or client culture in CCRs is incomplete and only partially realized. Whatever the intention of the teachers or coaches, the cultural learning that call centers afford and often require are viewed less as necessitating a wholesale transformation of subjectivity and more as a game in which cultural identities can be performed. Such a view tends to treat immersion in client cultures as a mode of professionalization, something that comes with the job and as such can be let go of, just as one can choose to stop working at call centers. The adoption of different personae also helps CCRs deflect abusive or cantankerous calls, rants, innuendos, threats, and groundless complaints by viewing them as directed not at themselves but at the created persona who interacts with callers. This distancing from a personal, more intimate sense of self from the customized, work-required identity enables CCRs to develop strategies for coping with job stress, while solidifying the notion that work identity is more a matter of professional demeanor, style, or a work-related requirement than a clear assault on or perversion of one's social and cultural tradition or sense of self: "it is their professional identity that is traumatized while their personal identity still remains intact."[40] The emerging use of such skills in manipulating cultural identity should be seen in the context of high turnover rates in call centers owing to the significant level of stress created by adjustment challenges to night employment and to the tension generated in a performance-oriented work culture.

In a country where other economic sectors find it difficult to compete with the IT sector, national and state governments are actively implementing new policies and funding infrastructure to woo foreign companies and businesses to set up operations in India. The social and cultural impact of call centers in certain segments of Indian society presents a complicated picture in which women's insertion into the new IT industry via call centers leads to both familial economic betterment and a kind of individual agency through financial independence or earning—and, in some instances, to a greater subjection to established social strictures on female behavior that also overlap with the regimentation of work behavior in call centers. Jaya Pradhan and Vinoj Abraham point out that "in India's patriarchal society, the emergence of call centers is nothing less than a social reform movement as far as economic, social and cultural empowerment is concerned."[41] The emphasis on education to improve one's chances as a bride in the marriage marketplace and the pressure on women to view marriage as a form of maturity, at the expense of pursuing other interests or professional careers, are offset by the salaries that female call center employees bring to their families. Call centers are appealing to families and women as a means of earning a second income, or even single income. Compared to opportunities in other economic sectors, call center employment is appealing, especially to young, unmarried women because, as Preeti Singh and Anu Pandey point out, "there appears to be no other area of employment in India which gives its employees an attractive pay package *at such a young age and with minimum qualifications.*"[42] Jobs such as teaching, nursing, and office administration were traditionally viewed as favorable occupations for women, and call center work is nontraditional employment whose pay scales compare favorably with those of traditional jobs. Singh and Pandey further note: "Call centers are one of the most sought after workplaces for young graduates and undergraduates as it provides them with a good environment to work in, decent emoluments and financial incentives, transportation both during day and night, and meals and refreshments. No other job allows the entry of employees with minimum education (school pass) at such attractive perks."[43]

Vasavi also notes that "for a large pool of graduates with basic degrees, who lack opportunities to be integrated into professional or higher education programmes or to be absorbed into regular and established employment, ITES [Information Technology Enhanced Services] flags their employability."[44] To women from low-income families that cannot support their pursuit of higher education, and to women interested in supplementing their spouses' incomes, call centers represent promising opportunities. The fact that most families now accommodate women working in call centers stands in sharp contrast to the high level of reluctance in the period before the sharp growth of the IT industry, because it was "taboo for girls to travel alone out of the house after dark."[45] Given the largely negative view of women working late nights or primarily in the nights, call center employment for women comes with the risk of being "sexually stigmatized."[46] A common tendency is to view night employment as creating opportunities for high earnings but with the accompanying risk of an increase in female assertiveness in domestic affairs, and as creating situations requiring that women interact frequently with male co-workers, which could also induce them to relax moral inhibitions or at least make them more vulnerable to male advances. Night work for women also signals the inability of families or spouses to fully monitor female behavior outside of the home, and, not surprisingly, female employees at call centers have to reckon with greater pressure to adjust to prevailing social mores, as their entry into these jobs generates social anxieties. For instance, in Hyderabad, an important technopolis, the city's major English newspaper, the *Deccan Chronicle*, reported in early 2006 that several taxi businesses petitioned the police and call center managers to mandate a dress code for their women workers.[47] The reasons for the petition included the ostensibly provocative nature of women's clothing, and their naiveté in seeking to work at night, which could be easily misconstrued as a sign of lax sexual morals. In response to such petitions, many call centers have started providing taxi service to pick up and drop off their female employees. But such arrangements also tend to reduce the amount of control that women may have over their working lives, since from the time of their departure from the house till their return, they are liable to be scrutinized for their interaction with other people, including fellow CCRs, and to have their behavior and sartorial styles monitored in order to ensure compliance with prescribed modes of female behavior.

Women's position in the IT labor market is fraught with sociocultural and economic contradictions. Although call center jobs certainly enable them to complement men's income in their families, they continue to face significant social pressure to conform to codes of behavior whose transgression would invite familial opprobrium and unwanted amorous interest in public spaces. The idea that their new role as wage earners is a clear indication of an increase in social status, which would eventually lead to greater female empowerment, financially and socially, cannot account for such fundamental contradictions in the gendered and classed nexus of IT globalization. However, the argument about the biopolitical dimension of the transnationalization of affective labor and its careful management of American culture is not rendered moot. To the contrary, what we have here is a "complex hieroglyphic" of a "hybrid contemporaniety,"[48] whose social and cultural morphologies are shaped by the disjoined dynamics of global cultural flows, which create what Appadurai calls a "globally variable synaesthesia" from which emerge dislocations of effects, mismanagement of desire, manipulations of identities, and appropriations to suit local or personal needs.[49]

In conclusion, to grapple with the complex changes engendered by globalization, it is both urgent and necessary to examine the role of culture in international contexts. As this analysis of call centers demonstrates, culture is hardly the icing on the cake of business work, or something people engage in after doing their work or after gaining financial security, or once the organizational structures for businesses are set up. Also, it would be a mistake to view culture as the aesthetic dimension of economic activity, one that has a dependent, subordinate relationship to labor and business. On the contrary, the notion of the other and the idea of cultural difference and how this difference can be examined and understood to enhance work management and productivity have become increasingly central to business practices, especially as their operations are stretched and mediated electronically across barriers of time and space, and across borders of nation and ethnicity. In a transnational economy, a noteworthy aspect of global cultural flows is their ability to engender large-scale social transformations, and call center cultures are only one important manifestation of the biopolitical dimension of such changes.

One promising way in which we can both examine and counter the psychosocial effects of such IT globalization is to draw models, concepts, and ideas from the humanities. They can not only enable us to study the new information economy in larger sociocultural contexts, but they can also help us develop a humanistic orientation toward global conditions and processes so that the question of human dignity, the labor of human activity, and the work of the human imagination can avoid becoming "cultural manicure," in Bill Readings' words, for those practices of globalization that are organized primarily around principles of profit and values of customer satisfaction generated by market needs and desires.[50] Although the biopolitics of transnational cultural flows continue to be central to the operations of the call center sector, the crucial point is that they cannot be viewed simplistically as a new dispensation of empire that serves the interests of powerful countries and corporations. Rather, their influence, economic viability, social utility, and cultural caché are transvalued by various players who have some stake in the new global economy.

＝{ NOTES }＝

INTRODUCTION

1. Immerman, *Empire for Liberty*, 12.
2. Johnson, *Blowback*, 4.
3. U.S. Department of Defense, *Base Structure Report.* According to the Stockholm International Peace Research Institute's *Background Paper on SIPRI Military Expenditure Data, 2010*, in 2010 Europe spent $382 billion (of which Western Europe spent $268 billion, Eastern Europe $65.5 billion, and Central and South Eastern Europe $48.3 billion); Central America and the Caribbean spent $6.5 billion; South America spent $63.3 billion; Africa spent $30.1 billion, Asia and Oceania spent $317 billion (China spent $119 billion); the Middle East spent $111 billion; Canada spent $22.8 billion; and the United States spent $698 billion. The dramatic difference between the expenditures of the United States and the other countries and regions (the rest of the world spent $932 billion) points to America's commitment to maintaining a global military network.
4. Johnson, *Blowback*, 5.
5. Johnson, *Dismantling the Empire*, 14.
6. Johnson, *Blowback*, 12.
7. Jefferson, *The Papers of Thomas Jefferson*, 237.
8. Ibid., 238.
9. Immerman, *Empire for Liberty*, 5.
10. Jefferson, *Republic of Letters*, 1586.
11. Immerman, *Empire for Liberty*, 15.
12. Bogues, *Empire of Liberty*, 11–12.
13. Pease, *National Identities and Post-Americanist Narratives*, 4.

1. EMPIRE AND DISSENT

1. Limón, "Translating Empire," 31. Limón seeks to "translate empire" by rethinking empire as a space of overlaps and disjunctions. See Mark Bauerlein's *Literary Criticism* for an incisive critique of the excessive zeal to make the study of literary and culture relevant to other worldly concerns. His point is not that such studies should not be conducted, but that very often both the way in which they are conceptualized and the way in which an array of

methodologies and categories are deployed without a sustained examination of their appropriateness for the task at hand pointlessly support particular political and ideological orientations. Slippery terms, loosely defined concepts, inadequate understanding of how terms are used in other disciplines, the subordination of exegetical labor by the zeal to develop predetermined lines of argument that deliberately discount contradictory tensions—these are some of the problems Bauerlein addresses.

2. A. Kaplan, "Violent Belongings and the Question of Empire Today," 8.
3. Ibid., 9.
4. Ibid., 10.
5. Giles, "Response to the Presidential Address to the American Studies Association," 20.
6. Limón, "Translating Empire," 30.
7. Ibid., 31 (emphasis added).
8. May, "Echoes of the Cold War," 38.
9. Ibid., 39–40.
10. Young, "Ground Zero," 14.
11. Ibid., 16–17 (emphasis added).
12. Butler, "Explanation and Exoneration, or What We Can Hear," 182.
13. Bérubé, *The Left at War*, 43.
14. Ibid., 7, 12, 39.
15. Jay, "White Out," 781.
16. Bauerlein, *Literary Criticism*, 36.
17. Benhabib, *The Claims of Culture*, 95–100. In 1989 three girls in France were expelled from school for wearing headscarves; this issue sparked off a national debate about secularism, multiculturalism, and religion that lasted well into the mid-1990s, with the French Supreme Court weighing in with a ruling that school authorities could make decisions they considered reasonable (95–98). See also "French Government Approves Curfew Powers."
18. Jay, "White Out," 784.
19. Ibid.
20. Ibid., 782–84 (emphasis added).
21. Cushman, "The Reflexivity of Evil," 84.
22. Geddes, Introduction, 3.
23. Gaddis, "And Now This," 5 (emphasis added).
24. Power, *"A Problem From Hell,"* xiii (emphasis added).
25. Ibid., xvii.
26. Quoted in Jacquard, *In the Name of Osama Bin Laden*, 259–61.
27. Kadir, "Defending America against Its Devotees."
28. Ibid., 142.
29. La Foy, *The Chaco Dispute and the League of Nations*, 1, 134.
30. Garner, *The Chaco Dispute*, 26.
31. del Vayo, "The Chaco War," 150.
32. La Foy, *The Chaco Dispute and the League of Nations*, 9–11. See also Farcau, *The Chaco War*, 7.
33. Garner, *The Chaco Dispute*, 33.
34. Rout, *Politics of the Chaco Peace Conference*, 16–17.

35. Ibid., 45, 67.
36. McCormack, "A Historical Case for the Globalization of International Law," 294.
37. Del Vayo, "The Chaco War," 159.
38. Ibid., 157.
39. Garner, *The Chaco Dispute*, 25.
40. Ibid., 25–26.
41. Zook, *The Conduct of the Chaco War*, 62.
42. Farcau, *The Chaco War*, 87–88; Zook, *The Conduct of the Chaco War*, 126, 149.
43. Farcau, *The Chaco War*, 46, 12.
44. Roy, "The Algebra of Infinite Justice," in *Power Politics*, 122 (emphasis added).
45. Ibid., 120.
46. M. Mann, *Incoherent Empire*, 9.
47. Ross and Ross, introduction, 1.
48. Ibid., 2.
49. Ibid., 1.
50. Ibid., 4 (emphasis added).
51. Ibid., 10.
52. Harvey, *The New Imperialism*, 26.
53. Even Harvey succumbs to the temptation to indulge in momentary displays of conspiratorial thinking when he notes that U.S. interests in Iraq are driven by those "as numerous as the Christian fundamentalists who now wield such a sinister influence in government" (ibid., 211). How to distinguish such a conspiracy theory from those that posit a Jewish conspiracy, which is especially popular among certain sections of the hard Left and orthodox Islamic communities, is an issue Harvey should have addressed, but he does not because doing so would lead him deeper into the labyrinthine world of dizzying conspiracies that leave little room for historical analysis.
54. Ibid., viii, 29.
55. Todd, *After the Empire*, 13.
56. Ibid., 193.
57. Ibid., 35.
58. Ibid., 45.
59. Fukuyama, "A Reply to My Critics," 22.
60. Todd, *After the Empire*, 51.
61. Fukuyama, "The End of History," 4.
62. Todd, *After the Empire*, 44 (emphasis added).
63. Ibid., 39.
64. Ibid., 176 (emphasis added).
65. Ibid., 3.
66. Giddens, *The Consequences of Modernity*.
67. Ibid., 14.
68. Ibid., 21.
69. Ibid., 27, 38.
70. Ibid., 21 (emphasis added).

71. Power, *"A Problem From Hell,"* 247, 334.
72. Ibid., xx–xxi.
73. Lévy, *War, Evil, and the End of History*, 356.
74. Power, *"A Problem From Hell,"* 121.
75. Ibid., xx.
76. Ibid. 512.
77. Ibid. xxi.
78. Kadir, "America and Its Studies," 16.
79. R. Kaplan, "America and the Tragic Limits of Imperialism," 56.
80. Power, *"A Problem From Hell,"* 504 (emphasis added).
81. Hardt and Negri, *Empire*, 18.
82. Djelal Kadir, "Defending America against Its Devotees," 136.
83. Ibid., 138, 150.
84. A. Kaplan, "The Tenacious Grasp of American Exceptionalism," 156.
85. Dawson and Schueller, "Introduction," 21.
86. O'Hara, *Empire Burlesque*, 12 (emphasis added).
87. Ferguson, "Clashing Civilizations or Mad Mullahs," 120.
88. A. Kaplan, "Violent Belongings and the Question of Empire Today," 10.
89. Ibid., 7.
90. Ibid., 10.

2. DWELLING IN AMERICAN

1. Fernández-Armesto, *The Americas*, 1, 4.
2. Kroes, "Imaginary Americas in Europe's Public Space," 299.
3. Ceaser, *Reconstructing America*, 2, 17.
4. Ibid., 17.
5. Ibid., 19.
6. Robin, "The Exhaustion of Enclosures," 370.
7. Ibid., 371.
8. Ceaser, *Reconstructing America*, 245 (emphasis added).
9. Ibid., 5.
10. Gould, "Entangled Histories, Entangled World," 780.
11. Ibid., 768.
12. Ibid., 766. In offering this explanation, Gould draws on the work of Jürgen Kock, Michael Wener and Bénédictine Zimmerman, and Deborah Cohen and Maura O'Connor.
13. Bright and Geyer, "Where in the World Is America?," 72.
14. Giles, *Virtual Americas*, 2.
15. Giles, *Atlantic Republic*, 50.
16. Ibid., 49–60.
17. Ibid., 50 (emphasis added).
18. Ibid., 112.
19. Kroes, "Imaginary Americas in Europe's Public Space," 17.
20. Ibid., 13, 15.
21. Ibid., 10–11.
22. Ibid., 16.

23. Revel, *Anti-Americanism*, 25.
24. Hollander, "Introduction," 6–7.
25. Ibid., 7.
26. Ibid.
27. Ibid., 9.
28. Ibid., 12.
29. Guerlain, "A Tale of Two Anti-Americanisms," 3.
30. Ibid., 3, 14, 16.
31. Ibid., 16, 11.
32. Bender, *A Nation Among Nations*, 61.
33. Shaw, "The Political Structure of a Global World" 25.
34. Ibid.
35. Ibid.
36. Ibid., 26.
37. Hardt and Negri, *Empire*, xii–xiii.
38. Ibid., xiv-xv.
39. Hardt and Negri, *Multitude*, xiv.
40. Ibid., xv.
41. Ibid., 100.
42. Hardt and Negri, *Commonwealth*, 110.
43. For criticisms of Hardt and Negri's construction of a grand narrative of power, resistance, and empire, see Balakrishnan, *Debating Empire* in general, and in particular Arrighi, "Lineages of Empire"; E. Wood, "A Manifesto for Global Capitalism?"; Brennan, "The Italian Ideology"; Callinicos, "Toni Negri in Perspective."
44. Hardt and Negri, *Multitude*, 109.
45. Hira and Hira, *Outsourcing America*, 151–56; Sheshabalaya, *Rising Elephant*, 103–6.
46. Murthy, "Making India a Significant IT Player in This Millennium," 224.
47. C. Mann, *Accelerating the Globalization of America*, 53.
48. Hira and Hira, *Outsourcing America*, 2, 47.
49. Pradhan and Abraham, "Social and Cultural Impact of Outsourcing."
50. Davies, *What's This India Business?*, 45.
51. R. Chengappa and M. Goyal, "Housekeepers to the World," *India Today*, November 18, 2002.
52. Naeem Mohaiemen, "India: The Dark Side of the Outsourcing Revolution," *CorpWatch*, January 25, 2004 (http://www.corpwatch.org/article.php?id=10048).
53. Foucault, "Right of Death and Power over Life," 266 (emphasis added).
54. Hardt and Negri, *Empire*, 23.
55. Vasavi, "'Serviced from India,'" 11.
56. McMillin, "Outsourcing Identities: Call Centers and Cultural Transformation in India," 235.
57. J. Ferguson and Gupta, "Spatializing States," 994.
58. Gitlin, *The Intellectuals and the Flag*, 129–40.
59. Ibid., 144.
60. Ibid., 143.

61. Ibid., 140.
62. Ibid., 139.
63. Ibid., 140.
64. Wolfe, "Anti-American Studies," 26.
65. L. Marx, "On Recovering the 'Ur' Theory of American Studies."
66. Lipsitz, "Our America." 139.
67. L. Marx, "On Recovering the 'Ur' Theory of American Studies," 126–28. Ian Tyrrell makes a good point when he says that "exceptionalism has varied in its impact over time and that it operates within the confines of political and legal institutions that shape the practice of American interactions with global systems" ("American Exceptionalism and Uneven Global Integration," 64). These "interactions with global systems" is just what dwelling in American seeks to examine in its critique of American empire. For example, the Pledge of Allegiance—written in 1882 by Francis Bellamy, a Baptist minister, to mark the Columbian quincentennial—was modified to say "the flag of the United States of America" rather than "my flag," and, in 1954, to add "under God." "America the Beautiful" was written by Katharine Lee Bates in 1893. The Arlington National Cemetery Memorial gained increasing significance as a national symbol after 1910, and the Tomb of the Unknown Soldier was dedicated in 1920 as another site for national rituals. In the nineteenth and early twentieth centuries, the large-scale migration of Catholics, Jews, and other groups to the United States could be accommodated through the use of such patriotic and nationalistic rituals and images. Given the vast abundance of natural resources on the frontier—whose closing in 1890 the historian Frederick Jackson Turner registered as a momentous event in American history—the United States could maintain independence as a nation by sustaining its economic self-sufficiency and thus achieve freedom from a debilitating dependence on other states. But by the end of the twentieth century, the explosive growth of the United States as an industrial and global power also led to an increase in dependence on other countries—close to half of the oil used in the United States in the 1990s was imported (Tyrrell, "American Exceptionalism and Uneven Global Integration," 65–75). This is why critiquing American exceptionalism only in its ideological manifestation—without examining its imbrication at varying moments in time in the material realities of population growth, use of recourses, industrialization, and so forth—leads to ahistorical analyses in which "culture" is just another word for "politics." To argue that culture and politics are interrelated is fundamentally different from assuming that the critique of culture is the same as, or will have the same effect as, critiquing the political. Undoubtedly, American exceptionalism has played and continues to play a powerful role in shaping how Americans view their country and how the United States as a nation-state interacts with the world, but critiquing it in the cultural and literary realms while making claims for the political valences of such critiques ends up conflating culture and politics.
68. A. Kaplan, "A Call for a Truce," 145.
69. Wolfe, Return to Greatness, 6.
70. L. Marx, "On Recovering the 'Ur' Theory of American Studies," 130.

71. Lipsitz, "Our America," 135.
72. A. Kaplan, "A Call for a Truce," 146.
73. Huntington, *Who Are We?*, xvii.
74. Renan, "What Is a Nation?," 19 (emphasis added).
75. Ibid., 11.
76. Limón, "Translating Empire," 31 (emphasis added).
77. The rise of cultural critique in the humanities, generally, over the last few decades is not without its problems. Gitlin points out that "in the prevailing schools of cultural studies, to study culture is not so much to grasp cultural processes but to choose sides or, more subtly, to determine whether a particular cultural process belongs on the side of society's ideological angels" (*The Intellectuals and the Flag*, 96). The focus on culture's relation to the world at large has led to easy conflations of culture as politics, rather than to a systematic explanation of how cultural processes work, and their interactions with other social processes in specific contexts of time and location. For a critique of cultural radicalism, see Fluck "Literature, Liberalism, and the Current Cultural Radicalism."

3. DISSENT ON THE BORDER

1. The terms "tribal" and "indigenous" are not necessarily synonyms in India. Referring to the *adivasis*—tribal people—as indigenous suggests that non-*adivasis* are not indigenous to India and are foreigners who conquered the Indian subcontinent, which is hardly the case. Rather, "tribal" refers to people outside dominant social structures, urban sites of power, or industrialized modernity, who have a tightly knit group identity. See Patel, "Resettlement Politics and Tribal Interests," 68.
2. JanMohamed, "Wordliness-without-World, Homelessness-as-Home," 101.
3. Ibid., 102. JanMohamed cites intellectuals like Edward Said, who are neither exiles nor immigrants, or are both, as practicing a "willed homelessness" (99) that affords Said, for example a "specular role" in which "he is able to provide in his writing a set of mirrors allowing Western culture to see their own structures and functions" (105). Said refers to "the ascetic code of willed homelessness" in his discussion of Eric Auerbach's "Philologie der Weltliteratur," which cites Hugo of St. Victor's *Didascalicon* in order to, says Said, "stress the salutary value of separation from home" ("Introduction," 7). Roy envisions herself and her role as a writer and intellectual along similar lines: "If protesting against having a nuclear bomb implanted in my brain is anti-Hindu and antinational, then I secede. I hereby declare myself an independent, mobile republic. I am a citizen of the earth. I own no territory. I have no flag. I'm female, but have nothing against eunuchs. My policies are simple. I'm willing to sign any nuclear proliferation treaty or nuclear test-ban treaty that's going. Immigrants are welcome. You can help me design our flag" ("The End of Imagination," in *The Cost of Living*, 109).
4. JanMohamed, "Wordliness-without-World, Homelessness-as-Home," 102.
5. Bose, "Critics and Experts, Activists and Academics," 136.
6. Ibid., 135–36.

7. Gramsci, *Selections from the Prison Notebooks of Antonio Gramsci*, 7.
8. Roy, "The Ladies Have Feelings, So . . . Shall We Leave It to the Experts?" in *Power Politics*, 11. Aware of her celebrity status and the media's emphasis on her good looks, Roy deliberately undermines her attractiveness by cropping her hair and wearing dresses that make her seem unglamorous. She also publicly rejected the 2005 Sahitya Academy Award, which the Indian government gave her in recognition of her work. Such examples show that Roy is not only aware of the risks of co-optation, but that she deliberately distances herself from media constructions of celebrities and personalities. These are attempts to avoid the cult of personality in order to bestow social legitimacy to her dissent, and make her dissent valuable as performing a civic function in the public commons of democracy (B. Ghosh, "Tallying Bodies," 127–9).
9. Said, *Representations of the Intellectual*, 83.
10. Ibid. 36.
11. Ibid., 33.
12. Roy, "The Greater Common Good," in *The Cost of Living*, 14.
13. Ibid., 44–46.
14. Roy, "On Citizens' Rights to Express Dissent," in *Power Politics*, 98.
15. Roy, "On Citizens' Rights to Express Dissent," in *Power Politics*, 87.
16. Roy, "The Ladies Have Feelings," in *Power Politics*, 24.
17. Mullaney, "'Globalizing Dissent'?," 114. How this squares with Roy's insistence on alternatives to capitalism and communism is hardly clear: "The alternative, if there is one, will emerge from the places and the people who have resisted the hegemonic impulse of capitalism and imperialism instead of being co-opted by it"; "The day capitalism is forced to tolerate non-capitalist societies in its midst and to acknowledge limits in its quest for domination, the day it is forced to recognize that its supply of raw material will not be endless, is the day when change will come"; and "The first step towards reimagining a world gone terribly wrong would be to stop the annihilation of those who have a different imagination—an imagination that is outside of capitalism as well as Communism" (*Broken Republic*, 212–14). Arguing against domination and the nondemocratic, environmentally destructive acquisition of raw materials is reasonable, but it is unclear if this is a clear alternative to capitalism in the sense in which Roy envisions the future. Is it a mix of capitalism and communism? Or socialism, or any other ism? What forms will it take, what new institutions need to be created, what cultures have to change or be invented, and at what social, economic, and political cost? These are extremely difficult issues that require major policy changes, laws, and cultural reorientations. Apart from their often legitimate criticisms of the government and the middle class—including of course, the prime instigator and mover of all things problematic in the world, America—these essays, unfortunately, do not to even attempt to explore the new vistas and possibilities that such dissent opens up.
18. Roy, "The Reincarnation of Rumpelstiltskin," in *Power Politics*, 36.
19. Todd Gitlin, "Myopia in the Name of the Weak," Outlookindia.com, October 17, 2001 (http://www.outlookindia.com/article.aspx?213455).

20. Roy, "The Greater Common Good," in *The Cost of Living*, 21.
21. Barsamian, *The Checkbook and the Cruise Missile*, 38.
22. Omvedt, "An Open Letter to Arundhati Roy."
23. Freire, *Pedagogy of the Oppressed*, 66–67 (emphasis added).
24. Roy, "The Loneliness of Noam Chomsky," in *War Talk*, 99.
25. Mullaney, "'Globalizing Dissent'?," 120.
26. Baneth-Nouailhetas, "Committed Writing, Committed Writer?," 96, 101.
27. Ibid., 93.
28. Roy, *War Talk* (C-SPAN video).
29. Siriyavan Anand, "'Holy' Cow and 'Unholy' Dalit," Outlookindia.com, November 6, 2002 (http://www.outlookindia.com/article.aspx?217815); Nonica Datta, "Politics of Cow Protection," *Hindu Online*, November 18, 2002 (http://www.hinduonnet.com/2002/11/18/stories/2002111800461000.htm).
30. Official and unofficial figures vary between 1,000 and more than 2,000 dead. See Sanghatana and the Committee for the Protection of Democratic Rights, "The Bombay Riots"; BBC News, "Gujarat Riot Death Toll Revealed"; Human Rights Watch, "India"; Coalition against Genocide, "Genocide in Gujarat"; Nussbaum, "Body of the Nation."
31. Arundhati Roy, "Ahimsa," *ZNet*, June 12, 2002 (http://www.zcommunications.org/ahimsa-by-arundhati-roy).
32. Roy, "The Reincarnation of Rumplestiltskin," in *Power Politics*, 37.
33. Roy, "The Ladies Have Feelings," in *Power Politics*, 2.
34. Roy, "The Reincarnation of Rumplestiltskin," in *Power Politics*, 83.
35. Roy, "Democracy: Who's She When She's at Home," in *Field Notes on Democracy*, 42–43.
36. Roy, "Peace Is War," in *An Ordinary Person's Guide to Empire*, 13.
37. Ibid., 7.
38. Ibid., 9.
39. Ibid., 7.
40. Roy, "The Ordinary Person's Guide To Empire," in *An Ordinary Person's Guide to Empire*, 38.
41. Roy, "The Algebra of Infinite Justice," in *Power Politics*, 122–23.
42. Roy, "Baby Bush, Go Home," in *Field Notes on Democracy*, 119.
43. Barsamian, *The Checkbook and the Cruise Missile*, 90–91.
44. Ibid., 93.
45. Buruma, "The Anti-American."
46. Roy, "The Ordinary Person's Guide to Empire," in *An Ordinary Person's Guide to Empire*, 37–38 (emphasis added).
47. J. Wood, *The Politics of Water Resource Development in India*, 20, 58.
48. Ibid., 113.
49. Ibid., 115.
50. Dwivedi, "Displacement, Risks, and Resistance," 48.
51. World Commission on Dams, "Dams and Development."
52. J. Wood, *The Politics of Water Resource Development in India*, 133–37, 141–43.
53. Leslie, *Deep Water*, 46.

54. J. Wood, *The Politics of Water Resource Development in India*, 176–77.
55. Ibid., 43–51.
56. Ibid., 165.
57. Ibid., 149–52, 162.
58. Iyer, *Towards Water Wisdom*, 120–22.
59. Roy, "The Reincarnation of Rumplestiltskin," in *Power Politics*, 70.
60. Iyer, *Towards Water Wisdom*, 130.
61. Khagram, *Dams and Development*, 5.
62. J. Wood, *The Politics of Water Resource Development in India*, 142.
63. Ibid., 197–202. Since most of these methods require constant maintenance not only by individuals but by communities, both large and small, creating communal responsibility and sustaining it over time is a major challenge. The proliferation of NGOs has also made the poor, *adivasis*, and farmers dependent on them, and it will take considerable time to make them more independent. Wood points out that although alternate solutions to dams are conceivable and practicable, they might not easily translate into social reality (203–4).
64. "Chomsky and Other Intellectuals on Nandigram," *Hindu Online*, November 22, 2007 (http://www.thehindu.com/2007/11/22/stories/2007112255861300.htm) (emphasis added).
65. Nussbaum, "Violence on the Left: Nandigram and the Communists of West Bengal."
66. "A CPI (M) Public Relations Coup," Outlookindia.com, November 25, 2007 (http://www.outlookindia.com/article.aspx?236082).
67. Ibid.
68. George, "Susan George Withdraws Her Signature From Statement," Sanhati.com, November 27, 2007 (http://sanhati.com/news/526). Another signatory, Vijay Prashad, explains his position well in his article "Fat Cats and the Left Rupture" (Pragoti.org, January 1, 2008, [http://www.pragoti.org/hi/node/475]), as he backtracks on the open letter's point that there is no basis for division: "But perhaps the basis for division is more foundational than we had assumed. The rupture, the casus, is so deep that it is impossible to lay out the facts without challenge." In this insightful piece, Prashad goes on to identify the role of the state, capitalism, and progress in forming the "structural gulf within the Indian left": the state is viewed as a necessary but imperfect apparatus by some, while others take a postnational and poststate position, arguing for a clear alternative to capitalism; still others rely too much on cultural politics and ignore material realities, an effect of the nexus of poststructuralism and postcolonialism; and critics of the state, whose opposition to it is valid, nonetheless fail to offer clear policies for development as if opposition were an end in itself. Also see the point-by-point rebuttal by Kunal Chattopadhyay to Tariq Ali, another signer, in "An Open Letter to Tariq Ali," Sanhati.com, November 21, 2007 (http://sanhati.com/news/522/#1).
69. "In Solidarity with Its [CPI(M)'s] Left Critics," Outlookindia.com, December 4, 2007 (http://www.outlookindia.com/article.aspx?236181).
70. Bhabha, *The Location of Culture*, 42.

71. Roy, "Walking with the Comrades," in *Broken Republic*, 123–24 (emphasis added).

72. Roy, "Azadi," in *Field Notes on Democracy*, 183.

73. Roy, "Whither Kashmir?"

74. Quoted in "Sedition versus Free Speech," *Hindu Online*, October 27, 2010 (http://www.hindu.com/2010/10/27/stories/2010102753601200.htm).

75. Roy, "Democracy's Failing Light," in *Field Notes on Democracy*, 2.

76. Ibid., 16.

77. Ibid., 11.

78. Roy, "Listening to Grasshoppers," in *Field Notes on Democracy*, 167.

79. Fanon, *The Wretched of the Earth*, 93.

80. Roy, "Listening to Grasshoppers," in *Field Notes on Democracy*, 68 (emphasis added).

81. Kumar, "The Un-Victim."

82. Roy, "Walking with the Comrades," in *Broken Republic*, 154.

83. Roy, "Listening to Grasshoppers," in *Field Notes on Democracy*, 61.

84. Roy, "Trickledown Revolution," in *Broken Republic*, 205.

85. Roy, "Walking with the Comrades," in *Broken Republic*, p. 94.

86. Ibid., 119–20.

87. Ibid., p. 121.

88. Arundhati Roy, "Arundhati Roy Replies," Outlookindia.com, June 7, 2010 (http://www.outlookindia.com/article.aspx?265619).

89. Ibid.

90. Ibid.

91. Roy, "Trickledown Revolution," in *Broken Republic*, 208.

92. Arundhati Roy, "Knocks on the Door: It's the Newspaper Boy," Outlookindia.com, June 21, 2010 (http://www.outlookindia.com/article.aspx?265790).

93. Jefferess, "The Limits of Dissent," 174.

94. Ghose, "Face the Nation with Arundhati Roy."

95. Ibid.

96. Arundhati Roy, "Absolutely Inexcusable," Outlookindia.com, May 19, 2010 (http://www.outlookindia.com/article.aspx?265483).

97. Mullaney, "'Globalizing Dissent'?," 119.

98. Ram, "Interview," 189.

99. Neera Chandhoke, "The Conceits of Representation," the *Hindu*, February 7, 2001 (http://www.hindu.com/2001/02/07/stories/05072523.htm).

100. R. Ghosh, "Epilogue," 184.

101. Jefferess, "The Limits of Dissent," 167.

102. Baneth-Nouailhetas, "Committed Writing, Committed Writer?," 100.

103. Ibid.

104. Limón, "Translating Empire," 31.

4. CULTURE, EMPIRE, AND REPRESENTATION

1. Dimock, "Literature for the Planet," 177.

2. Nafisi, *Reading Lolita in Tehran*, 6 (emphasis added).

3. Ibid., 42.

4. Fluck, "The Modernity of America and the Practice of Scholarship," 348
5. Fluck, "Literature, Liberalism, and the Current Cultural Radicalism," 215, 220.
6. Negar Mottahedeh, "Off the Grid: Reading Iranian Memoirs in Our Time of Total War," iranain.com, September 21, 2004 (http://www.iranian.com/Books/2004/September/Writers/).
7. Roksana Bahramitash, "The War on Terror, Feminist Orientalism and Orientalist Feminism," 222.
8. Ibid., 233.
9. The inner flap of the jacket of Shirin Ebadi's *Iran Awakening: A Memoir of Revolution and Hope* has a blurb written by Nafisi that contains this sentence: "One of the staunchest advocates for human rights in her country and beyond, Ms. Ebadi, herself a devout Muslim, represents hope for many in Muslim societies that *Islam and democracy are indeed compatible*" (emphasis added). This is not an endorsement that one presumed to be intent on demonizing Islam would make.
10. Nafisi, *Reading Lolita in Tehran*, 257.
11. Hamid Dabashi, "Native Informers and the Making of the American Empire."
12. Ebadi, *Iran Awakening*, 144–47.
13. Dabashi, "Native Informers and the Making of the American Empire."
14. Ibid.
15. Azar Nafisi, "Q & A," *Asia Society*, January 20, 2004 (http://asiasociety.org/arts-culture/literature/azar-nafisi-literature-celebration-and-refuge).
16. Dabashi, "Native Informers and the Making of the American Empire."
17. Foaad Khosmood, "Lolita and Beyond," ZNET, August 4, 2006 (http://www.zmag.org/content/showarticle.cfm?ItemID=10707).
18. Behdad, "Critical Historicism," 292.
19. Rowe, "Reading *Reading Lolita in Tehran* in Idaho," 254.
20. Ibid., 253–54.
21. Ibid., 255.
22. Ibid., 255–56.
23. Nafisi, "Q & A," *Asia Society*.
24. Azar Nafisi, "Interview with Robert Birnbaum," Identitytheory.com, February 5, 2004 (http://www.identitytheory.com/interviews/birnbaum139.php).
25. Rowe, "Reading *Reading Lolita in Tehran* in Idaho," 266.
26. Nafisi, *Reading Lolita in Tehran*, 1.
27. Ibid., 8 (emphasis added).
28. Ibid., 18 (emphasis added).
29. Ibid., 42.
30. Rowe, "Reading *Reading Lolita in Tehran* in Idaho," 262.
31. Bahramitash, "The War on Terror, Feminist Orientalism and Orientalist Feminism," 223.
32. Americanists—including the German Winfried Fluck, Russian Tatiana Venediktova, Indian Kousar Azam, and Turkish Gonul Pultar, to name a few—have long argued that American studies as conceptualized and practiced outside the United States ought to be examined less in terms of organic

links between U.S. American studies and international American studies and
more in terms of disjunctions, lag effects, reversals, and so on. Also see Muthyala, "'America' in Transit." The danger of treating all the isms that have dominated humanities scholarship in the United States as the golden standard by
which to evaluate how people in other countries read, teach, think, and write
about the arts and the humanities is compellingly explored in Afary and Anderson, *Foucault and the Iranian Revolution: Gender and the Seductions of
Islamism.* It is a sobering account of how a much admired and cited theorist
of power and knowledge in U.S. academia—Michel Foucault—succumbed to
the "seductions" of Islamism, despite the sophisticated nature of his ideas. It
is a history that has been suppressed, marginalized, or ignored by his readers,
and Afary and Anderson recover this subjugated knowledge about Foucault,
a knowledge that calls into question the assumed universal relevancy of contemporary theory.
33. Nafisi, "Q & A," *Asia Society.*
34. Nafisi, *Reading Lolita in Tehran,* 10.
35. Ibid., 19.
36. For this group of women readers, the connections among reading, abstrac-
    tion, and the cultivation of civil society become evident in their responses
    to books like *Lolita,* notes Simon Stow; he interprets the memoir to argue
    that Martha Nussbaum and Richard Rorty's emphasis on the role of litera-
    ture in liberal democracies tends to circumscribe interpretation by focusing
    on the text rather than the discussions about the text that are made by spe-
    cific individuals positioned differently in society ("Reading Our Way to De-
    mocracy?").
37. Rowe, "Reading *Reading Lolita in Tehran* in Idaho," 271.
38. Ibid., 263.
39. As Rowe points out, Berman does not focus on the aesthetic or cultural work
    that the text is doing in terms of legitimating an Anglo-American canon in
    the Great Books tradition. Berman's central argument, though, is less about
    literature and culture and more about how they foreground what to him are
    important shifts in the American Left—a critical rejection of specific ideolo-
    gies about power and revolution in favor of liberal individualism and imagi-
    nation. But this only makes Rowe's point more significant since it is clear that
    there is a certain sympathy and affection for this canon that is not easily ap-
    parent in the ruminations of writers outside of this canon about *Reading Lol-
    ita in Tehran.*
40. Rowe, "Reading *Reading Lolita in Tehran* in Idaho," 272.
41. Ibid.
42. Keshavarz, *Jasmine and Stars,* 3.
43. Ibid., 110.
44. Ibid., 73.
45. Ibid., 117 (emphasis added).
46. Nafisi, *Reading Lolita in Tehran,* 23.
47. Ibid., 74.
48. Ebadi, *Iran Awakening,* 103.
49. Keshavarz, *Jasmine and Stars,* 154.

50. Ibid.
51. Ibid., 136.
52. Ibid., 130.
53. Ibid., 129.
54. Ibid., 115.
55. Nafisi, *Reading Lolita in Tehran*, 206.
56. Keshavarz, *Jasmine and Stars*, 8.
57. *Jasmine and Stars* shows the significance of Persian culture in Iranian so-
    ciety as a counterpoint to *Reading Lolita in Tehran*'s focus on Western lit-
    erature. But Keshavarz spends so much time in the book trying to persuade
    the reader that her memoir is an alternative to Nafisi's text that the terms
    and range of its narrative exploration become dependent on the very book
    it is critiquing. There are memorable scenes in *Jasmine and Stars*: Keshavarz
    visits Iran to see her mother, who is recovering from a stroke. She reads po-
    etry by Sa'di to her mother, who—despite having difficulty speaking after her
    stroke—responds by affirming Sa'di's unique gifts as a poet. At the end of the
    book, Keshavarz reminisces about her father, his passion for poetry, and an
    incident involving the rescue of two kittens from a dry well. Discussions of a
    verse from the poet Hafez between father and daughter are interwoven into
    the activity of rescuing kittens in such a way that the poetry becomes part
    of the very fabric of everyday life. Several such moments in the text are un-
    fortunately punctuated by sections of literary criticism of Nafisi and *Read-
    ing Lolita in Tehran*. Had Keshavarz kept her focus on scenes and memories
    like these and allowed herself more freedom to go beyond a narrow focus on
    Nafisi and *Reading Lolita in Tehran*, given Keshavarz's deft writing and ex-
    tensive knowledge of Persian culture, *Jasmine and Stars* would have worked
    more persuasively as a counternarrative to what she perceives to be the New
    Orientalism. Similar criticisms of Nafisi, but without such a dismissive tone,
    are made by Amy DePaul in "Re-Reading *Reading Lolita in Tehran*." In "Why
    Americans Love Azar Nafisi's *Reading Lolita in Tehran*," Anne Donadey and
    Huma Ahmed-Ghosh offer a balanced view of the memoir's appeal to Ameri-
    can readers as they argue that Nafisi is reluctant to criticize U.S. foreign poli-
    cies that have affected Iran over the last half-century, and that she does not
    explore in detail the legacy of the shah's regime and the nexus of social class,
    religion, and modernity that brought about the revolution, or the manner in
    which it established its power and the many struggles against it launched by
    women from secular, religious, and working or poor classes. Although taking
    note of the many stringent criticisms of the memoir, Maurizio Ascari tem-
    pers them by emphasizing that the work is an "ambivalent text" that tends to
    lapse into moments of uncritical nostalgia but that also offers insightful anal-
    yses of a totalitarian regime's ability to control the bodies and imaginations
    of women, even as it dramatizes the power of literature and practices of read-
    ing to create alternate worlds to counter the regime and subvert its authority
    (*Literature of the Global Age*, 139).
58. Nafisi, *Things I've Been Silent About*, 240.
59. Ebadi, *Iran Awakening*, 210.

60. Association of American University Presses, "Nobel Peace Prize Winner Joins Battle against Treasury Department for Free Speech."

61. Ebadi, *Iran Awakening*, 51.

62. Ibid., 113–14.

63. Ibid., 122, 117.

64. Ibid., 210, 194.

65. Ibid., 180, 143.

66. Ibid., 121.

67. Dabashi, *Iran*, 163.

68. See Afary and Anderson, *Foucault and the Iranian Revolution*, chap. 2. In examining the many political uses to which Muharram (first month of the Islamic calendar, in which Shi'ites observe Ashura), was put by the clerics, Afary and Anderson point to how Karbala, where Caliph Hussein was martyred in 680, became a revolutionary place and time needing reenactment in the present, and martyrdom was turned into a social calling to effect political change.

69. Dabashi, *Iran*, 150.

70. Afary and Anderson, *Foucault and the Iranian Revolution*, 39.

71. Vakil, *Women and Politics in the Islamic Republic of Iran*, 50.

72. Parsa, *Social Origins of the Iranian Revolution*, 12.

73. Ibid., 9.

74. Ibid., 254 (emphasis added).

75. Lechner, "Global Fundamentalism," 21–23.

76. Marty and Appleby, introduction, 3.

77. Afary and Anderson, *Foucault and the Iranian Revolution*, 279.

78. Other traditions in Islam include Wahhabism, which emerged in the late nineteenth century and is characterized by an emphasis on literalism, intolerance of other traditions like Sufism, belief in transparent access to the laws of the divine, and anti-intellectualism; Salafism, which focuses on restoring the so-called golden age of Islam, the return to authority of the holy texts, and a reinterpretation of traditional Islam; and Salafabism, a merging of Wahhabaism and Salafism in the middle of the twentieth century, which is marked by a distancing from Western modernity and traditional Islam, viewing Islam only in opposition to the West, and growing alienation and resentment. The Khawarij, the Qaramites, and the Assassins are groups that have historically behaved violently toward other Muslims (Abou El Fadl, "9/11 and the Muslim Transformation," 86–94).

79. Mayer, "The Fundamentalist Impact on Law, Politics, and Constitutions in Iran, Pakistan, and the Sudan," 116.

80. Yeganeh, "Women's Struggles in the Islamic Republic of Iran," 35–37.

81. Azar Nafisi, "Interview with Robert Birnbaum," Identitytheory.com, February 5, 2004 (http://www.identitytheory.com/interviews/birnbaum139.php).

82. Tabari, "Islam and the Struggle for Emancipation of Iranian Women," 5.

83. Mayer, "The Fundamentalist Impact on Law, Politics, and Constitutions in Iran, Pakistan, and the Sudan," 81.

84. Nafisi, *Reading Lolita in Tehran*, 126.

85. Yeganeh, "Women's Struggles in the Islamic Republic of Iran," 32.
86. Naghibi, *Rethinking Global Sisterhood*, 56.
87. Khomeini, "Speeches," 99 (emphasis added).
88. Riesebrodt, *Pious Passion*, 205–7.
89. Nafisi, *Reading Lolita in Tehran*, 105.
90. Ibid., 106.
91. Kinzer's dissent privileges Americans and America even though its stated goal is to examine how an internationally planned coup unfolded in Iran. Along similar lines, there is much in Kermit Roosevelt's *Countercoup: The Struggle for the Control of Iran* that reduces the revolution to the handiwork of a few devious CIA operatives or to that of Britain and America, two powerful states. But despite this, the political and social climate that facilitated the success of the coup gains clarity: there was tremendous tension between the shah and Mossadeq, with each attempting to limit the other's power; there was disagreement about nationalizing Iranian oil reserves and renewing contracts with British companies; there was a dearth of technical knowledge and personnel in Iran to continue producing oil and managing its sale in international markets; there was dissension among numerous opposition groups, each of which—like the Tudeh Party which had Russian support—was reluctant or unable to join a coherent resistance movement against either the shah or America. There were also many people in the army and civil society who sympathized with the shah, although that sympathy should not be confused with hatred for democracy. The coup should be viewed in the context of constitutional monarchy (the legacy of the Constitutional Revolution of 1906–11), which recognized monarchic power while circumscribing it with the office of the prime minister and the parliament. Mossadeq's reliance on direct or indirect American financial aid compromised his government's ability to nationalize Iranian oil. Ayatollah Kashani, originally a supporter of Mossadeq, turned against him by cooperating with the coup planners to depose him. Generals like Zahedi and Gulianshah and Colonel Nassiry supported the shah, as several army and police units battled each other and the mobs in front of Mossadeq's house. All these actions form the contested terrain on which the coup's success needs to be examined.
92. Riesebrodt, *Pious Passion*, 101–20.
93. Dabashi, *Iran*, 147.
94. Duara, "Transnationalism and the Challenge to National Histories," 29.
95. The Persian Empire began with the Achaemenids (550–330 BC), the Seleucids (312–247 BC), the Parthians (247 BC–AD 226), and the Sassanids (AD 226–650). Following the emergence of Islam in the seventh century, new empires and dynasties arose, including the Umayyads (651–750), the Abbasids (750–1258), the Safavids (1500–1722), and the Qajars (1789–1926). This historical sketch is cursory and does not include numerous tribal and regional powers (Dabashi, *Iran*, 22–24).
96. Duara, "Transnationalism and the Challenge to National Histories," 30.
97. Dabashi, *Iran*, 141.
98. Ebadi, *Iran Awakening*, 23.

99. Sandra Mackey argues that Iran is a "tormented Janus" since it constantly seeks to reconcile the legacy of Persia with the legacy of Islam: "Like the shah's glorification of Persia, the Islamic Republic's exaltation of Islam *denies the two traditions existing within the Iranian national psyche*" (*The Iranians*, 5–9; emphasis added). This is why perspectives on Iranian history that privilege an American and Western vantage point, as Kinzer's text does, are unable to account for the utter disorderliness of Iran's historical archives and the cross-pollination and cohabitation of its cultures and religions, which make periodization itself less a marker of time, development, and transformation and more a chiasmatic site where the quest for a usable past must be narrated in two times at once; where the searcher for historical continuity is compelled to attend to the crisscrossing paths of Persian settlement and its religious and cultural legacies; where the coincidence of Arab tribal movements and the rise of Islam effect a rupture between temporal and divine authority, a rupture that makes visible other lines of contact, influence, and exchange—such as the transcontinental migration and reappropriation of European and Middle Eastern texts and writers, politicians and intellectuals, exiles and immigrants, and, more to the point, settlers.

100. Khomeini, *Islam and Revolution*, 200–208.

101. Dabashi, *Iran*, 140–41, 159.

102. In his declarations and speeches, Khomeini shows remarkable awareness of the political life of the monarchy, especially the manner in which it interacted with states like Britain, Russia, Israel, and the United States. When the parliament passed a resolution in support of the Vienna Treaty on Diplomatic Relations, Khomeini criticized it for giving immunity to American personnel even if, according to him, they committed crimes in Iran, whereas the shah himself, even as head of state, would not enjoy that kind of immunity if he "were to run over a dog belonging to an American" (*Islam and Revolution*, 182). The shah's government accepted a U.S. loan of $200 million for five years, to be repaid over ten years with a $100 million interest. The dependency of the Iranian economy, in this instance on America, created a colonized Iranian consciousness that crippled the government by turning it into a lackey for foreign powers. Khomeini sought to persuade Iranians that it was just these kinds of international treaties and economic deals that a government based on Islamic principles would annul or reject. However, nestled in his detailed, fiery rhetoric were hints of altering existing gender relations by preventing women and men from interacting in public places and from allowing women to teach boys and men to teach girls in schools, which he said would lead to moral decay (*Islam and Revolution*, 181–88). Once Khomeini came to power, woman—as material and discursive body and sign—became central for maintaining the purity of the Islamic nation. That use of woman would soon legitimate some of the most vicious practices of the theocratic state.

103. Arjomand, *The Turban for the Crown*, 138–39.

104. Ibid., 101 (emphasis added).

105. Arjomand, "Traditionalism in Twentieth-Century Iran," 223.

106. Arjomand, *The Turban for the Crown*, 152.

107. Afary and Anderson, *Foucault and the Iranian Revolution*, 40–41.

108. Dabashi, *Iran*, 249–51. Reformers in nineteenth-century Iran include Mirza Taqi Khan Amir Kabir, Mirza Hasan Khan Sepahsalar, Mirza Fath Ali Akhondzadeh, Mirza Aqa Khan Kermani, and Hajj Muhammad Ali Sayyah Mahallati. In the same century, the rise of Babism, premised on the millennial return of the imam, led to the creation of social movements that sought to resolve tensions between rural and urban Iranians. Various scholars—including Sheykh Ahmad Ahsa'i, Seyyed Kazem Rashti, Seyyed Ali Muhammad, Mulla Husayn Boshruyeh, and a woman by the name of Tahereh Qorrat al-Ayn—styled themselves as reformers because they interpreted Islamic theology in different ways (56–59).

109. Afary and Anderson, *Foucault and the Iranian Revolution*, 64; Dabashi, *Iran*, 147.

110. Afary and Anderson, *Foucault and the Iranian Revolution*, 64.

111. Ebadi, *Iran Awakening*, 36–37.

112. Dabashi, *Iran*, 166–68.

113. Ebadi, *Iran Awakening*, 85.

114. Nafisi, *Reading Lolita in Tehran*, 82 (emphasis added).

115. Ibid.

116. Ibid., 86 (emphasis added).

117. Ibid., 89.

118. Nafisi, "The Stuff That Dreams Are Made Of," 1.

119. Nafisi, *Reading Lolita in Tehran*, 281.

120. Ibid., 312.

121. Ibid., 282.

122. Rastegar, "Reading Nafisi in the West," 123.

123. Keshavarz, *Jasmine and Stars*, 118.

124. Naghibi, *Rethinking Global Sisterhood*, 63.

125. Hay, "Why Read *Reading Lolita*?," 17 (emphasis added).

126. Nafisi, "The Stuff That Dreams Are Made Of," 7.

127. Rowe, "Reading *Reading Lolita in Tehran* in Idaho," 266 (emphasis added).

128. Nafisi, *Reading Lolita in Tehran*, 64.

129. Bahramitash, "The War on Terror, Feminist Orientalism and Orientalist Feminism."

130. Nafisi, *Reading Lolita in Tehran*, 67.

131. Tahereh Khanoom tells Nafisi that she was held hostage by the Revolutionary Guards, who used her gender to justify their use of her as a human shield, since the man they were pursuing would most likely not risk shooting her, a woman. Although Nafisi assumes that she can "speak their language" and has something in common with them, it is a commonality that is undone primarily on account of her gender. Here, class identification is fractured by gender difference.

132. Nafisi, *Reading Lolita in Tehran*, 339.

133. Rushdie, *Imaginary Homelands*, 10.

132. Nafisi, *Reading Lolita in Tehran*, 342.

134. Ibid., 329 (emphasis added).

136. Ibid., 7.
137. Ibid., 42.
138. Bhabha, "Introduction," 4.
139. Nafisi, *Reading Lolita in Tehran*, 6.
140. Dimock, "Literature for the Planet," 177.

5. *THE WORLD IS FLAT*

1. Hira and Hira, *Outsourcing America*, 151; Sheshabalaya, *Rising Elephant*, 103–6.
2. NASSCOM, "Executive Summary." The fact that the IT sector of the economy has become a vital part of the Indian government's plans for large-scale economic restructuring is borne out by the fact that in *India Vision 2020*, a report issued by the Planning Commission of India in 2002, the second chapter—right after the introductory one—is about the knowledge economy and the IT industry, and their importance to India.
3. Mann, *Accelerating the Globalization of America*, 53.
4. Hira and Hira, *Outsourcing America*, 2, 47.
5. Corbett, *The Outsourcing Revolution*, xv.
6. Sheshabalaya, *Rising Elephant*, 5, 57.
7. Friedman, *The World Is Flat*, 7.
8. Ibid., 152.
9. Ibid., 168.
10. Ibid., 179.
11. Ibid., 205–6.
12. Friedman, "Remarks by Thomas L. Friedman on the Flattening World."
13. Thomas L. Friedman, "Flat World Fears," interview with Nayan Chanda, Outlook India.com, February 24, 2006 (http://www.outlookindia.com/article.aspx?230308).
14. Kroeber and Kluckhohn, *Culture*, 106–7.
15. Eliade, *Myth and Reality*, 5–8, 135.
16. Lincoln, *Theorizing Myth*, xii.
17. Quoted in Friedman, *The World Is Flat*, 3.
18. Ibid., 4–5.
19. Quoted in ibid., 3 (emphasis added).
20. Columbus, *The Four Voyages of Columbus*, 1:4–6, 14.
21. Ibid., 2:30, 34, 40.
22. Ibid., 2:48 (emphasis added).
23. Ibid., 2:92, 110.
24. Benjamin, *Illuminations*, 96.
25. Held, McGrew, Goldblatt, and Perraton, *Global Transformations*, 3.
26. Andrew McLaughlin, "Google in China," *Google Blog*, January 27, 2006 (http://googleblog.blogspot.com/2006/01/google-in-china.html).
27. Thomas L. Friedman, "Flat World Fears," interview with Nayan Chanda, Outlook India.com, February 24, 2006 (http://www.outlookindia.com/article.aspx?230308) (emphasis added).
28. McClintock, "The Angel of Progress," 292 (emphasis added). For chapter-

by-chapter counterperspectives to Friedman culled from various critical responses to *The World Is Flat*, see Aronica and Ramdoo, *The World Is Flat?*

29. Friedman, *The World Is Flat*, 332.
30. Ibid., 348.
31. Ibid., 364.
32. Ibid., 277–92.
33. Ibid., 367 (emphasis added).
34. Ibid., 380 (emphasis added).
35. Ibid., 387 (emphasis added).
36. Ibid., 411.
37. Quoted in ibid., 236.
38. Ibid., 234.
39. Ibid., 465 (emphasis added).
40. Lincoln, *Theorizing Myth*, 207, 17. Lincoln and Eliade exemplify what could arguably be referred to as the modern and postmodern orientations, respectively, toward the study of myth: Eliade emphasizes the realm of the sacred and the idea of prehistoric time, while Lincoln grounds his study in discourse and attends to myth's ideological force. Rather than searching for or attempting to create a "uniform definition" of myth (Nagy, "Can Myth Be Saved?," 240), we should pay attention to how the term has been used in varied contexts and situations. Its meanings could range from oral discourse and the opposition among *mythos*, logos, *fabula*, and history (Fulk, "Myth in Historical Perspective," 227); narratives that "represent large cultural and natural issues, in contradistinction to local reminiscence or mundane entertainment" (Toelken, "Native American Reassessment and Reinterpretation of Myths," 90); and specific genres in narrative form, concerned with origins, the sacred, and the social role of rituals (Hansen, "Meanings and Boundaries," 20–21). Because they register the existential anguish of human beings struggling to understand nature and the world's utter indifference to their predicament, myths mediate between humanity and divinity; they represent humanity's unconscious motives, fantasies, dreams, desires (Segal, "Does Myth Have a Future?").
41. Marx and Engels, *The Communist Manifesto*, 9 (emphasis added).
42. Roberto Gonzalez, "Falling Flat," review of *The World Is Flat*, by Thomas L. Friedman, *San Francisco Chronicle*, May 15, 2005, http://www.sfgate.com/cgi-bin/article.cgi?f=/c/a/2005/05/15/RVGHLCL11V1. DTL.
43. Hazony, "His World Is Flat."
44. Gugler, introduction, 6.
45. Ibid., 10.
46. Ibid., 16.
47. Janaki Nair. *The Promise of the Metropolis: Bangalore's Twentieth Century* (New Delhi: Oxford University Press, 2005), 334.
48. Heitzman, *Network City*, 210. For a comparative perspective, see Gifford "The Silicon Valley of China."
49. Heitzman, *Network City*, 209.
50. Keniston, "Introduction," 13–17.

51. Ibid., 17.
52. Ibid., 18.
53. Saxenian, *The New Argonauts*, 5–7.
54. Ibid., 276.
55. Bellah et al., *Habits of the Heart*, 72.
56. Ram-Prasad, "India's Middle Class Failure."
57. Saxenian, *The New Argonauts*, 276–77.
58. Ibid., 299.
59. Upadhya, "A New Transnational Capitalist Class?"
60. Singhal and Rogers, *India's Communication Revolution*, 158.
61. Upadhya ("A New Transnational Capitalist Class?") seems to include POIs (persons of Indian origin) in the NRI category. In India, POIs tend to get a more favored treatment than NRIs since POIs are "on the whole . . . much richer than NRIs" (Davies, *What's this India Business?*, 128).
62. Upadhya, "A New Transnational Capitalist Class?"
63. Ibid.
64. "Community Focus," *Indian Reporter*, July 21, 2006.
65. Upadhya, "A New Transnational Capitalist Class?," 5145–56.
66. Ibid., 5148.
67. Singhal and Rogers, *India's Communication Revolution*, 156.
68. Ibid., 162 (emphasis added).
69. Hashmi, "Outsourcing the American Dream?," 244.
70. Ibid., 242.

6. CALL CENTER CULTURES

1. Hardt, "Affective Labor."
2. Appadurai, "Disjuncture and Difference in the Global Cultural Economy," 10.
3. Poster, "Who's on the Line?"; Mirchandani, "Practices of Global Capital"; R. Chengappa, and M. Goyal, "Housekeepers to the World," *India Today*, November 18, 2002. However, cost effectiveness is not the only criterion for offshoring. British Telco recently announced that it was moving around 4,000 customer service jobs back to England from India. Although a depressed British economy and the need to provide jobs in the company's country were cited as main reasons, complaints about customer service and difficult accents were also considered ("BT Returns Call Center Work From India"). Companies like Delta Airlines and Sallie May have also announced that they were moving jobs from overseas to the United States (Brad Dorfman,"Delta Stops Using India Call Centers," Reuters.com, April 18, 2009 [http://www.reuters.com/article/domesticNews/idUSTRE53H1PN20090418]).
4. Hardt and Negri, *Empire*, 293.
5. Hardt, "Foreword," xi.
6. Ibid, ix.
7. Gill and Pratt, "In the Social Factory?," 15.
8. Hardt and Negri, *Empire*, 290.
9. Ibid., 292–93.

10. Hardt, "Foreword," xi.

11. Brian Massumi points out that affects are different from emotions in that "an emotion is a subjective content, the sociolinguistic fixing of the quality of an experience which is from that point onward defined as personal." There is an "irreducibly bodily and autonomic nature" to affects; they can also be viewed as "a suspension of action-reaction circuits and linear temporality in a sink of what might be called 'passion,' to distinguish it from passivity and activity" (*Parables for the Virtual*, 28). The meanings of these terms are far from settled, and it is beyond the scope of this book to review or synthesize them. For further discussion linking these terms to *operaismo, autonomia*, socialized worker, precariousness, Marx's "real subsumption," and Tronti's "social factory," see Thoburn's *Deleuze, Marx, and Politics*; Gill and Pratt's "In the Social factory?"

12. Poster, "Who's on the Line?," 299.

13. Stitt, *Diverted to Delhi*. 14. Shome, "Thinking through the Diaspora," 107.

15. Hardt, "Affective Labor," 96.

16. Foucault, "Right of Death and Power over Life," 266 (emphasis added).

17. Vasavi, "'Serviced from India,'" 11 (emphasis added).

18. McMillin, "Outsourcing Identities," 235. This ethnographic study is based on direct observation of two call centers and detailed interviews with forty employees working in six locations in Bangalore, India, a burgeoning global technopolis. Seeking to counter the inordinate emphasis on individual agency in discourses of globalization that celebrate IT globalization as unproblematically signifying individual and social empowerment in developing countries, McMillin contends that agency is "structured within domination," since the systemic functions of call centers in the global IT economy position call center employees in distinctly disadvantaged positions—professional excellence requires effective manipulation of another adopted identity, which is not required of the clients or customers whose needs these offices are set up to service (236–37). This is a good instance of the imbalanced positioning of customers and CCRs in the IT-enhanced network of work interaction.

19. Ferguson and Gupta, "Spatializing States," 994. This point is made in the context of examining the procedures by which the state legitimizes vertical encompassment, a hierarchical and horizontal mode of governance. Instead of understanding civil society as a sphere little influenced by the state, Ferguson and Gupta see civic and nongovernmental organizations as often reifying, in their modes of operation in civil society, state-sanctioned models of social organization.

20. Shome, "Thinking through the Diaspora," 110.

21. McMillin, "Outsourcing Identities," 237 (emphasis added).

22. Ibid., 236.

23. Poster, "Who's on the Line?," 276.

24. Ibid., 291.

25. Larry King, "John Kerry Addresses Supporters," *CNN Live Event/Special*, January 27, 2004, transcript no. 012702CN.V54 (http://157.166.226.115/TRANSCRIPTS/0401/27/se.02.html).

26. Poster, "Who's on the Line?," 281.

27. S. Mitra Kalita, "Hope and Toil at India's Call Centers," *Washington Post*, December 27, 2005 (http://www.washingtonpost.com/wpdyn/content/article/2005/12/26/AR2005122600852_pf.html).

28. Krishnamurthy, "Resources and Rebels," 11. With its focus on "identity management," Krishnamurthy's study is based on fieldwork and interviews with call center employees between eighteen and twenty-five years old, working in Pune, Bangalore, and Gurgaon, India.

29. Kamdar, *Planet India*, 148.

30. Vandana Shiva, "The Suicide Economy of Corporate Globalization," Countercurrents.org, April 5, 2004 (http://www.countercurrents.org/glo-shiva050404.htm).

31. Pradhan and Abraham, "Social and Cultural Impact of Outsourcing."

32. Carol Upadhya, liner notes for Uphadya and Sonti, *Coding Culture*, 15. Uphadya and Sonti's three-documentary series examines the differences in workplace cultures in an Indian-owned software company, an offshore outsourced office of an American company, and an Indian startup. These films present a nuanced approach to the study of IT globalization as they attend to culture not just as a variable category but in terms of how these companies' "positions in the global economy and to the kinds of work they perform" create specific workplace cultures that "shape the subjectivities of employees and managers."

33. Ramesh, "'Cyber Coolies' in BPO," 495. Ramesh bases his analysis on data gathered from six call centers in the technopolis of Noida, near Delhi.

34. Ibid., 496 (emphasis added)

35. Vasavi, "'Serviced from India,'" 10.

36. Winiecki, "Shadowboxing with Data," 88. Winiecki focuses on U.S.-based call centers. In a related context, Peter Bain and Phil Taylor—in their analysis of call centers at Telcorp UK, part of a U.S. multinational corporation—make a good case for questioning the absolute power of the electronic panopticon by studying how, for instance, worker resistance via unionization was possible in Telcorp. Union-management negotiations became more transparent with the use of recording technology, and the interests of supervisor and supervised overlapped, making it less likely in some instances for established protocols to be followed ("Entrapped by the 'Electronic Panopticon'?")

37. Krishnamurthy, "Resources and Rebels," 15.

38. Ibid., 13–16.

39. Ibid., 11.

40. Pradhan and Abraham, "Social and Cultural Impact of Outsourcing."

41. Ibid.

42. Singh and Pandey, "Women in Call Centres," 686 (emphasis added). Their observations are based on a study of several call centers in Delhi, Gurgoan, and Noida, India, and on the participation of 100 female employees. Most of the women were between eighteen and twenty-five years old.

43. Ibid., 687.

44. Vasavi, "'Serviced from India,'" 7.

45. Singh and Pandey, "Women in Call Centres," 687.

46. Pradhan and Abraham, "Social and Cultural Impact of Outsourcing."
47. "Taxi Firms Want Dress Code for BPO Staff," *Deccan Chronicle*, February 13, 2006.
48. Krishnamurthy, "Resources and Rebels," 16, 10.
49. Appadurai, "Disjuncture and Difference in the Global Cultural Economy," 10.
50. Readings, *The University in Ruins*, 172. Elaborating on the idea of dwelling in the ruins of the university rather than pining for the return of the traditional institution, he writes: "The question that is raised by the analogy is how we can do something other than offer ourselves up for tourism: the humanities as cultural manicure, the social sciences as travelogue, the natural sciences as the frisson of real knowledge and large toys" (ibid.). By using an interdisciplinary approach to examine the various roles, levels, and impact of cultural practices in a global environment, the humanities can help us reimagine ourselves as scholars and citizens able to intervene substantially at the level of political economy.

─{ BIBLIOGRAPHY }─

Abou El Fadl, Khaled. "9/11 and the Muslim Transformation." In *September 11 in History: A Watershed Moment?*, edited by Mary L. Dudziak, 70–111. Durham, NC: Duke University Press, 2003.

Afary, Janet, and Kevin B. Anderson. *Foucault and the Iranian Revolution: Gender and the Seductions of Islamism*. Chicago: University of Chicago Press, 2005.

Anzaldúa, Gloria. *Borderlands/La Frontera*. San Francisco: Spinsters/Aunt Lute, 1987.

Appadurai, Arjun. "Disjuncture and Difference in the Global Cultural Economy." *Public Culture* 2, no. 2 (1990): 1–14.

Arjomand, Said Amir. "Traditionalism in Twentieth-Century Iran." In *From Nationalism to Revolutionary Islam*, edited by Said Amir Arjomand, 195–232. Albany: State University of New York Press, 1984.

———. *The Turban for the Crown: The Islamic Revolution in Iran*. New York: Oxford University Press, 1988.

Aronica, Ronald, and Mtetwa Ramdoo. *The World Is Flat? A Critical Analysis of Thomas L. Friedman's New York Times Bestseller*. Tampa, FL: Meghan-Kiffer, 2006.

Arrighi, Giovanni. "Lineages of Empire." In *Debating Empire*, edited by Gopal Balakrishnan, 29–42. New York: Verso, 2003.

Ascari, Maurizio. *Literature of the Global Age: A Critical Study of Transcultural Narratives*. Jefferson, NC: McFarland, 2011.

Association of American University Presses. "Nobel Peace Prize Winner Joins Battle against Treasury Department for Free Speech." Association of American University Presses, October 27, 2004. http://www.aaupnet.org/news-a-publications/news/archived-press-releases/365-nobelist-joins-battle-for-free-speech.

Bahramitash, Roksana. "The War on Terror, Feminist Orientalism and Orientalist Feminism: Case Studies of Two North American Bestsellers." *Critique* 14, no. 2 (2005): 221–35.

Bain, Peter, and Phil Taylor. "Entrapped by the 'Electronic Panopticon'? Worker Resistance in the Call Centre." *New Technology, Work and Employment* 15, no. 1 (2000): 2–18.

Balakrishnan, Gopal, ed. *Debating Empire*. New York: Verso, 2003.

Baneth-Nouailhetas, Emilienne. "Committed Writing, Committed Writer?" In *Globalizing Dissent: Essays on Arundhati Roy*, edited by Ranjan Ghosh and Antonia Navarro-Tejero, 93–104. New York: Routledge, 2009.

Barsamian, David. *The Checkbook and the Cruise Missile: Conversations with Arundhati Roy*. Cambridge, MA: South End, 2004.

Bauerlein, Mark. *Literary Criticism: An Autopsy*. Philadelphia: University of Pennsylvania Press, 1997.

Behdad, Ali. "Critical Historicism." *American Literary History* 20, nos. 1–2 (2008): 286–99.

Bellah, Robert N., et al. *Habits of the Heart: Individualism and Commitment in American Life*. Updated ed. Berkeley: University of California Press, 1996.

Bender, Thomas. *A Nation among Nations: America's Place in World History*. New York: Hill and Wang, 2006.

Benhabib, Seyla. *The Claims of Culture: Equality and Diversity in the Global Era*. Princeton, NJ: Princeton University Press, 2002.

Benjamin, Walter. *Illuminations*. Translated by Harry Zohn. New York: Harcourt, Brace, and World, 1955.

Bérubé, Michael. *The Left at War*. New York: New York University Press, 2009.

Bhabha, Homi. "Introduction: Narrating the Nation." In *Nation and Narration*, edited by Homi Bhabha, 1–7. New York: Routledge, 1990.

———. *The Location of Culture*. New York: Routledge, 1994.

Bogues, Anthony. *Empire of Liberty: Power, Desire, and Freedom*. Hanover, NH: University Press of New England, 2010.

Bose, Pablo S. "Critics and Experts, Activists and Academics: Intellectuals in the Fight for Social and Ecological Justice in the Narmada Valley, India." *International Review of Social History* 49, supplement 12 (2004): 133–57.

Brennan, Timothy. "The Italian Ideology." In *Debating Empire*, edited by Gopal Balakrishnan, 97–120. New York: Verso, 2003.

Bright, Charles, and Michael Geyer. "Where in the World Is America? The History of the United States in the Global Age." In *Rethinking American History in a Global Age*, edited by Thomas Bender, 63–99. Berkeley: University of California Press, 2002.

"BT Returns Call Center Work from India." *Business Week*. July 16, 2009 (http://www.businessweek.com/globalbiz/content/jul2009/gb20090716_304942.htm).

Buruma, Ian. "The Anti-American." *New Republic*, April 29, 2002. http://www.tnr.com/article/the-anti-american.

Butler, Judith. "Explanation and Exoneration, or What We Can Hear." *Social Text* 72, no. 3 (2002): 177–88.

Callinicos, Alex. "Toni Negri in Perspective." In *Debating Empire*, edited by Gopal Balakrishnan, 121–43. New York: Verso, 2003.

Ceaser, James W. *Reconstructing America: The Symbol of America in Modern Thought*. New Haven, CT: Yale University Press, 1997.

Chomsky, Noam. "The United States Is a Leading Terrorist State: Interview with David Barsamian." *Monthly Review*, November 2001, http://www.chomsky.info/interviews/200111-02.htm.

Coalition against Genocide. "Genocide in Gujarat: The Sangh Parivar, Narendra Modi, and the Government of Gujarat." March 2, 2005. http://www.sabrang.com/MODI/CAGModiDossier.pdf.

Columbus, Christopher. *The Four Voyages of Columbus: A History in Eight Documents, Including Five by Christopher Columbus, in the Original Spanish, with English Translations.* Translated and edited by Cecil Jane. Two vols. in one. New York: Dover, 1988.

Corbett, Michael F. *The Outsourcing Revolution: Why It Makes Sense and How To Do It Right.* Chicago: Dearborn, 2004.

Cushman, Thomas. "The Reflexivity of Evil: Modernity and Moral Transgression in the War in Bosnia." In *Evil after Postmodernism: Histories, Narratives, and Ethics,* edited by Jennifer L. Geddes, 79–100. New York: Routledge, 2001.

Dabashi, Hamid. *Iran: A People Interrupted.* New York: New Press, 2007.

——. "Native Informers and the Making of the American Empire." *Al-Ahram Weekly,* June 1–7, 2006. http://weekly.ahram.org.eg/2006/797/special.htm.

Davies, Paul. *What's This India Business? Offshoring, Outsourcing, and the Global Services Revolution.* London: Nicholas Brealey International, 2004.

Dawson, Ashley, and Malini Johar Schueller. "Introduction: Rethinking Imperialism Today." In *Exceptional State: Contemporary U.S. Culture and the New Imperialism,* edited by Ashley Dawson and Malini Johar Schueller, 1–35. Durham: Duke University Press, 2007.

Del Vayo, Alvarez. "The Chaco War." In *Problems of Peace, Ninth Series: Pacifism Is Not Enough; Lectures Delivered at the Geneva Institute of International Relations August 1934,* 150–73. New York: Oxford University Press, 1935.

DePaul, Amy. "Re-Reading *Reading Lolita in Tehran.*" *MELUS* 33, no. 2 (2008): 73–92.

Dimock, Wai Chee. "Literature for the Planet." *PMLA* 116, no. 1 (2001): 173–88.

Donadey, Anne, and Huma Ahmed-Ghosh. "Why Americans Love Azar Nafisi's *Reading Lolita in Tehran.*" *Signs* 33, no. 3 (2008): 623–46.

Duara, Prasenjit. "Transnationalism and the Challenge to National Histories." In *Rethinking American History in a Global Age,* edited by Thomas Bender, 25–46. Berkeley: University of California Press, 2002.

Dumas, Firoozeh. *Funny in Farsi: A Memoir of Growing Up Iranian in America.* New York: Villard, 2003.

Dwivedi, Ranjit. "Displacement, Risks, and Resistance: Local Perceptions and Actions in the Sardar Sarovar." *Development and Change* 30, no. 1 (1999): 43–78.

Ebadi, Shirin. *Iran Awakening: A Memoir of Revolution and Hope.* New York: Random House, 2006.

Eliade, Mircea. *Myth and Reality.* Translated by Willard R. Trask. New York: Harper and Row, 1963.

Fanon, Frantz. *The Wretched of the Earth.* Translated by Constance Farrington. New York: Grove, 1963.

Farcau, Bruce W. *The Chaco War: Bolivia and Paraguay, 1932–1935.* Westport, CT: Praeger, 1996.

Ferguson, James, and Akhil Gupta. "Spatializing States: Toward an Ethnography of Neoliberal Governmentality." *American Ethnologist* 29, no. 4 (2002): 981–1002.

Ferguson, Niall. "Clashing Civilizations or Mad Mullahs: The United States between Informal and Formal Empire." In *The Age of Terror: America and the World after September 11*, edited by Strobe Talbott and Nayan Chanda, 113–41. New York: Basic, 2001.

———. *Colossus: The Price of America's Empire.* New York: Penguin, 2004.

Fernández-Armesto, Felipe. *The Americas: A Hemispheric History.* New York: Modern Library, 2003.

Fluck, Winfried. "Literature, Liberalism, and the Current Cultural Radicalism." In *Why Literature Matters: Theories and Functions of Literature*, edited by Rüdiger Ahrens and Laurenz Volkmann, 211–31. Heidelberg: Universitätsverlag C. Winter, 1996.

———. "The Modernity of America and the Practice of Scholarship." In *Rethinking American History in a Global Age*, edited by Thomas Bender, 343–66. Berkeley: University of California Press, 2002.

Foucault, Michel. "Right of Death and Power over Life." Translated by Robert Hurley. In Michel Foucault, *The Foucault Reader*, edited by Paul Rabinow, 258–72. New York: Pantheon, 1984.

Freire, Paulo. *Pedagogy of the Oppressed.* Translated by Myra Bergman Ramos. New York: Herder and Herder, 1972.

"French Government Approves Curfew Powers." *ABC Evening News Online*, November 8, 2005, http://www.abc.net.au/news/stories/2005/11/08/1500753.htm.

Friedman, Thomas L. "Remarks by Thomas L. Friedman on the Flattening World." Speech at the Rising Asia, Flattening World policy forum hosted by the Progressive Policy Institute, Washington, May 19, 2005.
http://www.dlc.org/ndol_ci.cfm?kaid=108&subid=192&contentid=253503.

———. *The World Is Flat: A Brief History of the Twenty-First Century.* Expanded edition. New York: Farrar, Straus, and Giroux, 2006.

Fukuyama, Francis. "The End of History." *National Interest* 16 (Summer 1989): 3–18.

———. "A Reply to My Critics." *National Interest* 18 (Winter 1989): 21–28.

Fulk, R. D. "Myth in Historical Perspective: The Case of Pagan Deities in the Anglo-Saxon Royal Genealogies." In *Myth: A New Symposium*, edited by Gregory Schrempp and William Hansen, 225–37. Bloomington: Indiana University Press, 2002.

Gaddis, John Lewis. "And Now This: Lessons from the Old Era for the New One." In *The Age of Terror: America and the World after September 11*, edited by Strobe Talbott and Nayan Chanda, 1–21. New York: Basic, 2001.

Garner, William R. *The Chaco Dispute: A Study of Prestige Diplomacy.* Washington: Public Affairs, 1966.

Geddes, Jennifer L. Introduction to *Evil after Postmodernism: Histories, Narratives, and Ethics*, edited by Jennifer L. Geddes, 1–8. New York: Routledge, 2001.

Ghose, Sagarika. "Face the Nation with Arundhati Roy." *IBN Live*, CNN-IBN, April 15, 2010,

http://ibnlive.in.com/news/maoists-being-forced-for-violence-arundhati/
113285-37-64.html.

Ghosh, Bishnupriya. "Tallying Bodies: The Moral Math of Arundhati Roy's Non-Fiction." In *Arundhati Roy: Critical Perspectives*, edited by Murari Prasad, 126–56. Delhi: Pencraft International, 2006.

Ghosh, Ranjan. "Epilogue: Should We Leave It to the Writer?" In *Globalizing Dissent: Essays on Arundhati Roy*, edited by Ranjan Ghosh and Antonia Navarro-Tejero, 180–92. New York: Routledge, 2009.

Giddens, Anthony. *The Consequences of Modernity*. Stanford, CA: Stanford University Press, 1990.

Gifford, Rob. "The Silicon Valley of China." *Prospect*, December 2007. http://www.prospect-magazine.co.uk/article_details.php?id=9919.

Giles, Paul. *Atlantic Republic: The American Tradition in English Literature*. Oxford: Oxford University Press, 2006.

———. "Response to the Presidential Address to the American Studies Association." *American Quarterly* 56, no. 1 (2004): 19–24.

———. *Virtual Americas: Transnational Fictions and the Transatlantic Imaginary*. Durham, NC: Duke University Press, 2002.

Gill, Rosalind and Andy Pratt. "In the Social Factory? Immaterial Labour, Precariousness and Cultural Work." *Theory, Culture and Society* 25, no. 1 (2008): 1–30.

Gitlin, Todd. *The Intellectuals and the Flag*. New York: Columbia University Press, 2006.

Gould, Eliga H. "Entangled Histories, Entangled World: The English-Speaking Atlantic as a Spanish Periphery." *American Historical Review* 112, no. 3 (2007): 764–86.

Gramsci, Antonio. *Selections from the Prison Notebooks of Antonio Gramsci*. Edited and translated by Quintin Hoare and Geoffrey Nowell Smith. Hyderabad, India: Orient Longman, 1996.

Guerlain, Pierrre. "A Tale of Two Anti-Americanisms." *European Journal of American Studies* 2 (2007):1–22 (http://ejas.revues.org/1523).

Gugler, Josef. Introduction to *World Cities beyond the West*, edited by Josef Gugler, 1–24. Cambridge: Cambridge University Press, 2004.

Hansen, William. "Meanings and Boundaries: Reflections on Thompson's 'Myth and Folktales.'" In *Myth: A New Symposium*, edited by Gregory Schrempp and William Hansen, 19–28. Bloomington: Indiana University Press, 2002.

Hardt, Michael. "Affective Labor." *boundary 2* 26, no. 2 (1999): 80–100.

———. "Foreword: What Affects Are Good For." In *The Affective Turn: Theorizing the Social*, edited by Patricia Ticineto Clough and Jean Halley, ix–xii. Durham: Duke University Press, 2007.

Hardt, Michael, and Antonio Negri. *Commonwealth*. Cambridge: Harvard University Press, 2009.

———. *Empire*. Cambridge: Harvard University Press, 2000.

———. *Multitude: War and Democracy in the Age of Empire*. New York: Penguin, 2004.

Harvey, David. *The New Imperialism*. New York: Oxford University Press, 2003.

Hashmi, Mobina. "Outsourcing the American Dream? Representing the Stakes of IT Globalization." *Economic and Political Weekly*, January 21, 2006. http://www.hoover.org/publications/policy-review/article/6276.

Hay, Simon. "Why Read *Reading Lolita*? Teaching Critical Thinking in a Culture of Choice." *Pedagogy* 8, no. 1 (2007): 5–24.

Hazony, David. "His World Is Flat." Review of *The World Is Flat*, by Thomas L. Friedman, *Policy Review*, August 2005. http://www.hoover.org/publications/policy-review/article/6276.

Heitzman, James. *Network City: Planning the Information Society in Bangalore.* New Delhi: Oxford University Press, 2004.

Held, David, Anthony McGrew, David Goldblatt, and Jonathan Perraton. *Global Transformations: Politics, Economics and Culture.* Stanford, CA: Stanford University Press, 1999.

Hira, Ron, and Anil Hira. *Outsourcing America: What's behind Our National Crisis and How We Can Reclaim American Jobs.* New York: AMACOM, 2008.

Hollander, Paul. "Introduction: The New Virulence and Popularity." In *Understanding Anti-Americanism: Its Origins and Impact at Home and Abroad*, edited by Paul Hollander, 3–42. Chicago: Ivan R. Dee, 2004.

Human Rights Watch. "India: Communal Violence and the Denial of Justice." April 1, 1996. Human Rights Watch. http://www.unhcr.org/refworld/publisher,HRW,,IND,3ae6a84f0,0.html.

Huntington, Samuel P. *Who Are We? The Challenges to America's National Identity.* New York: Simon and Schuster, 2004.

Immerman, Richard H. *Empire for Liberty: A History of American Imperialism from Benjamin Franklin to Paul Wolfowitz.* Princeton, NJ: Princeton University Press, 2010.

Iyer, Ramaswamy. *Towards Water Wisdom: Limits, Justice, Harmony.* New Delhi: Sage, 2007.

Jacquard, Roland. *In the Name of Osama Bin Laden: Global Terrorism and the Bin Laden Brotherhood.* Translated by George Holoch. Durham, NC: Duke University Press, 2002.

JanMohamed, Abdul R. "Wordliness-without-World, Homelessness-as-Home: Towards a Definition of the Specular Border Intellectual." In *Edward Said: A Critical Reader*, edited by Michael Sprinker, 96–120. Cambridge, MA: Blackwell, 1992.

Jay, Gregory. "White Out: Race and Nationalism in American Studies." *American Quarterly* 55, no. 4 (2003): 781–95.

Jefferess, David. "The Limits of Dissent: Arundhati Roy and the Struggle against the Narmada Dams." In *Globalizing Dissent: Essays on Arundhati Roy*, edited by Ranjan Ghosh and Antonia Navarro-Tejero, 157–79. New York: Routledge, 2009.

Jefferson, Thomas. *The Papers of Thomas Jefferson.* Edited by Julian Boyd. Vol. 4. Princeton, NJ: Princeton University Press, 1951.

———. *The Republic of Letters: The Correspondence between Thomas Jefferson and James Madison, 1776–1826.* Edited by James Morton Smith. Vol. 3. New York: Norton, 1995.

Johnson, Chalmers. *Blowback: The Costs and Consequences of American Empire.* New York: Metropolitan, 2000.

———. *Dismantling the Empire: America's Last Best Hope.* New York: Metropolitan, 2010.

Kadir, Djelal, ed. "America and Its Studies." Special issue, *PMLA* 118, no. 1 (2003).

———. "Defending America against Its Devotees." *Comparative American Studies* 2, no. 2 (2004): 135–52.

Kamdar, Mira. *Planet India: How the Fastest-Growing Democracy Is Transforming America and the World.* New York: Scribner, 2007.

Kaplan, Amy. *The Anarchy of Empire in the Making of U.S. Culture.* Cambridge, Massachusetts: Harvard University Press, 2002.

———. "A Call for a Truce." *American Literary History* 17, no. 1 (2005): 141–47.

———. "The Tenacious Grasp of American Exceptionalism." *Comparative American Studies* 2, no. 2 (2004): 153–59.

———. "Violent Belongings and the Question of Empire Today." *American Quarterly* 56, no. 1 (2004): 1–18.

Kaplan, Robert D. "America and the Tragic Limits of Imperialism." *Hedgehog Review* 5, no. 1 (2003): 56–67.

Keniston, Kenneth. "Introduction: The Four Digital Divides." In *IT Experience in India: Bridging the Digital Divide,* edited by Kenneth Keniston and Deepak Kumar, 1–36. New Delhi: Sage, 2004.

Keshavarz, Fatemeh. *Jasmine and Stars: Reading More Than* Lolita *in Tehran.* Chapel Hill: University of North Carolina Press, 2007.

Khagram, Sanjeev. *Dams and Development: Transnational Struggles for Water and Power.* Ithaca, NY: Cornell University Press, 2004.

Khomeini, Ayatollah Ruhullah Al-Musavi. *Islam and Revolution: Writings and Declarations of Imam Khomeini.* Translated by Hamid Algar. Berkeley, CA: Mizan, 1981.

———."Speeches." In *In the Shadow of Islam: The Women's Movement in Iran,* edited by Azar Tabari and Nahid Yeganeh, 98–103. London: Zed, 1982.

Krishnamurthy, Mathangi. "Resources and Rebels: A Study of Identity Management in Indian Call Centers." *Anthropology of Work Review* 24, nos. 3–4 (2004): 9–18.

Kinzer, Stephen. *All the Shah's Men: An American Coup and the Roots of Middle East Terror.* Hoboken, NJ: John Wiley and Sons, 2003.

Kroeber, A. L., and Clyde Kluckhohn. *Culture: A Critical Review of Concepts and Definitions.* New York: Vintage, 1963.

Kroes, Rob. "Imaginary Americas in Europe's Public Space." In *Straddling Borders: The American Resonance in Transnational Identities,* edited by Rob Kroes, 3–21. Amsterdam: VU University Press, 2004.

Kumar, Amitava. "The Un-Victim." *Guernica,* February 2011. http://www.guernicamag.com/interviews/2356/roy_2_15_11/.

La Foy, Margaret. *The Chaco Dispute and the League of Nations.* Ann Arbor, MI: Edwards Brothers, 1946.

Lechner, Frank. "Global Fundamentalism." In *A Future for Religion? New Paradigms for Social Analysis,* edited by William H. Swatos Jr., 19–36. London: Sage, 1993.

Leslie, Jacques. *Deep Water: The Epic Struggle over Dams, Displaced People, and the Environment*. New York: Farrar, Straus and Giroux, 2005.

Lévy, Bernard-Henri. *War, Evil, and the End of History*. Translated by Charlotte Mandell. Hoboken, NJ: Melville House, 2004.

Limón, José E. "Translating Empire: The Border Homeland of Rio Grande City, Texas." *American Quarterly* 56, no. 1 (2004): 25–32.

Lincoln, Bruce. *Theorizing Myth: Narrative, Ideology, and Scholarship*. Chicago: University of Chicago Press, 1999.

Lipsitz, George. "Our America." *American Literary History* 17, no. 1 (2005): 135–40.

Mackey, Sandra. *The Iranians: Persia, Islam, and the Soul of a Nation*. New York: Dutton, 1996.

Mann, Catherine L., with Jacob Funk Kirkegaard. *Accelerating the Globalization of America: The Role for Information Technology*. Washington: Institute for International Economics, 2006.

Mann, Michael. *Incoherent Empire*. New York: Verso, 2003.

Marty, Martin E., and R. Scott Appleby. Introduction to the *Fundamentalism Project*, vol. 3, *Fundamentalisms and the State: Remaking Polities, Economies, and Militance*, edited by Martin E. Marty and R. Scott Appleby, 1–9. Chicago: University of Chicago Press, 1993.

Marx, Karl, and Friedrich Engels. *The Communist Manifesto*. New York: Monthly Review, 1998.

Marx, Leo. "On Recovering the 'Ur' Theory of American Studies." *American Literary History* 17, no. 1 (2005): 118–34.

Massumi, Brian. *Parables for the Virtual: Movement, Affects, Sensation*. Durham: Duke University Press, 2002.

May, Elaine Tyler. "Echoes of the Cold War: September 11 at Home." In *September 11 in History. A Watershed Moment?*, edited by Mary Dudziak, 35–54. Durham, NC: Duke University Press, 2003.

Mayer, Ann Elizabeth. "The Fundamentalist Impact on Law, Politics, and Constitutions in Iran, Pakistan, and the Sudan." In *The Fundamentalism Project*, vol. 3, *Fundamentalisms and the State: Remaking Polities, Economies, and Militance*, edited by Martin E. Marty and R. Scott Appleby, 110–51. Chicago: University of Chicago Press, 1993.

McClintock, Anne. "The Angel of Progress: Pitfalls of the Term 'Post-colonialism.'" In *Colonial Discourse and Post-Colonial Theory*, edited by Patrick Williams and Laura Chrisman, 291–304. New York: Columbia University Press, 1994.

McCormack, Brian. "A Historical Case for the Globalization of International Law: The Chaco War and the Principle of *Ex Aequo et Bono*." *Global Society* 13, no. 3 (1999): 287–312.

McMillin, Divya. "Outsourcing Identities: Call Centers and Cultural Transformation in India." *Economic and Political Weekly*, January 21, 2006, 235–41.

Mignolo, Walter D. *Local Histories/Global Designs: Coloniality, Subaltern Knowledges, and Border Thinking*. Princeton, NJ: Princeton University Press, 2000.

Mirchandani, Kiran. "Practices of Global Capital: Gaps, Cracks, and Ironies in Transnational Call Centers in India." *Global Networks* 4, no. 4 (2004): 355–73.

Mullaney, Julie. "'Globalizing Dissent'? Arundhati Roy, Local and Postcolonial Feminisms in the Transnational Economy." In *Arundhati Roy: Critical Perspectives*, edited by Murari Prasad, 110–25. Delhi: Pencraft International, 2006.

Murthy, Narayana R. "Making India a Significant IT Player in This Millennium." In *India: Another Millennium*, edited by Romila Thapar, 212–40. New Delhi: Penguin, 2000.

Muthyala, John. "'America' in Transit: The Heresies of American Studies Abroad." *Comparative American Studies* 1, no. 4 (2003): 395–420.

Nafisi, Azar. *Reading Lolita in Tehran: A Memoir in Books*. New York: Random House, 2003.

———. "The Stuff That Dreams Are Made Of." In *My Sister, Guard Your Veil; My Brother, Guard Your Eyes: Uncensored Iranian Voices*, edited by Lila Azam Zangeneh, 1–11. Boston: Beacon, 2006.

———. *Things I've Been Silent About*. New York: Random House, 2008.

Naghibi, Nima. *Rethinking Global Sisterhood: Western Feminism and Iran*. Minneapolis: University of Minnesota Press, 2007.

Nagy, Gregory. "Can Myth Be Saved?" In *Myth: A New Symposium*, edited by Gregory Schrempp and William Hansen, 240–48. Bloomington: Indiana University Press, 2002.

Nair, Janaki. *The Promise of the Metropolis: Bangalore's Twentieth Century*. New Delhi: Oxford University Press, 2005.

National Association of Software and Service Companies. "Executive Summary: The IT-BOP Sector in India: Strategic Review 2011." http://www.nasscom.in/.

Nussbaum, Martha C. "Body of the Nation: Why Women Were Mutilated in Gujara." *Boston Review*, Summer 2004. http://bostonreview.net/BR29.3/nussbaum.html.

———. "Violence on the Left: Nandigram and the Communists of West Bengal." *Dissent*, Spring 2008. http://dissentmagazine.org/article/?article=1157.

———. and Richard Rorty. "Reading Our Way to Democracy? Literature and Public Ethics." *Philosophy and Literature* 30, no. 2 (2006): 410–23.

O'Hara, Daniel T. *Empire Burlesque: The Fate of Critical Culture in Global America*. Durham: Duke University Press, 2003.

Omvedt, Gail. "An Open Letter to Arundhati Roy." Narmada.org, June 1999. http://www.narmada.org/debates/gail/gail.open.letter.html.

Parsa, Misagh. *Social Origins of the Iranian Revolution*. New Brunswick, NJ: Rutgers University Press, 1989.

Patel, Anil. "Resettlement Politics and Tribal Interests." In *The Dam and the Nation: Displacement and Resettlement in the Narmada Valley*, edited by Jean Drèze, Meera Samson, and Satyajit Singh, 68–92. Delhi: Oxford University Press, 1997.

Pease, Donald E. *National Identities and Post-Americanist Narratives*. Durham, NC: Duke University Press, 1994.

Pease, Donald E., and Amy Kaplan, eds. *Cultures of United States Imperialism*. Durham: Duke University Press, 1993.

Pease, Donald E., and Robyn Wiegman, eds. *The Futures of American Studies*. Durham: NC: Duke University Press, 2002.

Planning Commission of India. *India Vision 2020*. New Delhi: Planning Commission of India, 2002. http://planningcommission.nic.in/reports/genrep/pl_vsn2020.pdf.

Poster, Winifred R. "Who's on the Line? Indian Call Center Agents Pose as Americans for U.S.-Outsourced Firms." *Industrial Relations* 46, no. 2. (2007): 271–304.

Power, Samantha. *"A Problem from Hell": America and the Age of Genocide.* New York: Basic, 2002.

Pradhan, Jaya Prakash, and Vinoj Abraham. "Social and Cultural Impact of Outsourcing: Emerging Issues from Indian Call Centers." *Harvard Asia Quarterly,* January 2006. http://asiaquarterly.com/2006/01/28/ii-122/.

Ram, N. "Interview: A Writer's Place in Society." In *Arundhati Roy: Critical Perspectives,* edited by Murari Prasad, 177–97. Delhi: Pencraft International, 2006.

Ramesh, Babu P. "'Cyber Coolies' in BPO: Insecurities and Vulnerabilities of Non-Standard Work." *Economic and Political Weekly,* January 31, 2004, 492–97.

Ram-Prasad, Chakravarthi. "India's Middle Class Failure." *Prospect,* September 2007.
http://www.prospectmagazine.co.uk/2007/09/indias-middle-class-failure/.

Rastegar, Mitra. "Reading Nafisi in the West: Authenticity, Orientalism, and 'Liberating' Iranian Women." *Women's Studies Quarterly* 34, nos. 1–2 (2006): 108–28.

Readings, Bill. *The University in Ruins.* Cambridge: Harvard University Press, 1996.

Renan, Ernest. "What Is a Nation?" In *Nation and Narration,* edited by Homi Bhabha, 8–22. New York: Routledge, 1990.

Revel, Jean François. *Anti-Americanism.* Translated by Diarmid Cammell. San Francisco: Encounter, 2003.

Riesebrodt, Martin. *Pious Passion: The Emergence of Modern Fundamentalism in the United States and Iran.* Translated by Don Reneau. Berkeley: University of California Press, 1993.

Robin, Ron. "The Exhaustion of Enclosures: A Critique of Internationalization." In *Rethinking American History in a Global Age,* edited by Thomas Bender, 367–80. Berkeley: University of California Press, 2002.

Roosevelt, Kermit. *Countercoup: The Struggle for the Control of Iran.* New York: McGraw Hill, 1979.

Ross, Andrew, and Kristin Ross, eds. *Anti-Americanism.* New York: New York University Press, 2004.

———. Introduction to *Anti-Americanism,* edited by Andrew Ross and Kristin Ross, 1–14. New York: New York University Press, 2004.

Rout, Leslie B., Jr. *Politics of the Chaco Peace Conference, 1935–1939.* Austin: University of Texas Press, 1970.

Rowe, John Carlos. *Literary Culture and U.S. Imperialism.* New York: Oxford University Press, 2000.

———. *Post-Nationalist American Studies.* Berkeley: University of California Press, 2000.

———. "Reading *Reading Lolita in Tehran* in Idaho." *American Quarterly* 59, no. 2 (2007): 253–75.

Roy, Arundhati. *Broken Republic.* New Delhi: Penguin, 2011.

———. *The Cost of Living.* New York: Modern Library, 1999.

———. *Field Notes on Democracy: Listening to Grasshoppers.* Chicago: Haymarket, 2009.

———. *An Ordinary Person's Guide to Empire.* Cambridge, MA: South End, 2004.

———. *Power Politics.* Cambridge, MA: South End, 2001.

———. *War Talk*. Cambridge, MA: South End, 2003.

———. *War Talk*. West Lafayette, IN: C-SPAN Archives, May 13, 2003. Video no. 175133.

———. "Whither Kashmir? Freedom or Enslavement." Lecture presented at "Whither Kashmir? Freedom or Enslavement," a seminar sponsored by the Jammu and Kashmir Coalition of Civil Society, Srinigar, India, October 24, 2010. http://www.youtube.com/watch?v=H3zrrozUhJIe.

Rushdie, Salman. *Imaginary Homelands*. Harmondsworth, Middlesex, England: Penguin, 1991.

Said, Edward. *Representations of the Intellectual*. New York: Vintage, 1994.

———. "Introduction: Secular Criticism." In Edward Said, *The World, the Text, and the Critic*, 1–30. Cambridge: Harvard University Press, 1983.

Sanghatana, Lokshai Hakk, and the Committee for the Protection of Democratic Rights. "The Bombay Riots: Myths and Realities." Centre for the Study of Culture and Society Archives, March 1993 (http://www.cscsarchive.org:8081/MediaArchive/liberty.nsf/%28docid%29/24 E086CA63A6FDCCE5256A4800291354).

Satrapi, Marjane. *The Complete Persepolis*. New York: Pantheon, 2007.

Saxenian, AnnaLee. *The New Argonauts: Regional Advantage in a Global Economy*. Cambridge: Harvard University Press, 2006.

Segal, Robert A. "Does Myth Have a Future?" In *Myth and Method*, edited by Laurie L. Patton and Wendy Doniger, 80–97. Charlottesville: University Press of Virginia, 1996.

Shaw, Martin. "The Political Structure of a Global World: The Role of the United States." In *The Paradox of a Global USA*, edited by Bruce Mazlish, Nayan Chanda, and Kenneth Weisbrode, 16–30. Stanford, CA: Stanford University Press, 2007.

Sheshabalaya, Ashutosh. *Rising Elephant: The Growing Clash with India over White-Collar Jobs and Its Meanings for America and the World*. Monroe, ME: Common Courage, 2005.

Shome, Raka. "Thinking through the Diaspora: Call Centers, India, and a New Politics of Hybridity." *International Journal of Cultural Studies* 9, no.1 (2006): 105–24.

Singh, Preeti, and Anu Pandey. "Women in Call Centres." *Economic and Political Weekly*, February 12, 2005, 684–88.

Singhal, Arvind, and Everett M. Rogers. *India's Communication Revolution: From Bullock Carts to Cyber Marts*. London: Sage, 2001.

Stitt, Greg. *Diverted to Delhi*. New York: Filmakers Library, 2002.

Stockholm International Peace Research Institute. *Background Paper on SIPRI Military Expenditure Data, 2010*. Solna, Sweden: Stockholm International Peace Research Institute, April 11, 2011.

Stow, Simon. "Reading Our Way to Democracy? Literature and Public Ethics." *Philosophy and Literature* 30, no. 2 (2006): 410–23.

Tabari, Azar. "Islam and the Struggle for Emancipation of Iranian Women." In *In the Shadow of Islam: The Women's Movement in Iran*, edited by Azar Tabari and Nahid Yeganeh, 5–25. London: Zed, 1982.

Thoburn, Nicholas. *Deleuze, Marx, and Politics*. New York: Routledge, 2003.

Todd, Emmanuel. *After the Empire: The Breakdown of the American Order.* New York: Columbia University Press, 2003.

Toelken, Barre. "Native American Reassessment and Reinterpretation of Myths." In *Myth: A New Symposium,* edited by Gregory Schrempp and William Hansen, 89–105. Bloomington: Indiana University Press, 2002.

Tyrrell, Ian. "American Exceptionalism and Uneven Global Integration: Resistance to the Global Society." In *The Paradox of a Global USA,* edited by Bruce Mazlish, Nayan Chanda, and Kenneth Weisbrode, 64–80. Stanford, CA: Stanford University Press, 2007.

Upadhya, Carol. "A New Transnational Capitalist Class? Capital Flows, Business Networks, and Entrepreneurs in the Indian Software Industry." *Economic and Political Weekly,* November 27–December 4, 2004, 5141–51.

Upadhya, Carol, and Gautam Sonti. *Coding Culture: Bangalore's Software Industry.* 3 films. Bangalore, India: National Institute of Advanced Studies, 2006.

U.S. Department of Defense. *Base Structure Report.* Washington: U.S. Department of Defense, 2009. http://www.defense.gov/pubs/pdfs/2009baseline.pdf.

Vakil, Sanam. *Women and Politics in the Islamic Republic of Iran: Action and Reaction.* New York: Continuum, 2001.

Vasavi, A. R. "'Serviced from India': The Making of India's Global Youth Workforce." In *In an Outpost of the Global Economy: Work and Workers in India's Information Technology Industry,* edited by Carol Upadhya and A. R. Vasavi, 1–20. New Delhi: Routledge, 2007.

Wilson, Rob. *Reimagining the American Pacific: From South Pacific to Bamboo Ridge and Beyond.* Durham: Duke University Press, 2000.

Winiecki, Donald J. "Shadowboxing with Data: Production of the Subject in Contemporary Call Centre Organizations." *New Technology, Work and Employment* 19, no. 2 (2004): 78–95.

Wolfe, Alan. "Anti-American Studies." *New Republic,* February 10, 2003, 25–32.

———. *Return to Greatness: How America Lost Its Sense of Purpose and What It Needs to Do to Recover It.* Princeton, NJ: Princeton University Press, 2005.

Wood, Ellen Meiksins. "A Manifesto for Global Capitalism." In *Debating Empire,* edited by Gopal Balakrishnan, 61–82. New York: Verso, 2003.

Wood, John R. *The Politics of Water Resource Development in India: The Narmada Dams Controversy.* New York: Sage, 2007.

World Commission on Dams. "Dams and Development: A New Framework for Decision Making." London: Earthscan, 2000. http://www.internationalrivers.org/files/world_commission_on_dams_final_report.pdf.

Yeganeh, Nahid. "Women's Struggles in the Islamic Republic of Iran." In *In the Shadow of Islam: The Women's Movement in Iran,* edited by Azar Tabari and Nahid Yeganeh, 26–74. London: Zed, 1982.

Young, Marilyn B. "Ground Zero: Enduring War." In *September 11 in History: A Watershed Moment?,* edited by Mary L. Dudziak, 10–34. Durham, NC: Duke University Press, 2003.

Zook, David H., Jr. *The Conduct of the Chaco War.* New Haven, NY: Bookman, 1960.

Auerbach, Eric, 199n3
Austen, Jane, 107–8, 111
authenticity, 62–65, 79–83, 126–27
Azam, Kousar, 204–5n32

Bahramitash, Roksana, 110–11, 117, 145
Bain, Peter, 215n36
Baneth-Nouailhetas, Emilienne, 66, 104
Bangladesh, 95
Barsamian, David, 63, 74
Bauerlein, Mark, 7–8, 194–95n1
Behdad, Ali, 114, 116
Belgium, 14
Bellah, Robert N., 166
belligerence, 11
belonging, 1–2
Benador, Eleana, 110, 113
Bender, Thomas, xvi, 41, 43
Benjamin, Walter, 58, 157
Berman, Paul, 120, 205n39
Bérubé, Michael, xvi, 6–7
Bhabha, Homi, 88
Bhatia, Sabeer, 169
biopower, xviii–xix, 45, 178–79, 190–91
birth control, 19–20
blowback (resentment to U.S. imperialism).
    See anti-Americanism
Bogues, Anthony, xv, xvi
Bolivia, 11–16
border intellectuals: Arundhati Roy
    distortion of, 63, 65–67, 70–71;
    globalization and, xviii; mobilization
    of antiglobal dissent and, 55; syncretic
    vs. specular border intellectuals, 53, 56,
    60–61, 70–71
Bose, Pablo S., 56
Bosnian war, 10, 22, 27
Braudrillard, Jean, 34
Brazil, 11
Bright, Charles, 37
Brooks, Geraldine, 110–11
Buffon, Georges Louis Leclerc, Count de,
    34
Buruma, Ian, 75
Bush, George W.: "banality of evil"
    phenomenon and, 113–14; global
    totalitarianism and, 73–74; Osama bin
    Laden and, 16, 98; unilateralist foreign
    policy of, 17, 195n53; war on terror and,
    3, 9, 17, 59; war policy of, 5
Bushan, Prashant, 60

Butler, Judith, 6, 113
Byron, George Gordon (Lord Byron), 38–39

call centers: as affective labor, 173–75;
    biopolitical reproduction of culture
    and, xviii–xix, 178–79, 190–91, 214n18;
    cultural and language training,
    174, 176–79; as instruments of
    modernization, 69–70; role of women
    in, 188–90; in Slumdog Millionaire,
    171–72; Western call centers, 213n3,
    215n32, 215n36; work conditions, 185–
    90, 215n32; worker hybrid identities
    in, 181–82, 190; worker surveillance in,
    186–88, 190. See also IT globalization;
    outsourcing
Cambodia, xiii, 22, 25, 27, 95
capitalism: capitalist imperialism, 17–18,
    200n17; industry-oriented urban
    planning, 164; Iranian Revolution and,
    137–38; oil companies as Chaco War
    interest, 12–13, 15–16
Ceaser, James, xvii, 33–35
censorship, 128, 130. See also control;
    surveillance
Chaco War (Bolivia-Paraguay), 11–14
Chanda, Nayan, 157–58
Chandhoke, Neera, 103–4
Cheney, Dick, 62
Chile, 11–16
China, xiii, 95, 150, 157–58
Chomsky, Noam, xi, 53, 61, 84–88, 101–2,
    202n68
civil disobedience, 71–72, 81–82. See
    also dissent; resistance; violence/
    nonviolence
civil liberties: consumer vs. citizen in global
    cities, 164; New Americanists and,
    49–50; war on terror and, 3. See also
    democracy; empire of liberty; freedom
class: anti-IT globalization "American
    worker" class, 169–70; class
    consciousness in Reading Lolita,
    145–46, 210n131; transnational digerati
    class, 161–62, 165–69, 182–83
Clinton, Bill, 5, 58, 62, 69
Clough, Arthur Hugh, 38–39
Cold War military structure, xii, 65–67
Cole, Juan, 110
colonialism: defined, xi; absence of
    postcolonialism in Nafisi, 117; call